Paperless Publishing

Paperless Publishing

Colin Haynes

Windcrest®/ McGraw-Hill
New York   San Francisco   Washington, D.C.   Auckland   Bogotá
Caracas   Lisbon   London   Madrid   Mexico City   Milan
Montreal   New Delhi   San Juan   Singapore
Sydney   Tokyo   Toronto

©1994 by **McGraw-Hill, Inc**.
Published by Windcrest, an imprint of McGraw-Hill, Inc.
The name "Windcrest" is a registered trademark of McGraw-Hill, Inc.

1 2 3 4 5 6 7 8 9 0   DOH/DOH   9 9 8 7 6 5 4

Library of Congress Cataloging-in-Publication Data
Haynes, Colin.
   Paperless publishing / by Colin Haynes.
      p.   cm.
   Includes index.
   ISBN 0-07-911895-X (pbk.)
   1. Electronic publishing—United States.   I. Title.
Z479.H39   1994
686.2'2544536—dc20   94-13362
                                                   CIP

Acquisitions editor: Jennifer Holt DiGiovanna
Editorial team: Joanne Slike, Executive Editor
                 David M. McCandless, Managing Editor
                 Marianne Krcma, Book Editor
                 Joann Woy/Colin Haynes, Indexers
Production team: Katherine G. Brown, Director
                 Lisa M. Mellott, Coding
                 Wanda S. Ditch, Desktop Operator
                 Kelly S. Christman, Proofreading
                 Toya Warner, Computer Artist
Design team: Jaclyn J. Boone, Designer
             Brian Allison, Associate Designer
Cover design: Carol Stickles, Bath, Pa.   911895X
Cover copy: Cathy Mentzer   WK2

To librarians everywhere as they face the challenges and opportunities of a new age of publishing.

Contents

Introduction

This is the first book to provide all writers with a complete turn-key package to publish over the information highways, by modem, on floppies, and CDs. You hold in your hand information about the cultural revolution made possible by paperless publishing, plus the essential tools to participate fully in these exciting developments. The playing field of publishing suddenly becomes more level for all writers who can produce competent works. You can publish electronically without an agent or a commercial publishing imprint.

This book celebrates, for me, 40 years as a professional writer. I have written millions of words over four decades, but none have so excited me as the opportunities for writers, photographers, poets, and artists described on the pages that follow. My enthusiasm for these wonderful new ways of expression and communication grew with every page I wrote. I hope that your enthusiasm to participate will grow also as you read.

1

Publishing directly from your personal computer

ELECTRONIC publishing empowers all writers in ways that no technology has ever done before. Whatever you write—fiction, poetry, news, how-to books, or business documents—there are exciting things happening that will directly affect how you write and distribute your work. As readers, too, all of us are entering a new era of rapid cultural and social change resulting from this new technology. Artists, photographers, and other creative people will be similarly affected.

This book is not about some high-tech fad that will come and go, or be limited only to a small niche market. The cultural adventure on which we are embarking is something of direct concern to you. Unlike the Renaissance some five centuries ago that followed the invention of the printing press with movable type, this "Renaissance 2" is a revolution in which almost everyone in the industrialized nations can participate. It can truly become another Age of Enlightenment.

Already a wide range of nonfiction and fictional works are being published without paper. There will probably be over 15,000 commercial titles on compact disks alone by the middle of this decade. Even more titles will be circulating on floppy disks, or being distributed via bulletin boards and over telephone lines as computer files. Whatever you write, you can also publish for pennies through these new media.

⇨ What is electronic publishing?

Electronic publishing covers a broad spectrum of media, formats, and methods for creating and distributing works. The common element is that the publications exist as computer files that can be read and distributed without needing to be published in the conventional sense as hardcopies on paper. It is virtual publishing, with the words and pictures having no recognizable physical form until they reach the reader, where they can be read or viewed in a variety of ways depending on the needs of the reader—including being printed out onto paper.

The most visible forms of electronic publishing are the methods used by organizations to disseminate information internally, and CD-ROM, with titles on compact discs similar to those used for playing recorded music. In addition to these high-profile, much-hyped forms of electronic publishing, there is a grass-roots movement by writers and artists to cost-effectively exploit less-advanced computer technology to reach both mass and niche markets. Many authors, small independent publishers, institutions, and corporations publish on floppy disks, rather than the expensive and technically complex multimedia CD-ROM, and transmit their works via modem to bulletin boards, on-line services, or directly to their target audiences.

Is it difficult—and expensive—to become an electronic publisher? Turning a manuscript into a presentable electronic book is remarkably easy, and does not require expensive equipment. You can do it on very basic personal computing hardware using low-cost, even free, software. If floppy disks are your publishing medium, the unit cost can be literally pennies. Publishing on-line can be done for the cost of the telephone calls and perhaps modest charges by the bulletin boards or on-line services that you use.

Even if you have no computer at present, you can get into electronic publishing for as little as $300 by renting or buying used equipment, and still produce acceptable work, with the hypertext and other features that enable you to compete with titles from big corporations with massive resources and skilled staff. This book shows you how to do this, and the enclosed disk contains programs that enable any writer to publish electronically to a potentially high standard.

The cost obviously increases if you wish to add sound, animation, or other multimedia features to your publications. Limited animation can be achieved on basic systems, but really requires a 486-level PC or a System 7 Macintosh. In that case, expect to spend around $2,000 to get the memory, processing power, and storage needed. If, like millions of computer users, you already have such a system, the good news is that powerful and easy-to-use multimedia authoring software is available for street prices of around $100.

 # Low cost and easy entry

The low cost and ease of entry into the new media ensures electronic publishing an important place in mainstream publishing. Electronic publishing has evolved further in a decade, in many respects, than conventional print publishing has developed over five centuries.

Some experts of this phenomenon predict that electronic media will surpass conventional paper books in both range and volume within a few years. Already there are strong indications that the days of conventional textbooks in schools and colleges are numbered. Hundreds of thousands of people rely more on electronic news services than on printed newspapers—and those services are operating profitably.

 # Viable alternatives to smearing ink on dead trees

As Nathan Myhrvold, the head of advanced technology for Microsoft Inc., the world's largest software publisher, puts it, "We still communicate mainly by smearing ink across dead trees." Now the pace of the change from print to electronic communications is being accelerated because of the shortage and cost of the trees that must be killed, and the expense, slowness, and environmental impact inherent in the "ink-smearing" process.

Anyone concerned about the environment must welcome the trend towards electronic publishing. In addition to the enormous savings in cost and scarce resources, electronic media have other socially important attributes that make them impossible to ignore. These include making the written word readily accessible to millions of visually handicapped people who are denied the use of printed communications, but who can readily magnify the type of digitized texts, or change them to the spoken word.

Electronic publishing is already starting to fulfill its promises of leveling the playing field for young people from disadvantaged

backgrounds, and helping adults with limited financial resources start and operate businesses, advance careers, and obtain higher education.

⇨ Cultural and social impact

Electronic publishing has a particular cultural and social importance because it gives added dimensions and power to the written word. The new media may prove to have the strengths that print publishing lacks in providing powerful leisure alternatives to television.

Television—and radio—are becoming dominated by junk material as they steadily encroach on print's traditional role of entertaining and informing us. The emergence of electronic publishing in its different guises at least offers a hope of maintaining channels of communication and ways of imparting knowledge in which important issues are treated in a comprehensive, responsible way, and clear distinctions can be maintained between reality and illusion.

This book explores these culturally important aspects of electronic publishing that open up such wonderful new opportunities for those who write, or who can communicate with visual images. You will see that, although some forms of electronic publishing might share the same screens as television broadcasting, they are very different media.

⇨ Words enter another dimension

Particularly intriguing are the ways in which the very physical structure of text might change. We have been dominated for centuries by the belief that words forming sentences, paragraphs, chapters, and publications exist only in the two dimensions to which print is limited.

When you use a highly technical reference book, for example, you might find it difficult, at least initially, to understand the relevance of its different sections and how they relate. You are limited to seeing

the contents of the book in two dimensions, with only two pages of it open at any one time. When evaluating the usefulness of a book you plan to buy, you try to overcome these problems by flicking through the pages, essentially trying to get it to dynamically interact with you.

The better electronic reference books are inherently dynamic. They reach out to help you use them. They are now also starting to enter a fascinating third dimension, sometimes with the help of portable devices like the one shown in Fig. 1-1.

Figure 1-1

It has taken five centuries for words to escape from the physical confines of the printed page, but only a few years to be liberated from the computer screen. With this Virtual Vision unit, words and images appear to float in space. You can read a book or watch a video program while walking or relaxing on the beach or refer to a manual while fixing the car. One of the first applications helps patients relax in the dentist's chair while having their teeth drilled!
Virtual Vision Inc.

At Xerox PARC (the Palo Alto Research Center in California), which has been the source of so much advanced information processing technology, researchers are making text function efficiently in three dimensions, to give assemblies of words a physical depth. In the Xerox Information Theater project, you can browse through a text database on screen almost as a virtual reality experience. The words and phrases are not changed into graphics, but are set out in three-dimensional trees and other structures so that you can almost literally move into the text and explore it physically, just as scientists are using virtual reality to be able to move around inside models of molecular structures, notably the DNA helix, to understand them better.

Hypertext links take on a new substance and usefulness when this third dimension opens, becoming far more dynamic when they break away from the paper metaphors of one two-dimensional page leading sequentially to another. Developments in artificial intelligence, working with linked and embedded computer-created objects and other information-processing technology, will let you create and use words in ways that you cannot even conceive of now.

On-line and CD-ROM text databases are already becoming so huge that established methods of using them are breaking down. We can only go so far in refining better and faster ways of searching for specific information. The next phase (which is already here) involves computers that help create relationships between you, your documents, and the information they contain, consequently making documents really give up their information. Such computers learn quickly as you begin a search on what information you are really seeking. They interpret, rather than just slavishly follow, the keywords and other search parameters that you provide.

When you enter these large text resources, you might not even know what you really want among all the riches there. But the computer will note, as you grope around, what you accept and reject, alternately enlarging and then refining your searches, making suggestions, and steadily guiding you to the knowledge you seek.

Words must be published electronically to exploit these developments, which represent a quantum leap in the power of the written word to influence our cultural, as well as technological, evolution. Consequently, for those who love words, literature, and the wonders of the human mind, the prospect of electronic publishing replacing much of print publishing is not a doomsday scenario, but one offering marvelous new creative and cultural opportunities.

Crashing through linguistic barriers

Another of many culturally important developments made possible by electronic publishing is the way it is starting to demolish linguistic barriers. One of my previous books has just been published in Japan in a long, complicated, and ridiculously expensive process. However,

as I write these words, the UPS delivery truck arrived; the driver handed me, in a small brown package, software offering almost everything I need to produce an electronic version of this and any future books in Kanji, Hiragana, and Katakana (the various Japanese writing systems). Not only can it save months of work and thousands of dollars, it creates publishing opportunities in other languages that never existed before. Later in this book, you will see how easy and practical it is now to publish directly from a modest desktop to the furthest corners of the global marketplace.

All this does not mean the end of conventional books, those attractive, indeed sensuous, objects that impart knowledge and take us on the most exotic adventures. Books, wonderful books, will always be with us, but now they are joined by other exciting additions to the publishing spectrum. Existing printed works, and a veritable avalanche of new titles, are now available in more flexible, economical, and practical forms. Usually they will be read on computer screens— particularly the new generation of portable, pocketable information processors, the handheld *personal digital assistants* (PDAs) that are about to become almost as ubiquitous as pocket calculators, and as convenient for reading as a paperback (Fig. 1-2).

Just as some books today are borrowed, and others purchased, so electronic books will be selected and used by readers as temporary disposable—or more permanent durable—consumer items. They will increasingly be read in their paperless, digitized form as society becomes more computer-conscious, but they can also be read in a more traditional manner by printing out all or part as conventional hardcopies on paper, using hardware readily available at home or in the office. The cost of the individually created hardcopy will be competitive with buying a trade paperback—usually less.

Nor need we lose all the physical and visual appeal of printed books when they are transferred to disk. The self-publishing author and the small press going into electronic media have great opportunities for creative packaging and presentation to give real-life substance to a virtual publication. Although on-line distribution of electronic publications through the Internet and other services is very important, you will see how to give the new publishing media the visual and tactile appeal to make them desirable consumer objects.

Figure 1-2

Personal digital assistants are making e-books as convenient to read as paperbacks, and much more powerful. You can carry in a pocket or handbag the contents of a whole bookcase of reference works or your favorite collections of novels. The cost is much less, and information can be located far more easily.
Sharp Electronics Corporation

⇨ Hybrid formats for books and magazines needing shelf-appeal

A particularly effective publishing format is the book-disk hybrid combination—combining some of the physical substance and point-of-sale features of a printed book, with all of the flexibility and cost-efficiency of a floppy or CD-ROM disk. These hybrids are becoming the mainstay of some authors and publishers, with the hardcopy proportion of the package decreasing as readers come to accept that the real value lies in the information on the disk. The popular book-CD combination *From Alice to Ocean* is one such work. The illustration in Fig. 1-3 is a still from the CD, showing how readers can interact with the CD or use it for teaching purposes.

These hybrids are an excellent packaging format for magazines and journals—and for many types of self-publishing also. Combining print and electronic media overcomes many marketing problems. For example, both a popular magazine from Belgium and the Indize business economic data service from Mexico use techniques well

Figure 1-3

Books and disks can make impressive combinations, as demonstrated in From Alice to Ocean, *the coffee-table book and accompanying CD about Robyn Davidson's journey by camel across the Australian Outback.*
Claris Corporation

within the reach of almost any desktop personal computer to appeal to their audiences.

Hybrids have particular appeal for academic and scientific publishing—and are the media of the future for school and college projects, theses, doctorates, and conference papers.

⇨ Powerful forces at work

The economic and environmental forces behind this revolution in written communications are very powerful. Electronic books are far, far cheaper and easier to produce and distribute than print—and they are very kind to the environment. These methods of publishing are expanding very rapidly and fast becoming a feature of everyday life, driven forward both by big-money investment and by the forces of individual entrepreneurship and creativity that are the main focus of this book.

Even the established print media can hardly contain their enthusiasm, despite the challenges they face.

"Books have made their way to your computer's screen—and people are actually reading them," said *Newsweek*, the first major news magazine to produce a CD (Fig. 1-4) in a story on electronic publishing. "Electronic books are popping up everywhere . . . . Some are already more popular than their print counterparts."

Print metaphors are being carried over to the new media as readers make the transition from print to screen. Newsweek Interactive was the first CD-ROM produced by a major news magazine, with each quarterly issue adding impressive multimedia features to three months of archival text from Newsweek *and* The Washington Post, *all searchable far more easily than the originals or microfilm archives.* Newsweek Communications

Figure 1-4

"The technology adds to the printed word a whole new dimension—interaction," said *Business Week*.

"The electronic book represents the start of a publishing revolution," declared the *Los Angeles Times*. "Reading will never be the same."

The *Washington Post* described the electronic books put out by the Voyager publishing company as being "in the vanguard of a fast-growing new field that is about to revolutionize the publishing industry."

Mac, DOS, Unix, Windows, OS/2—e-books are everywhere!

Voyager alone has developed a list of over 50 titles for the Macintosh computing environment. The DOS/Windows computing community, with over 100 million compatible systems worldwide, is expanding its electronic publishing activities at a far greater rate. Electronic publications can be created to move easily between these computing environments, and to Unix, OS/2, and other platforms. Therefore, almost everything in the following pages is relevant to you, whatever kind of system you use. Some of the authoring programs mentioned are specific to a particular platform, but many of these will soon be available in other versions.

Learning to use good authoring and publishing software is not very difficult; once pointed in the right direction, you will be off and running in no time. Actually doing it, rather than reading detailed instructions, is far more fruitful, and a lot more fun. The most important benefits you should obtain from this book are learning about the many opportunities offered by electronic publishing.

Many works are now disseminated to substantial readerships only as electronic files on floppy disks or on-line services. This book will get your creative and entrepreneurial juices flowing by examining the stories behind some of them, including previously printed books that have metamorphosed into electronic forms featuring sound, moving pictures, and other multimedia features.

Readers adapt to the new media

Electronic publishing will become more prestigious and satisfying for authors, and more acceptable to readers, as public attitudes and perceptions of computing change. This is happening already at an increasing pace. Soon, an electronic text on a floppy will be almost as acceptable as a printed one to over 200 million people around the world who have ready access to a personal computer in their homes and at work. That demographic category includes the entire target readership for many publications. Children, frequently more comfortable with computers than their parents, might come to regard electronic media as more natural than print. Already, a generation has largely abandoned newspapers.

Reference books represent an example of such changing attitudes. For generations, encyclopedia sets have been marketed with strong visual imagery of their physical bulk, emphasizing that the volumes constitute a large and valuable source of information. We have all been exposed to the advertisements, fliers, and mailings picturing shelves groaning under the weight of 20 volumes that will "enhance your home and demonstrate your investment in your children's future."

In a very few years, consumer perceptions have changed so that significant numbers of people now accept that those same values are contained in a tiny CD-ROM disk that looks the same as a music CD you can buy for as little as $5. The total sales of electronic encyclopedia on disks are approaching their first million as I write, and sales are rapidly accelerating. Even *People* magazine, the epitome of popular print publishing, launched a CD edition in 1994.

 Hardware developments

Computer hardware technology is a powerful driving force also. The Apple Newton, shown in Fig. 1-5, and a whole new generation of other practical, yet very portable personal computers, is stimulating the publishing of all kinds of electronic books, not just reference works.

Figure 1-5

Powerful economic forces—including some of the biggest corporations in print and entertainment media—are driving electronic publishing forward. Some of the top titles are appropriate for release in even the smallest electronic media, as illustrated here by topical business information on the hand-held Apple Newton. Apple Computer, Inc.

The situation is similar to what happened following the introduction of early personal computers into the business and consumer markets. These computers were at first regarded as having limited usefulness for most people, mainly operating specific software—spreadsheets, databases, and word processors—for particular tasks. But human creativity generated a wide range of software applications, enabling the personal computer to evolve into a multipurpose machine that launched a revolution in all forms of information processing and communications.

Similarly, the software—with all kinds of electronic literature as a major player—will power the success of the hand-held PDAs comprising this new wave of hardware. The multibillion-dollar global enterprise that is driving hardware development must stimulate, as well as benefit from, an explosion in electronic publishing from the desktops of thousands of individual authors. The two go hand-in-hand, like the ubiquitous audiocassette tape and Walkman tape player.

To help those of us not fully computer literate, the book metaphor is being carried over into the new PDAs, since it is so familiar to those for whom keyboarding and on-screen cues to interfacing are alien. Computing is changing to become a mass medium, and moving information from print to virtual electronic forms becomes not so much revolutionary, as evolutionary.

For example, AT&T's EO hand-held computer is a very high-tech device, but still reflects its paper ancestors by presenting itself as a notebook, with table of contents and tabs like file dividers. You can write into it and read electronic publications from it by just tapping on the screen, to use it as easily as physically turning pages. Right in your hand you have a device that works like a book, but also has a stubby aerial providing you with a gateway to the Internet (Fig. 1-6) and other on-line services—without the need even to plug into an electrical or telephone socket. With the developments taking place in satellite radio links and the cable "information highways," such PDA devices carry with them substantial amounts of published material, and are always within reach of some of the world's best libraries and publishers when you want to download more.

Create your own books and other publications

This quick introduction to a vast new field of human activity, demonstrates that you cannot ignore electronic publishing if your business, professional, or leisure interests concern words, pictures, and information. It is real, here, now—and very exciting. Everyone who can read can use and enjoy the publications becoming available on disk—and those of us who write can become more actively involved as publishers.

Figure 1-6

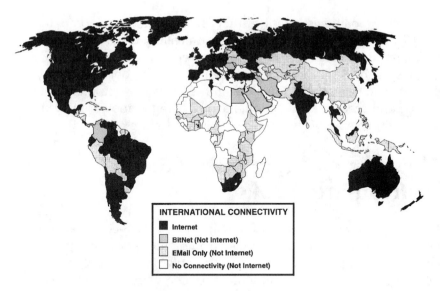

INTERNATIONAL CONNECTIVITY
- Internet
- BitNet (Not Internet)
- EMail Only (Not Internet)
- No Connectivity (Not Internet)

One of the main reasons that electronic publishing has become viable is the growth of The Internet, an informal global network for digital communications. Between 15 and 30 million people were believed to be using "The Net" in 1994, and it now reaches around the English-speaking world and into all industrialized nations.
©1993 Larry Landweber and the Internet Society.

⇨ Writers become publishers

Anyone with a PC can now create and publish electronically to high professional standards, using very affordable software and hardware. Examples of some of the best programs are described in this book, or included on the accompanying disk. They enable anyone who can create text on a computer to compile their manuscripts into easy-to-use on-disk presentations that can include such features as hypertext, graphics, and executable programs.

Distribution, packaging where appropriate, and marketing are also covered in the following pages to help you participate in other major electronic publishing functions. You will learn the resources available now to liberate writers from the frustrations and inhibiting aspects of the traditional book- and periodical-publishing business.

The really good news is that, if their content matter is competently put together and meets a need, electronically self-publishing authors can generate revenue, advance their careers, promote their businesses, or achieve whatever other publishing objectives they seek without purchasing additional outside services or equipment. Authors, artists, and other creative people are all being empowered by this new technology in ways never conceivable before.

New ways of marketing and distributing books

Creativity and enterprise will flourish in this new medium—but it is not all good news. The ease of electronic publication brings challenges and problems also. It solves only one of the three main difficulties of authorship, "to write anything worth the authorship, to find honest men to publish it, and to get sensible men to read it," defined by the 19th century English writer C.C. Colton.

Self-publishing authors will encounter increasing competition for the attention of readers, so they must be even more certain that what they write is worth reading. Writers are being challenged also to adapt to radically different methods for the production, marketing, and distribution of their intellectual property, with the problem of appropriate pay for their work not yet resolved.

How do we get paid?

Receiving payments for works distributed electronically is a particularly difficult issue, discussed in detail later in this book. There must be new incentives for the end users—the readers—to pay, and for authors to be rewarded. The existing financial systems for print often do not work well for authors, and individual creative talent might fare even worse in the electronic media, where ease of copying is an inherent feature of the technology.

Consequently, the author of electronic books might have to accept, as thousands of shareware software program authors have done already, that most of those readers who benefit from your electronically

published work will never pay you a penny for your efforts. For example, we are already seeing developments such as the on-line library bulletin boards that offer "all you can read for $5 a month." Electronic texts are copied and circulated through rapidly expanding formal and informal networks, which authors and publishers cannot monitor or control as they do the conventional book trade and public libraries.

⇨ New ways of selling

The publishers of nonfiction reference works must depend increasingly for their revenues on "the second sale," as is the case now for many software publishers. They may give away, or heavily discount, their titles to generate a loyal base of subscribers who will pay to lock into an update or new edition service.

The authors and publishers of fiction—together with most other nonfiction categories—who cannot adopt these "second sale" marketing policies will need to be very imaginative in how they generate revenues. They might need legislative and financial assistance similar to the Public Lending Rights concepts that operate successfully in European countries.

One encouraging development is in electronic catalogs, distributed free, in which a summary of your book can entice a reader to decide to buy it with just a telephone call, paying by credit card for a code that unlocks your text and pictures. If you have created a worthwhile reference work, that might be only the first of many payments you receive from that same reader, who may buy your book a piece at a time as he or she needs particular information from it.

If your publishing motives do not include generating income, electronic publishing has enormous appeal with very few disadvantages. Most of us need a financial return for our efforts, however—hopefully a better one than the majority of writers obtain from a traditional publishing industry notorious for the way it treats the suppliers of its raw material. Rewarding authors remains one of the biggest challenges for electronic publishing, but you will find in these pages that there is good news in this respect also.

Quality still counts

There are bound to be quality-control problems in such an easily accessed and open media as electronic publishing, where self-publishing writers are free to downplay the editing function. Editors have always tended to be maligned by writers. American author Elbert Hubbard got a lot of sympathy from his fellow writers when he defined an editor as "a person employed on a newspaper, whose business is to separate the wheat from the chaff, and to see that the chaff gets printed."

He was wrong. Editors have always protected readers from an awful lot of rubbish that authors sought to impose on them, as well as disciplining writers worthy of publication into honing their work to higher standards. You need to have been an editor to comprehend also how they have protected readers from the carelessness with grammar, spelling, and accuracy displayed by even some of the best-known literary names.

Books with inferior writing or content don't deserve to be published in any format, but we will be exposed to lots of them from electronic sources where there are no active editors to filter them out. Consequently, authors will need to display more self-discipline.

Readers might download your book by telephone, or get a copy on disk for a nominal duplication fee, but they won't spend much time on it if it does not deliver acceptable standards. Readers will be helped to be selective as more electronic books are reviewed by qualified critics, but there will always be a need for writers to be very conscious of quality standards if the new media are not to be swamped by chaff, and worthy work lost among the rubbish.

Catering for minority interests and niche markets

Despite these problems, electronic publishing must, on balance, be good news for everybody. Among those who will benefit most are

authors who have not been able to release worthwhile works of specialist or minority appeal because of the cost structures of conventional publishing and distribution. Now they will find many of their problems solved, and new opportunities for their enterprise created, particularly by exploiting database marketing techniques to reach niche markets.

For those who adapt to the changing times, publishing can become much more adventurous and fun with the availability of electronic media. The formats for electronic books are becoming even more varied than those of the paperbacks and hardcover volumes in different shapes, colors, and bindings that line today's bookstore or library shelves.

You will use your hand-held portable computer to read the electronic equivalent of a paperback novel or self-help book, with the pages entirely text, or with some simple line drawings or diagrams if appropriate. But there will also be lavish, full-color productions—books that are really multimedia programs incorporating such features as animated and live-action video, graphics, and advanced audio, such as the example in Fig. 1-7. A new generation of authors and publishers capable of producing these sophisticated electronic publications is being educated now, as illustrated by IBM experiencing a strong demand from schools for its advanced, and expensive, multimedia publishing system.

⇨ Multimedia in perspective

The overwhelming majority of the books sold after centuries of book publishing are physically very basic—black text in a few popular fonts printed onto sheets of cheap white paper stapled, stitched, or glued together. Similarly, despite all the hype, complex multimedia works are unlikely to dominate electronic publishing because of the computing and personal resources they require, their cost to produce, the large size of the computer files required, and the hardware needed to play these complex files satisfactorily. Most books on disk do not need lots of color, graphics, sound, or other multimedia features, although many will benefit from some of these features, and

Figure 1-7

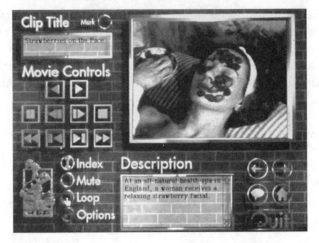

The range of electronic publications is already enormous. Many of the multimedia titles reflect creative collections of archival video and movie clips and still images. This is a shot from MPI Multimedia's entertaining Wild, Weird & Wacky CD-ROM. MPI Multimedia

incorporating color and graphics need add nothing to production costs.

There is an enormous pent-up demand to publish information that can be conveyed satisfactorily just as text. Read any of the magazines for writers and you get just a sampling of the burning desire by so many writers to be published. Consequently, self-publishing on disk will expand to satisfy the needs of thousands of writers, irrespective of the demand or lack of it from their readers. As is the case with some print publishing of poetry, writers will still publish to other writers if their work does not find a general market.

The amateur novelist will seize these new opportunities to break through the publishing logjam and get his or her work duplicated and distributed in the hope that it will succeed on its own merits. Nonfiction authors will exploit the ease with which they themselves can add graphic illustrations such as charts, graphs, diagrams, or line drawings to augment their texts. Many writers of nonfiction will be motivated to publish on disk because they know their niche markets

well and can cost-effectively target books on disk to their readers in ways just not practical or affordable for printed works.

⇨ The death of the rejection slip

It is so fast and easy to get the computer to turn a manuscript into a book on a disk that we will see a boom in such schemes as the electronic publisher who recently promised "the death of the rejection slip." He invited authors to send their written work as straight text files on disk, which he would convert into a properly formatted book on disk. If the publisher thought it of high-enough quality, or with sufficient potential readers, the title would be listed in his catalog and distributed on a royalty basis.

In this scheme, even if your works were "rejected" for commercial distribution, your creative effort would not automatically die. The publisher returns your disk with the formatted book on it in a finished form, professional title screens, chapters, and an index, that you can copy as required and distribute at minimum cost. Although not accepted for commercial distribution, you might still be able to make your book a financial success through your own knowledge of the market for your work and the effort you can put into promoting to that market.

Much of the frustration, heartache, and disappointment in writing of all kinds will be eased by the fact that electronic self-publishing offers an alternative to the very long odds of your work being accepted by a commercial publisher, broadcaster, or theatrical producer. Even now, print publishing's rejection slip is not the end of the publishing road, as demonstrated by the author of Star Trek scripts rejected by Paramount who has released them via bulletin boards to get reactions from his fellow Trekkers.

Self-help and self-improvement books are just one field in which authors will release their manuscripts on disk—either before publication to get advance input from others with relevant experiences, or to share their words and boost their prestige after their manuscript has been rejected by commercial publishers.

Scientific and academic publishing transformed

A scientist who needs to publish to advance his or her career, but is frustrated by the restrictions and overload of the scientific and academic publishing system, can now circulate up-to-date copies of research electronically more efficiently and cheaply than through established journals. Internet and other communications networks and bulletin boards already link millions of scientists and academics around the world. The distribution channels are in place to disseminate technical, scientific, and academic publications of various kinds. There are specialist writers and researchers who have even started their own bulletin boards to disseminate and enhance their work.

Increasingly, researchers, academics, and others who write to further professional interests or careers will package the files for downloading by their peers, colleagues, and critics into more sophisticated electronic book form. These will come complete with hypertext facilities and a wealth of cross-references, sources, and executable code to extend the written word into computerized demonstrations or presentations. Such works not only present their authors as impressively as possible, but can transform publications into practical working tools. For example, I am preparing an electronic book including the code-breaking programs that Penn Leary used to research the printed book he wrote about Francis Bacon being the true author of Shakespeare's plays. Academics will be able to evaluate this research better—and pursue it themselves—in ways impossible from Penn's original print publication.

I have just edited another text to be released electronically that will make available to thousands of medical professionals the findings of important new research on nitrous oxide gas therapy for recovering alcoholics and patients with drug dependencies. Although my author friend Dr. Mark Gillman has gained over 200 print publications in scientific journals, much of his work falls between the parameters set by individual highly specialized print publications, so electronic media enabled him to share his important findings with a large global audience with a definite need to know about it.

 # Separating substance from hype

Of course, the ability for researchers to publish so easily poses
dangers and problems in a world where getting in first and offering
quick-fix solutions are such great temptations. It will be more difficult
to differentiate substance from hype and reality from illusion in
research papers presented on disk or on-line.

The freer flow of research information made possible by electronic
publishing could bring greater benefits than the risks, however. In any
case, there must be alternatives to the present peer-review and
editorial selection processes. As you will see later, just one area of
research, the international Human Genome Project, is generating so
much material so fast that print simply cannot cope with it anymore.

 # Business, politics, and poets

Poets, politicians, and those who write to meet various professional
or business objectives are among the seemingly unlikely bedfellows
who will find that taking the electronic route offers previously
undreamed-of opportunities to be published. For example, the prime
motivation for many poets is to share their words rather than sell
them to generate income. Now they can do so on disk at minimal
cost and free themselves from the expensive and unsatisfactory
practices of vanity publishers.

Publishing a book can also be very effective in advancing a career or
achieving a political or business objective. The Clinton presidential
campaign used electronic publishing to advance its cause in ways that
will be widely applied in future elections.

If you are in business, you might be forced to become involved with
electronic publishing sooner or later, even if its possibilities do not
excite you now. Much of the business community has no choice but
to move from paper to electronic media now that the U.S. and
European governments are compelling their suppliers to produce
manuals and other documentation in electronic formats. As the
majority of internal corporate correspondence moves to electronic

mail by the mid-1990s, so the bulk of the business community's internal and external documentation will become digitized to reduce costs, increase efficiency, and cater for the growing demand by end-users to get their information in this more digestible and easily handled form.

 # Breaking the physical barriers of print

Once it moves off paper, information of all kinds displays a remarkable ability to become more dynamic. A company might start with straightforward document imaging for archival purposes, then move rapidly to exploit the far greater opportunities for cost savings and increased efficiency. An author who simply transfers a word-processed manuscript into a file that mimics a book is soon tempted to add hypertext, sound, or illustrations, using tools like TextArt in WordPerfect for Windows (Fig. 1-8). For several years I wrote a pulpy

Figure 1-8

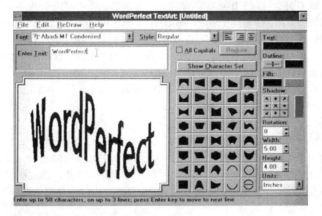

Word processing software now offers many sophisticated text- and image-manipulation features that can be fully exploited in the electronic media—and used to generate attractive printed packaging, also. Here, for example, is the text manipulation feature TextArt from WordPerfect for Windows. WordPerfect Corporation

romantic serial, and it would be fun to go back and add the sound effects of deep breathing, a trickling stream, and perhaps closing video clips of the sunsets into which my heroes and heroines walked hand-in-hand!

All the many new electronic publishing options—from the $10,000 IBM multimedia school system to $30 shareware running on an aging PC picked up in a yard sale—can break through the physical boundaries of the printed page to communicate more effectively. Graphics in color that enlarge a perspective or help to explain or entertain, audio samples and effects that add a sound dimension to pictures and written words, easy cross-referencing and footnotes through which you can take hypertext leaps into an author's original sources are just some of the options available already. This is not a look into the future. Electronic publishing is here and now.

Books that enlarge and talk

The giant Sony Corporation, which made an investment greater than the defense budgets of some nations so that it could get a headstart into electronic publishing, released a disk version of Ira Levin's novel *Sliver* that ends the reader's problems of tired eyes or failing light. When you no longer want to read the text, you can switch to the audio version on the same disk and have the book read aloud to you. Individual self-publishers are able to offer readers that facility also.

The handicapped and the elderly

Fiction and nonfiction works on disks are a boon to the visually handicapped and to the elderly—the latter being the fastest growing consumer group with particular needs that only electronic publishing can satisfy. The public library services on which so many senior citizens and others rely are in rapid decline because of the high cost of acquiring, storing, and handling print. Libraries can obtain and offer readers a much larger inventory of electronic books adaptable to aging eyes at far less cost than they can printed works that are bulky, expensive, easily stolen, and deteriorate rapidly.

When demand for a title exceeds the copies available, the library can create another copy in seconds, in large print if that's the way the reader needs it. Readers with their own hand-held computers who find ordinary-sized print difficult to read can just press a button and the electronic text doubles, triples, or quadruples in size.

Electronic books are a blessing to the visually handicapped because every book published in electronic form becomes accessible to the blind. Computers can convert almost any computerized text into talking books—at rapidly reducing cost and increasing efficiency. Authors benefit also. Audio books are one of the expanding areas of publishing, and the electronic book on disk is over half-way into this other medium. Also, you don't have to turn the pages of an electronic book—and such a simple reading task is difficult, painful, or impossible for millions of people.

Limitless opportunities

The variety of subjects for electronic publishing is virtually limitless. The categories available already extend from contemporary popular literature back to the classics. The million words in Shakespeare's plays and poetry are generating some of the most popular electronic publishing titles, giving a new high-tech dimension to *Life* magazine's comment, "Each new generation returns to Shakespeare to try to find, like any other whodunit reader, the truth within those wonderful words."

The Hypertext Hamlet available on floppies is not a gimmicky exploitation of a perennial favorite, but demonstrates how electronic publishing can make great literature more accessible and enriched by background information, comment, and sources for further information. Among the many searchers after literary truth who are tapping into electronic publishing's vast potential are the university researchers in California who can analyze, in ways never possible before, the disputed authorship of Elizabethan works, and probe into the mysteries of the Renaissance Golden Age of Literature.

A lawyer in Nebraska, an investigative journalist in Mexico, a schoolteacher in Singapore reflect the enormous range of

personalities and intellects being applied anew to Shakespeare, and able to benefit from him being electronically published on disk.

Sherlock Holmes is enjoying a similar revival in electronic books—he even has a bulletin board to himself. The medium is also generating new works unique to itself that can spread through the publishing/broadcasting environment, like the phenomenally successful Carmen San Diego series that has crossed from the computer to the television screen, and back again.

⇨ Xanadu comes closer

A short distance from San Francisco's Golden Gate Bridge, the father of hypertext works towards making electronic publishing's Xanadu a reality. Ted Nelson, who introduced me to this fascinating field, has developed a realistic business plan with, as its ultimate objective, putting all of the world's published literature into computer databases. In the near future, we may be able to walk into an electronic publishing outlet and order up a title, plus its associated source material, almost as easily as you can stroll into a McDonald's and get a hamburger. Just as you can custom-build a cassette tape of your favorite music, you will be able to shop on-line at an electronic bookstore and download onto floppy disks a bundle of fiction or nonfiction works to help on a research project, for school studies, or to take on vacation.

If Ted Nelson's Xanadu project succeeds, its best feature for authors will be that it contains an automatic royalty credit system. When anyone accesses your book, the computer pays a royalty into your account.

Books that are now just "a good read" will acquire additional dimensions to entertain, educate, and inform. Publishers who see the potential of the new electronic media will augment high-tech novels like Tom Clancy's *The Hunt for Red October* with maps, blueprints of the missiles and atomic submarines, and audio "telephone taps" and other material with which the reader can explore and participate. Electronic publishing can enable readers to move much closer to the author, even to share in the creative process, if that is what they and

the authors wish. Significant numbers of fiction authors are now meeting on-line with their readers, not just to promote their books but to get constructive feedback on already published works and suggestions for future titles.

⇨ Realizing writer's dreams

One of the best shareware programs with which to compile electronic books is named, appropriately, Writer's Dream, because it delivers on the dream of many writers who despair of ever being published in print. Just "being published," though, is only the first of Writers' Dreams becoming reality with electronic publishing. There is other software available enabling you to control the whole creative, production, and distribution processes. You can expand the horizons of your work both creatively and financially.

"The personal computer is becoming a liberating, creative tool," says an author on the creative frontier, Doug Millison. Jeff Napier, creator of the Writer's Dream book-compiling program, agrees. He sees the most dramatic and exciting aspect of electronic publishing to be the way it empowers authors with specialized knowledge or creative imaginations to disseminate their work to the widest possible audience. The opportunities—the right—to publish can no longer be denied.

The tools that the technology and the skills of programmers such as Jeff Napier and Ted Husted (the creator of the award-winning Dart electronic book compiler on your disk) are providing to empower authors are being used in some fascinating ways. The celebrated cyberpunk author William Gibson produced an electronic book titled *Agrippa* that can be run and read only once on a computer. Then it self-destructs into encrypted code. Because of its unique features, collectors paid as much as $1,500 a copy for *Agrippa* "first editions," a most unusual example of the potential for successful entrepreneurial self-publishing. Fans of this peer figure of hacker mythology immediately set about cracking his book's self-destruct encryption code. Gibson expects them to succeed and then release his text and their solutions to its coding mystery over thousands of bulletin boards—"and that will be a pretty interesting way to be published too," he comments.

Cooperative writing

The term *electronic book* is not new—it was first coined over 25 years ago by the distinguished software engineer Andries van Dam at Brown University to describe documents created and read through a computer. It has taken the intervening two decades, however, for electronic publishing to blossom into a universal medium. We have first had to go through a phase when personal computers were used to create hardcopy paper documents. Only now are they really starting to break out of these traditional restraints, to stop imitating paper media, and communicate to maximum effect in their own uniquely flexible and dynamic electronic medium.

One result is the now-frequent publication of texts that are always changing as both the original authors and their readers contribute to them. That is a prime business need, as you will see in the next chapter on how electronic publishing is transforming the way authors work. It can be fun also. A popular activity on bulletin boards has been the co-authoring of fictional electronic books. People take turns coming on-line to develop the plot, introduce or manipulate characters, and then hand the literary baton to another. Some of the results are fascinating examples of a literary collaboration that has never been possible before.

The concept of constantly evolving texts has been developed furthest and fastest in the business community, where electronic publishing is having a major cultural and economic impact. Every kind of corporate document, from the technical manuals for servicing a jumbo jet to the employee handbooks detailing medical benefits, can be compiled as true team efforts and then continually modified by new input, experience, and changing circumstances.

In the business world, electronic knowledge sharing, text processing, and publishing are creating what Raymond Cote and Stanford Diel, testing editors of *Byte* magazine's laboratory, described as "living knowledge." This is a new form of corporate "storytelling" as important to the evolution of business cultures as traditional storytelling has been to the development of human society's thinking processes and beliefs.

"This living knowledge emerges as people share their perspectives and defuse their collective prejudices, blind spots, and unfounded assumptions," the two editors maintain.

Most of this corporate storytelling and exchange of living knowledge takes place through local networks and electronic mail systems that vary widely. For more formal publishing, industry and governments created the *SGML* (Standard Generalized Markup Language) in 1986 as the international standard for electronic publishing through which documents can be exchanged. In much electronic publishing for business purposes, it will be essential to conform to this standard, so detailed information about it is presented later in this book.

Easy, economical publishing

There are also other easier, and more economical, ways to publish electronically simply by exploiting the universal personal computer operating systems, DOS and (to a lesser extent) the Macintosh. By using basic ASCII text, perhaps enhanced by file management software such as List, or easy-to-use publication formatting programs such as Writer's Dream or Illustrated Reader (Fig. 1-9), you can produce a book or journal on disk that is readily accessible by anyone with a PC or Mac.

More advanced electronic books—but still easy for authors to create and readers to use—feature sophisticated hypertext links. They can be compiled by programs such as Dart and Orpheus. Some programs, such as Storymaker, are particularly appropriate for younger readers. Other programs enable you to easily create magazines and newsletters on disk, write and publish poetry, or even create games, another valid electronic self-publishing medium.

The latest versions of almost all of these shareware authoring programs now do a good job of displaying graphics and running other programs, so that electronic books on disk can be enhanced visually and aurally with the animation, sound effects, and other features found in expensive commercial multimedia publications on CD-ROM.

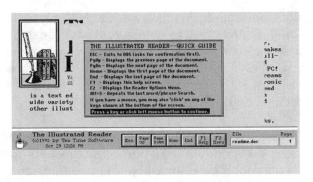

Figure 1-9

*Some of the most interesting electronic
publishing action is from the desktops of
individual authors using programs that will run
on basic PC systems. This screen is from* The
Illustrated Reader, *a shareware authoring
program that effectively blends pictures and text
into attractive screen combinations. These self-
published e-books can be distributed efficiently
and very cheaply by modem or on floppy disks.*
Tea Time Software

Thanks to higher density disks and file compression programs, large
texts or ambitious multimedia works can be self-published on a single
floppy. These multimedia books can feature graphics, sound, or
animation, or interactive programs such as tutorials. They can be
"read" on virtually any other personal computer without the need for
a CD drive by circulating, along with your publication, a run-time
playback module. The whole package unzips onto a hard drive from
which it can run faster and more smoothly than some CD-ROM
productions. Even the creating, mastering, and duplication of CDs is
now coming within the reach of a small business or an individual
author's desktop and bank balance. Consequently, this medium is
given appropriate attention in the following pages.

➪ **Future trends**

For a long time to come, the future of universal electronic publishing
will be linked to the average PC and Macintosh environments—

especially in their portable forms. We will see in the next few years a rapid growth of electronic devices compatible with those desktop standards, but about the size of a standard paperback book. Sony's Bookman shows what is possible, although, like the early personal computers, this particular hardware was a pioneer handicapped by lack of compatibility and high price.

There will be a continued rapid growth of electronic publishing on CD-ROM disks, but it is not yet the appropriate medium for most self-publishing, and may soon be eclipsed by the growth of on-line publishing opportunities as the information highways stretch into more homes and offices. Although it is now possible to create a master CD-ROM and duplicate it for substantially less than some conventionally printed books—under $2 each in quantity—the hardware to do this is still expensive, at around $3,000 for a basic system. Also, most independent publishing projects do not contain enough text or graphics to justify the enormous storage capacity of a CD—you can compress the files and put them onto one or two floppies which users can decompress to their hard disks.

Consequently, electronic books on CD-ROM will continue to be dominated for several years by commercial publishers with big budgets. Anyway, CD-ROM books can be read only by the minority of computer users who have the right playback hardware, which limits their potential readership considerably. CDs risk being leapfrogged in technology by both on-line services and *smart cards*, those miniaturized electronic devices the size of credit cards already displaying enormous potential for electronic publishing to the users of portable computers.

The floppy disk or the modem link remain the electronic publishing mass media of the present and the immediate future. They are cheap, universal, and readily accessible to both authors and readers. The floppy and the telephone lines are where you can take your first adventures in electronic publishing at minimum cost and to maximum effect.

"Electronic publishing is in its infancy, and radical developments can be expected in the next few years," says one of the leading pioneers in the medium, John Galuszka of Serendipity Systems. John forecasts

parallel development of the two main distribution channels—on-line and in "hard" electronic format on floppies, CD-ROMs, and the smart cards that could become the main medium in the second half of this decade.

Nothing is certain, but that need not deter you. Once you start creating your work in electronic, digital form, it will always be comparatively easy to develop and convert it to take full advantage of new opportunities as they arise.

The technology is fascinating, the cultural implications make it a great adventure. Let's get started!

Turn your work into multimedia

IF you intend to publish electronically, you now have no choice but to at least consider using multimedia. I would not have been so dogmatic about this just a year ago, but the economic and creative forces driving multimedia publishing forward have now become too strong to ignore.

Perhaps more significant than all the publicity that commercial interactive multimedia CD-ROM titles have been getting is that the on-line services have been gearing up to handle sound, video, and interactivity also. This will give an enormous boost to the grassroots creation of multimedia works by individual authors, artists, photographers, and other creative talents. Most of these individuals need to self-publish in the new media because of problems getting their works taken up by major publishers that mirror those being experienced in print.

The intellectual property rights issue (explored in depth in chapter 8) is another important factor that might force much of this individual creative effort to be circulated on-line rather than prettily packaged and marketed through retail outlets. Creating a title in multimedia can involve bringing in—and probably modifying—music, sound effects, and visuals. It can become an impossible task to track down which material might be in the public domain, who owns the rights, what permissions are needed, and then negotiating realistic fees to secure those permissions. Multimedia offers enormous creative and publishing opportunities, but it is also a legal minefield.

⇨ Growing fast

The expansion that is taking place in the market for multimedia materials is too big for you to ignore if any of your income comes from publishing. Over six million CD-ROM drives—the hardware that is the core of much multimedia publishing—are expected to be sold during 1994, and by the end of the decade we can expect around 50 million drives to be installed in personal computers, with probably many more than that in multimedia consumer devices of various kinds linked to television sets.

CD-ROMs are proving physically very acceptable and attractive to consumers, and have a high perceived value. Thanks largely to junk mail, printed material that might actually have cost more to produce than a CD is perceived by the consumer as having less value. Even older people with a lifetime of inhibitions about marking or tearing sections out of printed books and magazines are now junking and mutilating their hardcopy reading materials. In any library, bookstore, or flea market you will see how rapidly books depreciate, with clean volumes originally costing over $20 going for a dollar or less.

A CD-ROM, still in its novelty phase, is perceived as a premium durable product irrespective of its actual manufacturing cost. This can enhance the marketable value of its contents, offering authors and other creative people opportunities to generate additional income that might not be available to them in print.

These same factors make CD-ROMs powerful promotional tools for books, particularly those that are published electronically and can be incorporated in catalogs on disk from which they can be downloaded directly by telephone credit card order for the unlocking code. Surveys have shown that over 75 percent of new computer users are likely to spend a considerable amount of time browsing through a free CD-ROM software catalog, with perhaps a third actually making purchases from it.

What is multimedia?

Multimedia has ceased to be a precise term, and there are ongoing industry pressures to enforce its usage only in relationship to quite sophisticated publications. There are similar problems in defining *interactive multimedia*, because the degree to which readers are able to interact can vary so widely. To avoid confusion, multimedia in this book means any electronic publication that adds to text built-in features not found in traditional print. That's fair, because there is a precedent in the clear distinction between silent and talking movies, irrespective of the quality and complexity of the soundtrack or the picture. Plain text is the equivalent of the silent movie, while multimedia is like the talkie, no matter whether the movie is a small-

screen black-and-white production or a wide-screen color spectacular with advanced stereo sound.

Interactive multimedia refers to multimedia publications like the one shown in Fig. 2-1 that offer the reader the opportunity to actively participate and, to some degree, control the way that the publication performs, and not be just a passive observer of the words and pictures. Multimedia publications blend computer files, text, audio, and visual material in different combinations to create a publication or presentation that can be played back on a computer's monitor and speakers, or directly to a television set.

Figure 2-1

Interactive multimedia publications enable information to become dynamic. Text can be extended with sound and pictures through hypertext and other techniques, as demonstrated in this screen from The Archives of History. MPI Multimedia

The changing role of the writer

Writers need to move quickly to establish their roles as innovators in multimedia because we face far more direct competition from other creative people than we have in print. Authors might feel very underprivileged in their earning capacities in print, but our craft has enabled us to enjoy a special role in society. Even writers of somewhat questionable literary skills have been able to leverage this into lucrative academic positions, speaking engagements, and other secondary activities. Even an impoverished author with no profitable publishing successes tends to be more highly regarded in our money-conscious society than a blue-collar worker earning three times as much.

These perceptions could change as multimedia becomes more powerful than print, directly affecting the almost mythical status of the author and the aura surrounding writing in our culture. Inevitably, as information and original thought disseminate more widely and diffusely, they tend to become more and more isolated from their authorship sources. Fictional works in multimedia are affected also because they tend to be more collaborative and interactive, with coauthors, artists, programmers, and even readers participating in the creative process.

While these developments might seem to be threats to writers, the opportunities for writers to produce and sell should increase because of an explosion in demand for material to fuel the new media, similar but far bigger in scale to what followed the availability of cheap paper and movable type during the Renaissance. Nearly every production, presentation, or publication still originates with words on paper, expressing the creative concepts that writers are so well-equipped to capture in a tangible form. Right through the development process, words continue to define and be the vehicle to move multimedia projects forward, so there are essential roles that only proficient, imaginative, creative writers will be able to play.

 # Musicians and artists become authors also

We are already experiencing how artists and musicians can become authors in multimedia. Pop stars Peter Gabriel and David Bowie were among the first to demonstrate this with their pioneering CD-ROM discs. Gabriel's "Xplora" was the first interactive music video disc for the Macintosh, demonstrating how interactive multimedia publishing can bring performing artists and their audiences closer together.

Peter Gabriel researched the project in on-line discussions over the Prodigy service, then combined on disc the performances and supplementary multimedia information about eleven of his songs. The viewers/listeners/readers are guided by Gabriel through such activities as recording sessions at studios in England. They can even participate in the audio mixing process, and join in playing various instruments simply by clicking their mouse buttons.

Bowie's 1994 CD-ROM release "Jump They Say" allows fans to edit a video from his new album and participate in the music. Sega, the games publisher, and other musicians are creating CD-ROM releases that allow varying degrees of audience participation. Nobody knows yet how far this new use of the electronic media will go, but it is reasonable to expect that audiences will become more and more participative until they become performers themselves—a kind of karaoke that blends the media with the end-users so that each time one of these publications is opened it provides a unique experience.

These musicians demonstrate how writers, artists, and photographers can use similar techniques to create new publishing and marketing dimensions for their works. To do this effectively requires writing skills. Again, the perceived threat to the written word also yields new opportunities for writers prepared to grasp them.

Even plain text needs attractive packaging

If you are distributing fiction or a serious reference work containing only text to an audience with a definite need to know your information, your content might be strong enough to stand on its own without any multimedia trimmings. After all, some of the most important scientific and academic publishing in print succeeds despite ignoring basic principles of clarity and graphic design!

However, as a rule, almost *every* electronic publication benefits from at least modest multimedia features. At the least, it needs to be packaged attractively to enhance its chances of being noticed among all the other information clamoring for attention. You can easily, and without increasing the size of your files too much, add the equivalent of an attractive dust jacket or title page to your electronic book, as shown in Fig. 2-2. Software on the enclosed disk enables you to do this on basic PCs, so your multimedia opportunities are already within easy reach.

Extending your creativity into multimedia productions is made very easy with easy-to-use authoring software. This screen from the SST-Super Show & Tell program enables visuals to be sorted into sequence as an author would assemble and caption slides for a conventional book or feature article.
Ask Me Multimedia Center

Figure 2-2

Most subjects that have traditionally been tackled in books with little or no graphical illustration can gain new dimensions and extend their marketability if the words are enhanced with multimedia features. These need not be the elaborate visuals and sound effects becoming commonplace in mass-marketed games or CD-ROM titles. Add basic

search facilities, a little animation to your graphics, or just a few snippets of sound, and your title can be promoted as multimedia, having considerably increased perceived value compared to one that is just in plain text.

If you read the typical computing magazine—both editorial and advertisements—you will get the impression that you need powerful hardware and software to attempt multimedia publishing. That is just as untrue as claiming that you need a Porsche to get you to and from work. Nor do you need to know all the latest technological buzzwords or have any programming knowledge. You can add graphics—and even animate them—easily and economically using low-cost draw, paint, publishing, or presentation commercial or shareware programs. There are also many shareware programs that let you construct interactive tutorials without the need for programming knowledge. Turning a text manuscript into an interactive quiz takes some additional writing effort, but the software to do the job need not be any more difficult to use than a word processor.

Selecting authoring software

There are now over a thousand software programs available for use in multimedia authoring. If you have an older, less powerful system, you might do best to look at some of the shareware options available on a "try before you buy" basis. They tend to be less demanding in their system requirements. You can obtain them on-line, by mail through shareware distributors, or for under $5 a disk from the shareware retailers appearing in shopping malls everywhere.

The computer magazines hardly ever mention these shareware offerings, but programs such as Jeff Napier's MultiMedia Workshop and Orlando Dare's MultiMedia Maker should not be regarded as second-string products just because they do not have substantial corporations behind them and are not sold in pretty boxes. The best of these shareware programs reflect years of personal effort by dedicated authors. They are particularly appropriate if you want to publish on single self-contained floppies, or on-line in relatively small files that almost any system will run satisfactorily.

This approach opens up many publishing opportunities just not practical for more complex productions that must be distributed on a CD-ROM or as a handful of floppies. Among Orlando Dare's many suggestions for the use of his MultiMedia Maker is to generate talking resumes to give you an edge in the job market, as well as to create "a bang-up opening for your electronic publishing products."

If ease of use is a prime requirement for you rather than a wealth of advanced features, for around $100 there are some excellent commercial multimedia authoring applications for Windows and the Macintosh that enable you to create impressive results in an hour or two. They are very intuitive to use, and might well have all the features you will need for the foreseeable future.

How your multimedia title is built

Select an authoring program that uses a production method you are likely to be comfortable with. For example, some programs use a timeline or storyboard metaphor, onto which you patch the different elements of your production and coordinate when each starts and finishes. The precision with which this is achieved varies considerably between programs, and between versions of programs.

Other software functions like animated flowcharts. You start with the equivalent of a blank chart, then drag and drop into place icons representing each of the media being used, as in Fig. 2-3. This creates a framework or outline for your publication, which you then flesh out with all the different elements of text, sound, and visual material.

If you are familiar with HyperCard for the Macintosh, you might be more comfortable with an authoring program that adopts a card metaphor. If you already have material in HyperCard stacks, there are a number of programs that enable you to collate and enhance the cards into multimedia publications.

Whatever the friendly face they try to present on screen to make your authoring tasks easier, most of these programs rely on scripting languages that actually do the work. For really advanced multimedia

Figure 2-3

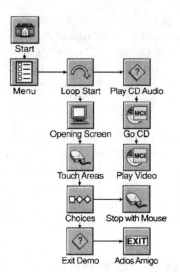

Compiling and editing a multimedia work is made much easier with programs such as HSC InterActive, in which you build flowchart structures using icons to represent different elements. The contents, such as graphics, text, or sound, are added to the icons. HSC Software

authoring, you need to get beyond the amiable icons and be able to tweak the programs to make them specific to your needs. The Grasp package from Paul Mace, who gave me my first demonstration of multimedia years ago in Oregon, is an example of such a professional program.

⇨ Plan for your skills and needs to expand

If your interest in multimedia is likely to grow and you will need to continue developing your skills and resources, select your entry-level software from a publisher with a stable of more advanced programs. MultiMedia Works from Lenel Systems International is one example. For under $100, it offers remarkable capabilities in its manipulation of objects in the Windows environment, and has modestly priced stablemates in the same software family if you want to move on to more ambitious projects.

If publishing commercially, rather than not-for-profit, is your objective, check the conditions imposed by the publisher of the software before making your final choice. Some include royalty-free runtime modules that can travel with your publication to enable it to

be read, while others do not offer this facility, or impose licensing fees for the necessary viewer software.

⇨ Don't do your own brain surgery

However advanced your multimedia productions become, there should never be any need to do your own programming. This is such an active field that something appropriate for your needs should already be available straight off the shelf.

In the early days of this medium, many authors tried to "do their own brain surgery" when creating interactive, tutorial, and multimedia titles by tackling the programming themselves. Now there is such a choice of good software that it is far more time- and cost-effective to use what is available and focus your efforts on the actual creation of the text, sound, and visuals, and on the marketing of the final product.

Jim Hood of Washington State, the successful author and self-publisher, is an example of this approach. He has the technical ability to write the programs to power his titles, but why should he when other people have already done so? He recognizes that his time and talents are better spent on the creative and marketing tasks.

"I now do little, if any, programming, and prefer to concentrate on preparing text and data which I then pour into existing menus, authoring systems, or specific software packages which I license from others," Jim explains.

He continues, "However, if you have the knowledge, you can achieve greater control and lower cost by using an authoring system which you can modify yourself. Programs such as Writer's Dream, MultiMedia Workshop, and LookBook provide the menu, shell and other structures for a product. You can add the interactive quiz part by such other shareware programs as Exam Bank or Coursemaster."

"You can also invest more by licensing sophisticated software," Jim says. "The choice is yours—whether you want to 'roll your own'

product with greater control plus saving on licensing fees, or go for a more polished package at a slightly higher cost."

Jim's advice is to make your choice market-driven: choose the method that best suits your current marketing objectives; you can always change the format later. His electronic publishing experience with his PC-Learn title is a good example. He launched this tutorial on personal computing a few years ago to test the demand, packaging it then as a basic, predominantly text, work using simple menus. The content met a real need, and PC-Learn became popular despite its primitive software. At that point, it needed greater sophistication to exploit fully the market that the first humble edition had identified.

"I needed a highly polished look to go with my information," says Jim, "so at that point I licensed from Eagle Systems a sophisticated menu system and retrofitted it to PC-Learn to make my title appeal to the large audience which I had identified as being ready to pay to cover these additional costs."

"But with another of my titles—Professor PC Laptop—I have decided to use the less costly, but still attractive, Writer's Dream menu system. One must strike a balance of what is appropriate for the title, the target readers, the finances available, and marketing considerations," he explains.

⇨ Learn by doing

If you have a CD-ROM drive, a fun and practical way to get the actual feel of multimedia, rather than just reading about it, is to try Professor Multimedia from Individual Software Inc. This single CD provides more demonstrations and information about multimedia and how it can be applied than you could expect to pick up at the most costly seminar or workshop. If you want to read and study the topic at an advanced level, *The McGraw-Hill Handbook of Multimedia*, edited by Jessica Keyes, provides the expertise of some of the best brains in the business.

One of the most economical ways to experiment with your own productions on even modest PC systems is to use Jeff Napier's MultiMedia Workshop, which is on the disk included with this book. Jeff says that he created MultiMedia Workshop "for anyone who has something to say . . . you'll find it easy to create disks that get your ideas to the public."

In addition to Jeff's usual emphasis on ease of learning and use, there are versions of this multimedia authoring program that are remarkable in requiring only 512K of RAM, and being able to run on systems with CGA or Hercules monitors, and just floppy disk drives. Consequently, this program also works well on portable computers with limited processing power.

Of course, you can take advantage also of higher-end hardware including SVGA displays and sound boards (Fig. 2-4), but this

Figure 2-4

Adding sound can be a very simple process—or taken to sophisticated levels of editing and reproduction. This 16-bit Roland Audio Producer card fits easily into a desktop computer to provide CD-quality recording. Roland Corporation U.S.

package is one of the few that gives you a taste of multimedia potential if you do not have the hardware to run the latest commercial software programs. It is also invaluable to take this comparatively low-tech approach if you need to distribute your publications to run on low-powered hardware, as is often the case with schools or international release.

MultiMedia Workshop's simple point-and-press search facility might be more appropriate for your publishing needs than advanced hypertext features. It incorporates comprehensive drawing and word processing programs, sound and music effects, and a wide range of visual effects. It even has a synthesized speech facility. It is also very efficient in its use of systems resources and disk space—you can get up to 100 pictures on a 360K floppy.

The Mshow.exe program that you distribute with your presentation to enable your readers to run it takes up only 45K. At a registration fee of only $29.95—including the rights to use the runtime program without paying royalties—this has to be one of the best bargains available in multimedia electronic publishing if it fits into your way of working.

The Workshop is one of the very few practical ways to get into electronic publishing if your system does not have a hard disk, because you can decompress the files on another system, then copy those files onto floppy disks and use them on a floppies-only system.

To get such universal compatibility, Jeff makes full use of the basic ASCII text and ASCII-Vector-Graphics formats. The trade-off is a lower quality of display, but the benefits are enormous if your prime concern is to create presentations that can be run by the vast majority of computer users. An equally important benefit is the way that large publications and presentations can be accommodated in very small files, even if they have graphics and sound effects. Consequently, you can distribute a substantial publication on a basic 360K floppy disk, or send it economically to a large number of bulletin boards and on-line services.

MultiMedia Workshop is an object lesson for the electronic publishing maxim that more is not necessarily better. Multimedia programs with greater sophistication can bring fewer results—and revenues, if that is your objective—because fewer computer systems can run them, and they generate large files that are difficult and expensive to distribute. At the same time, the MultiMedia Workshop program is very Windows-friendly, and comes with its own icon so that, after installation, you can start it with a couple of mouse clicks.

Don't forget the marketing

This book devotes considerable attention to "lower-end" programs because most author-publishers find it important to publish in formats that will reach the largest possible international markets, where comparatively primitive systems such as PCs and XTs are still common. There continues to be a massive user base of less-powerful systems that show no signs of being scrapped. You can have a considerable marketing edge if you publish multimedia works on floppies to these computer users, who are being ignored by the big commercial publishers pitching to CD-ROM owners.

Incredible things are being done with these older, less powerful, systems, and their users represent an enormous potential market for many electronic publications. If you create your publication or presentation in software that will run on CGA, EGA, or standard VGA displays, and does not need more than standard RAM, or much, if any, hard disk capacity, you can reach these markets most effectively.

Most of these millions of computer users around the world understand English—and authors and publishers should remember that important English-language markets are not confined to North America, the United Kingdom, and Australia. India, for example, has the largest English-speaking literate workforce in the world after the U.S., and over 500,000 personal computers.

Multimedia for small markets and small fry

The increased storage capacities of floppies, together with improved compression techniques and the ability to create one-off or short-run

CD-ROM discs, is making multimedia publishing for small niche markets far more viable. Multimedia might even be appropriate for important one-to-one communications, like submitting a book or television script proposal or a job application.

Michael O'Donnell, who founded the Ask Me Multimedia Center at the University of North Dakota, tells about a sound, pictures, and text publication on disk that he created for the smallest audience imaginable: his five-year-old son, Tyson.

"Tyson was very upset when we had to move homes," Mike recalls. "He had a really hard time figuring out where he is now in relation to where we used to live. The changes were proving quite traumatic for him, so I created a little interactive multimedia show about how and why we had moved homes. I showed where we used to live, the familiar things about our previous home, and where it was located in relation to our new address.

"My son was the main character in the story about our move, and he could replay the move from his own viewpoint by participating in the program as he ran it on the computer.

"It worked marvelously and Tyson ran the show over and over again himself, finding it far more interesting than watching television. This little multimedia production really helped him to adjust to the move, and to settle down happily in our new home. These are the kinds of applications of multimedia that I find so fascinating, and why I expect multimedia in various forms to become such an important part of writing, art, and other creative activities," Mike concludes.

 # Publishing through kiosks in public places

Mike O'Donnell is now an evangelist about the many ways that multimedia can enhance our lives, but he learned about this technology the hard way when he lost his shirt—along with his house and most of his possessions—as a pioneer of multimedia information kiosks for tourists in Virginia in the mid-1980s. Both the hardware

and the software were not sufficiently developed in those days to make such a venture viable. Now almost anything is possible as multimedia booms into a projected $25 billion business by 1995, but you still need to be very careful getting into tight market corners such as kiosks, where development costs can be high and, if a title doesn't work, it might be structured so rigidly for the medium that it is not easy to try it in another market niche.

However, publishing material for use in kiosks in malls, tourist locations, and other public places offers enormous potential, with particular opportunities to generate funding through sponsorship and on-screen advertising. If kiosk distribution is likely to figure in your plans, you might want to select a high-end authoring program that will enable you to publish on video laser disc, and also monitor usage of the kiosks and record any data that is entered by end-users. Macromedia's Director and Authorware Professional are the types of software that enable authors to meet such needs, but when you get into this kind of complexity, the learning curves tend to be much longer and steeper.

If you already have video material that you want to publish on laser disc, it can cost as little as $300 per disc to do the transfer. The Optical Disc Corporation (800-350-3500) maintains a list of certified recording centers providing these services in different parts of the U.S.

⇨ Keep it simple

Apart from demonstrating the impact that a simple interactive program can have on children as well as adults, the anecdote about little Tyson shows how quick and easy it is to author a multimedia publication. Mike O'Donnell used his own Super Show & Tell (SST) multimedia software running under Windows. This type of program typically costs less than $200 and is categorized and reviewed as being intended for home or amateur use, with the inference of being inferior to more expensive and complex multimedia authoring software targeted primarily at the business presentation markets. As mentioned earlier in this chapter, that is not necessarily true.

If you are venturing into multimedia for the first time, before laying out a lot of money on so-called professional software—and maybe having to upgrade your hardware to run it—take a look at programs like SST. Even if you plan ambitious productions, such as full-motion video, you might well find that such "low-end" programs have all the features that you need. Their short learning curve is an even more attractive incentive to go this route than the low cost.

If your content is of high quality, the tools with which you assemble it might become less critical as long as they do a competent job within their limitations. Indeed, try to be too clever and you can fall flat on your face, particularly when using multimedia in business situations.

There is an obvious temptation, once you have the tools and the skills, to over-use multimedia's power to increase production values. It's natural to suppose that special effects will enhance your ability to communicate effectively. However, like the zoom button on a videocamera, multimedia's special effects are best used with style in moderation, and confined to appropriate situations where they really benefit the publication and are not incorporated just as a gimmick.

Beware of trying to be too complex, particularly if tempted by a wide range of features provided in the best animation, morphing, and other image-manipulation programs. The bold, simple image and sequence can be by far the most effective, and your publication's impact and aesthetic qualities might be reduced by incorporating too many production gimmicks. Instead of being judged on content, your efforts might be critiqued on how well you did the multimedia, and the importance of the content consequently diluted.

Particularly in professional and business environments, a classically simple, elegant desktop-published printed piece stands out from all the multi-font, clip art clutter that bombards us. The same principle applies as electronic publishing becomes more commonplace.

Multimedia hardware requirements

To create and use the more sophisticated multimedia effectively, you need hardware that is at least up to the industry's MPC Level 2 specification established in 1993. There is now a wide choice of MPC2 hardware systems available at retail outlets and by direct mail, with prices steadily falling.

The MPC2 specification calls for a personal computer with a 25 MHz 486SX central processing unit (CPU) or better—get a 486DX or Pentium processor if you can afford it. The system must have a minimum of 4M of RAM, with at least 8M recommended. A hard drive with a minimum of 160M is specified, but the cost difference of larger-capacity drives is now so small that at least 250M will be cost-effective. The more space and the faster the access speed, the better.

Your video display will need to be super VGA, 640×480 resolution, and able to display 65,536 colors. Sadly, some of the best programs and multimedia titles no longer support standard 16-color VGA, although there are many millions of those monitors still in use around the world. If you are publishing to a mass international market where standard VGA is the norm, bear this in mind.

In addition to the usual parallel and serial ports, the MPC2 specification calls for MIDI input and output ports (normally on the sound board) and a joystick port for playing games. The sound board must be capable of handling at least 16-bit digital sound, an eight-note synthesizer, and a MIDI player.

The CD-ROM drive should be an integral part of the system, be CD-ROM XA ready, and able to read multisession discs. A 300K-per-second transfer rate is specified for MPC2, with a maximum average seek time of 400 milliseconds. However, you should be able to buy significantly faster CD drives than this with little or no price premium over the basic MPC2 requirements.

Beware of buying outdated CD-ROM drives. They might look the same as the latest models, but the speed and efficiency with which drives can retrieve information is increasing all the time, creating a lot of outdated and redundant hardware that finds its way into the marketplace at apparently bargain prices.

Speed of access is particularly important for CD-ROM drives because they are inherently much slower in delivering data to your system than the typical hard drive. Even a comparatively fast CD-ROM drive might have an actual functional speed that is a tenth of the transfer rate of your hard drive. This can be very restricting when accessing a large database or running a complex multimedia presentation.

Over the two years between mid-1992 and mid-1994, the access speeds of some CD-ROM drives have increased by as much as 400%, often without obvious visual differences. So it is easy to get caught with an old, slower model version. Such dramatic increases in transfer rates are not likely to continue because of the practical problems of achieving acceptable error rates when accessing data on ever-faster spinning disks, as well as getting rid of the heat that the drive motors and mechanisms generate as rotation speeds increase. However, there will be a steady improvement in CD drive performance; monitor this before making a buying decision.

Advanced multimedia needs lots of system power. When running a high-end multimedia production program such as Adobe's Premiere, you need lots of RAM and other system resources. You just can't have too much in the way of system resources if you intend to use video, and it is a false economy not to have the most powerful hardware you can afford. Also, make provisions for easily and economically upgrading as improved hardware becomes available or your needs increase.

If your computing experience has been confined mainly to handling text, you will be amazed at how demanding graphics can be—and moving graphics, such as videos or animation, are the most demanding of all. A system that might tackle enormous text files with aplomb can fail dismally to cope with graphics because they consume such large amounts of memory and disk space.

Adding pictures and sound the easy way

You might decide, particularly if you are a corporate writer with a budget to dip into, to contract out all or part of your multimedia production requirements, particularly any video elements. (Although doing so can be very expensive and has wrecked the budgets of many a multimedia production.) Or you might decide that video and audio demand more system resources, time, and computing knowledge than you are able to devote to your multimedia publishing project.

In either case, consider first the large amounts of material now becoming available as video and audio clips that can be incorporated at low cost into multimedia productions. These work rather like clip art. A CD-ROM disk contains a selection of video, still photographic images, or audio material under different classifications. If you find something that would help your program, you just copy and patch it into the appropriate place.

If your electronic publication is for internal, non-profit uses, there is usually no fee above what you paid for the clip collection. If you are publishing commercially for profit, you probably have to get clearance and pay a royalty, but this can now be a simple and reasonably economical procedure. The compiler of that particular clip collection will (or should!) have tracked down the original copyright holders and established proper licensing arrangements.

Just a few segments of the appropriate video sequences can add enormous production values to your title at very little cost, leaving you more of your budget to spend on other multimedia features, and perhaps removing the need to contract out the production at all. You might be able to convert a manuscript into a multimedia title just by adding clip visuals and audio creatively.

 # Video points for publishers to ponder

Video production and editing for multimedia deserve a book on their own, but there are some key points directly related to video use in electronic publishing that need to be emphasized here:

> If sourcing from, or delivering to, an international market, remember that the video standards are far more diverse than the PC and Mac compatibilities that dominate international personal computing. Your hardware and software must support the North American and Japanese NTSC broadcast standards, as well as Europe's PAL, or you might need to spend considerable sums and risk losing quality to do conversions later.

> You might need to cater also for VHS, super VHS, and Hi-8 as well as professional video standards in one or more of these broadcast formats, even if you think you will be using only one of them. The added flexibility to capture and output video in various standards gives you far more scope to use video footage from a wide variety of sources, and to shop around to get the best deals on duplication.

> Compatibility problems often arise within your computer system when you upgrade it for multimedia production purposes. Your existing monitor and a new video capture card might not work well together, for example, or a sound card might conflict with your printer or mouse.

> There is a lot of hype for multimedia hardware and software that makes it appear to be a cinch, for example, to extend Windows into a full capacity to capture, edit, and create video material. The dream is far different from the reality, although you can get very good results quite easily if your expectations are reasonable (Fig. 2-5). Instead of aspiring to include long full-motion video sequences, use video sparingly to bring short clips or single frames displayed in small windows alongside the relevant text.

Figure 2-5

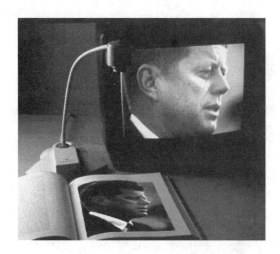

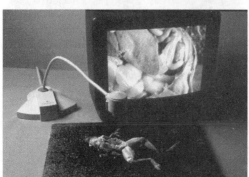

Both still and video cameras, as well as scanners, can be used to import visual material into e-books. Visuals can be taken from existing printed sources (a); the author or an interview subject can record audio and video segments to camera for direct recording on disk (b); and details from three-dimensional objects can be turned into informative illustrations (c). The camera used here is the FlexCam Document, a new generation of desktop miniature video cameras that are very easy to use. VideoLabs

 # Buyer beware!

If you do decide to contract out your video production needs, any major metropolitan area has lots of suppliers anxious to pitch for your business, including new ventures without a track record. To reduce the risk of making a bad choice, be sure to see examples of previous productions and follow up by seeking the opinions of those clients. Ensure that you will be given similar production values, within the constraints of your budget, to those you see in the demos—and that the contract protects you against budget over-runs and hidden costs.

Your contract should include a guaranteed completion date, as well as identify the key staff who will be deployed on your project. You might meet some impressive creative people while they are pitching for your business, and then find that your work is actually handled by more junior and less experienced staff, or has been subcontracted to freelancers who you know nothing about.

Be aware that video production is a creative process in which the personnel involved might have very limited understanding of the commercial or other objectives that you, as the client, seek. It's up to you to carefully coordinate the creative process that brings the words, pictures, and music together, with how you, as the publisher, have defined your target market.

For example, a sound engineer who lays on a rap music track might do a great job for a product aimed at the MTV youth market, but alienate a target group who you would expect to be watching PBS or A&E. The ability to cater for specific markets is very important in multimedia authoring, and does not automatically correlate with the professional competence of production specialists.

As a client, I once commissioned an important television commercial for screening in a major Third World market, and my advertising agency employed a high-powered television director from Canada. She was undoubtedly competent, but had little understanding for the distinctive culture of the audience I was trying to reach. She had to be removed from the project, and I finished the editing with a local

technician at a fraction of the cost, but many times the sensitivity for the market.

It is particularly important that you are happy with both the concepts and the detailed treatments as reflected in scripts and storyboards before allowing the project to go forward to the very expensive phases of shooting, or the development of computer-generated images. It is comparatively cheap and easy to modify scripts and storyboards, but difficult and expensive to make changes once the cameras are rolling.

Allocating resources

A typical ratio of time and money to be invested in a reasonably sophisticated multimedia production would be one-third of the resources to initial planning and scripting and two-thirds to development and final compilation. The time and budget required vary enormously, of course, but if the work is contracted out, be prepared to pay $1,000 or more per finished minute of a professionally produced title that uses video and has a significant amount of interactivity built in.

The cost factor is why learning to use the power of authoring software yourself can pay off handsomely. The learning period can extend from a few hours to several months. If you pick software appropriate to your needs and abilities, you should acquire the capacity to produce a short, effective presentation from existing material within a day or two.

Adding sound is easy and economical

New horizons open for audio use in all kinds of electronic publications with the advent of TrueSpeech for Windows, enabling sound files to be compressed to about a sixteenth of their original size, so that a minute of clear speech occupies about 60K of disk space. Compaq and Microsoft are among the industry leaders

adopting this system, with TrueSpeech incorporated in the Windows Sound System audio add-on kit.

However, as with other multimedia features, don't get too far ahead of the capabilities of the target markets for your works. By early 1994, the installed base of sound cards in personal computers in America alone was approaching eight million, so sound is becoming an important element for many computer users. But while the number of installed sound cards is increasing rapidly—by four million a year or more—the majority of PCs for many years to come will have only their tiny built-in speakers. Those users with sound cards that were purchased, often impulsively, to use with a game or a CD will spend a lot of their time with their enhanced sound systems inactive.

Your electronic publication might need to be compiled, therefore, with the knowledge that any audio functions you build into it might not be used to full effect by a significant proportion of your target audience. With this in mind, you might decide to include sound files that will work on just the internal speaker that almost every system has, or that you will double up (if you have sufficient disk space) and include files for both the internal speaker and the most widely installed sound cards.

Where to find your audio material

There is a wealth of audio material available on the shareware market that does not require a sound card—both programs to generate audio files and the sound equivalent of clip art. If the right audio clip is not available, you can create it yourself, or ask a specialist to do it for you.

Orlando Dare, president of Creative Software Engineering in Baltimore, Maryland, has been a pioneer in this field with his PC-Talk programs. Orlando is a digital design engineer who for years has been trying to improve the quality of sound through the PC speaker, while the main commercial thrust has been to exploit the large potential profits available from providing expensive hardware and software products to those who can afford higher-end systems. Orlando has made a significant contribution for the majority of users who rely on the restricted sound capabilities with which their systems were delivered. This will continue to include many portable computers sold with only the voice they were "born" with, and no space inside to add a sophisticated sound card to replace the internal speaker.

 # Squeezing sound

If you have a lot of audio to squeeze on to a disk, you might consider going mono rather than stereo for at least some of sections and using only the right or left channels. This technique was pioneered by audio books that double the capacity of compact cassettes by recording separate sections of the book on each of the four tracks. You can play these books only on stereo systems that permit you to turn one channel completely down or off. Similarly, only some sound cards and CD-ROM players permit the playback of such *discrete channels*.

If you want to hear how this technique works in multimedia, it is used to good effect in Sony's electronic version of the Mayo Clinic Family Health Book.

 # Sound by telephone

The telephone provides a cheap and convenient way to obtain audio input for multimedia publications. If your work includes quotes, particularly by well-known people in the field you are covering, you can record these (with the subject's permission) while interviewing by telephone as well as when face-to-face. When converting an existing manuscript to multimedia, you might go back to interview subjects and ask them to repeat particularly interesting quotes over the telephone for you to record and then incorporate in your multimedia production.

Spoken endorsements of your electronic publication can be very effective as sound files accompanying summaries of your publication in on-line or CD-ROM catalogs, or in other promotional material that you distribute.

We are entering an era in the expansion of telephone services when distributing electronic publications by telephone will be important

also. An interesting example of digital audio distribution by telephone is the new Digital Generation Systems network out of San Francisco, which transmits radio commercials from its computer to the computers of local radio stations around the country. This cracks one of the last barriers to radio stations switching almost entirely from analog to digital systems.

⇨ Binaural stereo could give you the edge

Binaural stereo is an interesting opening in the audio element of multimedia publishing that you might find worth exploring. It's not new, the concept having been invented in the 19th century by Frenchman Clement Ader, but binaural stereo is comparatively unknown, even among audiophiles. The British Broadcasting Corporation has used it very effectively in both radio drama productions and in a documentary about the hearing of blind people. Its commercial exploitation has been very limited, however, because most recorded material is designed for playing back through loudspeakers, whereas binaural audio only really works when heard through headphones. This could be appropriate for the personal way in which electronic publications are read by one person at a time in situations where headphones might be preferred.

Binaural recordings are made using a dummy head with a microphone in each ear. It is not absolutely essential to have a head, as long as the sound being recorded is separated into two distinct channels. The BBC positioned microphones on each side of a large disc to get the same results as a dummy head, and there are various alternative approaches to achieving this separation when feeding audio signals into a sound card.

By trying to create as far as possible a recorded sound exactly as it is received by each ear of someone on the spot, and then playing it back directly into each ear of the listener, you get really impressive results, particularly through high-quality headphones hooked into 16-bit sound cards. Headphones avoid the mixing and blurring of sounds from speakers.

Binaural sound is more than a gimmick, but you could use it effectively just as a gimmick to stimulate interest in your title. The technique might add sufficient production values and marketing appeal to certain electronic publications featuring audio to reduce or eliminate the need for incorporating visuals. Use it, for example, to demonstrate music, bird and animal sounds, or to give a richness to the human voice in poetry.

 Existing books that convert well to multimedia

The activity in multimedia publishing creates many opportunities for writers to sell material or be commissioned to work on projects. Many authors have existing works that will convert effectively to the new media. Major multimedia publishers such as Voyager already have on staff acquisitions editors seeking suitable works.

If you want to see hardcopy examples of the types of children's and adult books that transfer well to high-level CD-ROM multimedia productions, just go into your nearest bookstore and browse through the Dorling Kindersley titles there. Peter Kindersley, an Englishman who founded the imprint after a long career as a book packager, was one of the first publishers anywhere to switch his print production and layout operations to computers. Even those titles he produced in the '80s show the influence that his banks of Macs had on design, with crisp, colorful graphics and blocks of text laid out like icons on a clear white page.

Kindersley considerably advanced some of the design concepts pioneered in print by, among others, Reader's Digest how-to books, with their emphasis on stylized graphical images and easily digested short bites of text. Such books work really well as multimedia. Even on the printed page, the graphics in such Dorling Kindersley titles as David Macaulay's great *The Way Things Work,* almost invite you to press on them to make them become animated. That's just what does happen in the multimedia titles Dorling Kindersley is producing in conjunction with Microsoft. In the first of these, Microsoft Musical Instruments, a child or adult can enjoy learning about instruments

from all over the world, and call up an immediate playing demonstration of any of them.

This electronic book immediately became a big seller. If you take a look at it, you can see that it represents a substantial investment to achieve such high production values. Those up-front costs can be greatly reduced if there is an existing hardcopy illustrated text from which to build the multimedia title.

 ## Scope for self-help titles

Already, multimedia versions of the popular do-it-yourself home and car repair manuals are starting to appear, and almost any kind of self-help title has multimedia potential. It might merit the full sound and pictures treatment, or simply easy search facilities and perhaps an interactive quiz feature.

If you have already, or can generate, an appropriate title, explore sponsorship and advertising possibilities. For example, for home or car maintenance titles, sponsors might be found among tools, parts, and other hardware suppliers, as well as manufacturers and distributors of paints, timber, and other consumables. Hardware and motor parts stores offer attractive retailing opportunities when you have your multimedia title ready to market.

 ## Do-it-yourself medicine

Self-diagnosis medical publishing in multimedia formats is another potentially large growth area with plenty of room for additional titles in addition to the considerable number already available. Such major releases as Home Medical Advisor and the Mayo Clinic Family Health Book on CD-ROM disks might seem so comprehensive that there is no room for anything else, but they offer general advice and fairly basic search options. You might be able to reach larger potential markets by publishing more focused information on floppies, as well as zeroing in on special-interest groups. I wish I'd thought of these opportunities when I signed away without thinking the electronic rights to my book about computing-related health problems!

The ability offered by newer authoring programs to add greater interactivity and more capable search features such as fuzzy logic make medical advice and diagnostic multimedia titles far more capable. Health maintenance organizations love them because they can reduce doctor consultations and recommend non-prescription medication.

If you have access to, or can create, appropriate material, you might consider sponsored publication through an HMO, citing the successful experience that the Harvard Community Health Plan has had with its scheme. Patients able to tap into the Harvard medical database and advice program on-line made 5% fewer clinic visits than those without this facility. This experience indicates that specialist medical bulletin boards and on-line services could do well, and provide marketplaces for a variety of publishing enterprises. Diabetics, for example, are targets for much product advertising and publishing.

A significant number of hospitals use videodiscs to help patients already diagnosed with conditions such as breast or prostate cancer to learn about these diseases and evaluate their various options. Such valuable services can be made much more widely available by transferring the programs to CDs or distributing them on floppies to install on hard drives. There is a lot of scope to create new multimedia material based on texts and visuals that might already exist in print, and so could comparatively easily be computerized and made interactive.

⇨ Musical opportunities

You might need few or no visuals in your multimedia production if you have a text subject suitable for musical illustration. For example, an author with musical knowledge can produce impressive titles about individual instruments, performers or composers, detailed analyses of great works, profiles of orchestras, and similar musical titles with quite modest hardware and software resources. Publishing music by computer also becomes much more practical now that there is very affordable and functional music reading software, such as Midiscan for Windows, which can automatically convert sheet music to multitrack MIDI files.

Pop musicians who have grown familiar with computerized musical instruments might seem to be leading the way, but the attractions are so great that we can expect to see many electronic publications about classical, jazz, and other music forms also. They don't all need to go onto CD-ROM; for many purposes it might only be necessary to combine text with simple graphics, musical notation, and sound files, all of which can be compressed effectively to get a comprehensive multimedia publication onto floppy discs.

Using Midiscan is a revelation in how easy it is to score music directly into the computer and print out scores with almost the same ease and proficiency as word-processing text. Couple such developments with the amazing software and hardware additions that can turn even a modest personal computer into a powerful music machine, and it is inevitable that much original composing and arranging, as well as the publishing of works created in the traditional way, will in the future be digitized.

This is culturally a very important development that all who love music can welcome, even those for whom the sounds of electronically synthesized instruments are no substitute at all for the real thing. Much published music must be captured as dynamic information that evolves through the continuing input of composers, arrangers, and musicians, and at various stages needs to be duplicated for wider access. One can envisage the day when it will be the norm for the members of an orchestra or band to refer to scores on portable liquid-crystal displays. These scores will be truly active electronic documents, evolving during rehearsal as amendments and notations are made on them by everybody involved. Apart from the practical and time- and cost-saving benefits, the quality of performances might actually improve as such fleeting moments as a phrase of inspired improvisation during rehearsal can quickly be captured and recalled at will.

⇨ Morphing is a practical tool

Another technological software development with great potential in electronic publishing is *morphing*, a form of animation in which one image is transformed into another. Even low-cost morphing programs

such as MorphWizard and HSC Digital Morph can be used to add production values and aid comprehension. Industrial processes, or the evolution of product designs, can come to life by morphing in ways far more difficult to depict in words and conventional graphics.

For example, you can add impact by making the points around a visual of a mouth move to combine with a sound file and so create a talking head. A simple storyboard, or collection of slides, can become much more impressive by morphing between the images. A slow, gradual morphing can indicate the passage of time, while you can give impact to an individual image by freezing that particular frame.

Morphing effects between text and visuals can be very effective. I look forward to experimenting in my Lake Poets' project (described in detail in chapter 10) by trying to morph Wordsworth's words host of golden daffodils "fluttering and dancing in the breeze" into visuals of the flowers that inspired him.

⇨ Virtual reality as a publishing medium

Virtual reality might not yet be seen as a publishing medium, but in fact it has enormous potential for almost all genres. The applications in fiction and poetry are limited only by the imagination, as you create virtual worlds in which readers can directly interact with your characters, settings, and plots. In nonfiction, it must become commonplace to provide virtual reality simulations in a wide range of tutorials, and for research purposes.

Molecular scientists are able to invite colleagues to join them inside the interesting molecule they describe in the accompanying research paper. Together, author and readers can move around and examine the relationships of atoms, neutrons, and protons. Expect this kind of publishing to be applied extensively by researchers involved in The Human Genome Project, since they have the financial and computing resources to push this technology to its limits.

Virtual reality might be used to enhance text and two-dimensional drawings and photographs already published in other media. Delegates to the 1993 Imagina conference in Monte Carlo saw an impressive example of this. They walked around the Abbey of Cluny, once the cultural center of Europe and the world's largest Christian church. The Abbey was physically destroyed after the French revolution, but it was rebuilt in virtual imagery in Monte Carlo using the published and unpublished research of Professor John Kenneth Conant of Harvard, who devoted much of his life to excavating the site of the Abbey.

Students of the Ecole National des Arts et Metiers, with the help of IBM-France, were able to rebuild an amazingly realistic computer simulation of the cathedral. Now, wearing a virtual reality helmet and movement sensors, you can walk into the nearest equivalent we can ever have of one of the world's most architecturally and culturally significant buildings. Unfortunately, Professor Conant died in 1984, missing by only a few years the enjoyment of what must be the ultimate publishing experience.

While the computer reconstruction and simulation of the Abbey of Cluny is of immense importance to historians and archaeologists, it is also a milestone in electronic publishing. It shows just one way that texts can be republished electronically for results that the original authors could not even have dreamed were possible. The advent of multimedia makes it particularly important to preserve authors' original notes and research materials, as examined in more detail later in this book.

Games as a medium for authors

Games have become an important publishing category on the information superhighways, as well as being distributed on disk to stand-alone computer and game-playing hardware. The range is far beyond the combat video games for children that are generating so much controversy. Some of the writers involved in the games medium report that they find it just as challenging to develop meaningful characters with depth, and intricate plots and settings, as to create

fiction for print. Games deserve to be taken seriously as a significant publishing medium because they can be used to explore such a wide variety of human situations and needs in addition to just offering transitory entertainment.

Computer adventure games are obviously moving away from the text games that were once so popular to incorporate ever-more-ambitious graphical elements. The style and distinctive points of view of the original authors can still be preserved to a large extent, as was demonstrated with the game version of *Gateway,* by science fiction writer Frederick Pohl.

While creating complex electronic games is very much a team effort, with the role of the authors tending to be obscured, there is still scope for authors and designers to emerge as distinct creative artists developing their own loyal followings. The opportunities for publishing in game formats to niche markets have hardly been tapped yet. There are several competing, and usually incompatible, hardware platforms struggling for a slice of the lucrative electronic games market, so you need to be careful in choosing the format in which to publish if you go beyond the Macintosh and DOS/Windows environments.

The trend with the dedicated games hardware is toward greater processing power to enable the games to be more realistic, so the 32-bit and 64-bit systems such as 3DO and CD-I will expand at the expense of the older 8-bit and 16-bit formats. The user bases are enormous and create viable markets for a wide range of electronic publications. The Sega Genesis system alone has an estimated 18 million users, and reaching them becomes easier with the introduction in 1994 of the Sega Channel on cable television, and the joint venture with AT&T for games to be played by telephone.

There are particular publishing opportunities using games systems that will play Photo CDs, and many ways to promote your games titles through magazines, retail outlets, and the manufacturers of the hardware. These manufacturers are always looking for good promotional opportunities among the developers of new titles for their systems.

The ancient board game, chess, is a clear ancestor for the complex computerized war and business games, with substantial text elements, used to evaluate real-life military and corporate events. There are many opportunities to create games on computer for training purposes. These can be published electronically in their own right, or incorporated into other print or electronic publications to add an interactive games element to a predominantly text work.

Games can also be used to promote publications. Create a game to release as shareware or freeware to generate publicity and sales for your book. There is software available to help, so even with little or no programming experience, you can create powerful promotional tools for your self-published works.

A particularly interesting example of the role of games in the blurring and merging of the boundaries between media is Craig R. Hickman's *The Strategy Game*, which has three distinctive publishing "identities." It is an exercise in a kind of vertical multimedia marketing of a core creative concept that could prove to be a trend-setter.

Business McGraw-Hill published the book version, which is structured as well as possible in print to be similar to an interactive computer game. Readers can choose their paths through the text, react to prompts, and garner information much as children do with some of their video games. Instead of shooting down space invaders, readers interacting with the book take decisions as the chief executive of a mythical company. Depending on the quality of those decisions and how they apply the information available in the pages of the book, they and the company are winners or losers.

The computer game with the same core concept as the book is not, as one might expect, packaged with the book. Craig decided to make the software a distinctly different product, allowing the book version of *The Strategy Game* to incorporate the best and most appropriate features for its particular market, and then create the computer version to be the best that it could be for that particular medium. Each version is self-contained and complimentary to the others, so that satisfied buyers of one have a strong incentive to purchase the other also, which generates higher overall sales. With this packaging

and marketing approach, total revenues should be greater than if the book and the disk were packaged and sold together as a single product, like the book you are reading now.

This example of segmented multimedia publishing does not end there. Craig's concept in either the soft- or hardcopy forms (or both!) lends itself to business management training, so he produced another book as a guide to how to use *The Strategy Game* as training material.

Create your own multimedia publishing opportunities

You don't have to start from scratch to launch such a multifaceted multimedia project. You might already have manuscripts or other materials that you can develop in similar ways. Never before have there been such powerful tools to enable you to create your own publishing opportunities, and they coincide with a rapid expansion in alternatives to conventional publishing channels to market original works.

As H.G. Wells commented, printing enabled "the intellectual life of the world to enter upon a new and far more vigorous phase—it ceased to be a little trickle from mind to mind; it became a broad flood, in which thousands, and presently scores and hundreds of thousands of minds participated."

The first Renaissance of Western civilization seemed to Wells, writing early in this century, to have happened remarkably quickly after the Germans in the fourteenth century began making paper cheaply enough for the printing of affordable books to take off when Gutenberg invented movable type. Even Wells, that technology visionary, could not have anticipated the far greater speed with which multimedia developments are stimulating a "Renaissance 2." Developments that took decades now happen in months, and the new skills and knowledge that comes with them are affecting not just hundreds of thousands in Europe, but millions of people around the world.

That's why, to return to the theme of this chapter, writers and other creative artists cannot afford to ignore multimedia. There is a tendency among some authors to adopt a Luddite approach, distancing themselves from this technology. Perhaps they fear that the culture in which they have a defined role as writers is threatened by it, and their own positions consequently threatened.

To quote H.G. Wells again: "New and stirring ideas are belittled, because if they are not belittled, the humiliating question arises, 'Why then are you not taking part in them?'"

Electronic publishing is transforming business

THE paperless office has not arrived yet because desktop publishing gets in the way by creating a proliferation of paperwork that consumes vast resources. Desktop publishing enables businesses to produce more paper with greater speed and, generally, an improved appearance. It is largely an interim phase in the business community's long-term drift away from paper made possible by personal computing.

The computer industry's success in promoting desktop publishing has resulted in a business culture in which the form of paperwork—the typography and visual elements—now assume an importance that might even distract from the content. People have become so fascinated with fonts and fancy formatting that many companies are unnecessarily complicating their transition to internal and external electronic publishing, where it is even more important that content, not form, reign supreme. Document-imaging software, derisively called "page turners" by its competition, could establish standards for electronic publishing that inhibit the development of the new media.

Page turners, or basic document imagers, mimic paper. They can be impressive examples of software engineering, but they inhibit much electronic publishing because they are so deeply rooted in printing technology and attitudes. Especially for internal corporate publishing where a lot of material might exist only in hardcopy form, the temptations to replicate paper are strong.

Page turners are attractive because they can enable you to get a paperless system up and running quickly at reasonable initial cost with little initial opposition. The short-term savings might quickly fade, however, against the long-term disadvantages. For a start, most business documentation is in standard 8.5-x-11-inch (or A4) sheets in portrait format that just don't fit the squatter, wider computer screen configurations. Trying to fit pages laid out on vertical letter-size paper onto horizontal computer monitor screens makes little sense.

 # Many companies have no choice

There are some difficult transitional stages as the business community begins en masse to go digital with its documents. The pressures to make the change cannot be resisted. Hundreds of thousands of companies around the world have no choice but to adopt electronic "paperless" publishing technologies. If they fail to do so, they simply will not be able to sell to government agencies and other companies with specific timetables that impose dates by which service manuals and other essential documentation must be supplied in electronic formats.

Digitized documentation is fast becoming an essential capability for the 300,000 vendors doing business with the U.S. government and for individuals and corporations selling to other governments around the world that are also moving to electronic environments for assessing, ordering, and paying for supplies. This change has a far-reaching impact on the way business is done at all levels. Some companies have not even tried doing business with the federal government in the past; these businesses could not cope with government bureaucracy that can take up to 40 months just to reach the decision to buy a computer system—let alone pay for it! Under the impetus given to the paperless business environment by the Clinton Administration, and Vice President Al Gore in particular, the federal government will have a substantial part of its procurement activities computerized by mid-1995, with full implementation scheduled for early 1997, shortening a typical acquisition transaction from three weeks to five days.

 ## The SGML Standard

Companies dealing with the Department of Defense, aerospace, telecommunications, and other large high-tech industries have no effective alternative but to use electronic publishing and document-managing systems that support the Standard Generalized Markup Language (SGML) international standard. This standard promises to become ever more important for much corporate and technical

publishing. It has been adopted by many industry organizations—the Association of American Publishers being among the first.

SGML is part of the *Computer-aided Acquisition and Logistic Support* (CALS) program of the U.S. Department of Defense, which is setting the standards likely to be adopted for high-level technical publishing around the world, particularly in aerospace, telecommunications, automotive manufacturing, and armaments. The proficiency with which the different "commercial-strength" authoring programs cope with CALS compliance varies greatly, so this should be a major consideration if SGML is important in your publishing objectives.

The decision by federal and state governments to "go paperless" has many other implications. For example, major overhauls have been taking place in the Department of the Environment and the Occupational Health and Safety Administration. These are leading to new reporting procedures and the dissemination of much more information, which only digital documentation is able to cope with—both in terms of the volume of the information involved and the speed with which it has to be prepared and processed.

Fortunately, a great deal of software is being prepared to cope with this situation. There are, for example, very specific electronic publications on floppies dealing with various aspects of new regulations requiring organizations to create written injury and illness prevention plans. Floppy disks are a good medium for this kind of publishing because of the speed and economy with which specific information can be updated. It is far easier to ensure that you have the latest disk of, say, the Emergency Preparedness Plan than its 50-page paper equivalent. It might be difficult and expensive, on the other hand, to keep revising a collection of such works on CD-ROM. The best sources to keep up with what is available in these niches of electronic business publishing are the professional and specialized periodicals, dealing with such issues as waste management or occupational safety and health.

 # You might already be in the publishing business without knowing it

You might already unknowingly work for a company that is an active publisher. It might publish books and other publications to support its corporate manufacturing, distribution, or service functions. Managers often do not realize that the skills and resources to create books already exist within their organization and can be deployed very cost-effectively in switching to electronic document management.

Technology is advancing so rapidly and becoming so complex that paper can no longer cope in many business situations. Boeing Aerospace is, for example, one of the world's leading publishers. The weight of documentation, particularly the servicing and operations manuals, needed for a 747 exceeds that of the aircraft itself. No wonder Boeing is already involved in electronic publishing in a big way! The manufacturers of many other products must also publish extensive technical, servicing, and operational information that is increasingly going onto disk rather than paper.

 # Even if it can't be done, somebody's doing it!

Members of a business community steeped in a paper-based administrative culture keep protesting that particular forms of corporate publishing just cannot be digitized. However, every day someone, somewhere is proving them wrong—often a competitor. As author Elbert Hubbard declared, "The world is moving so fast these days that the man who says it can't be done is generally interrupted by someone doing it."

Despite the traumas involved in moving away from paper, the benefits can be enormous. When *Byte* magazine investigated the

corporate use of electronic publishing in its September 1993 issue, it found examples of companies that had slashed costs and increased productivity five-fold by switching from print to digitized information. *Byte's* Cary Lu comments, "Electronic publishing gives you the keys that unlock all the information in your documents, information that you couldn't find before or even knew that you had."

These benefits will not be enjoyed to the full, however, if business decision-makers fail to appreciate all the implications of making their words and pictures perform to maximum effect as they graduate from the page to the virtual environment.

Changes in the structure of corporations

Bill Gates, President of Microsoft Corporation, the world's largest software company, expects an acceleration in the ways that the new electronic media actually transform the structure of corporations, not just how information flows within the business world.

"The tools of the information age are prime agents of change for the business community," says Gates. "For example, the average size of companies must get smaller as a result of electronic media, because of the ease with which you can collaborate with people who don't work inside your company. The need to have particular expertise within a company will become very much less, and that is resulting in a scale change in our corporations."

"Although the economic news emphasizes that companies like IBM and GM are laying off people, this scale change is generating other jobs made possible outside the big corporations by the new electronic media," he concludes.

Microsoft itself is an example of this trend. While it has reduced its employee numbers in some areas during the early '90s, there has been phenomenal growth of employment among the 750 smaller software companies in the state of Washington. Many of them are new ventures, and the majority of them do contract work for

Microsoft, keeping in touch electronically. There was, therefore, a net gain in employment in Washington's software industry, despite the negative headlines about Microsoft's layoffs. A similar pattern is seen in other industries and in other states and nations.

Gates forecasts a business future with new ways of working and communicating that have never been done before. Already he has several hundred people on such projects, many of which will not come to full fruition before the end of the century. He is particularly bullish about developments in multimedia publishing of all kinds, media that he played a large part in creating when he invested heavily in CD-ROM software in the mid-1980s, at a time when hardly anyone else was predicting the present remarkable growth rates.

⇨ The new footloose industries

New highly mobile industries are being spawned by the information revolution. They are being dubbed "footloose industries," and are particularly attractive in scenic areas and rural communities because they are clean and undemanding of local resources. Their environmental impact is minimal because they do not need to extract minerals, dump waste, cut down trees, or consume natural resources. As electronic publishing in all its forms gathers momentum, these industries will increasingly run almost virtual offices and virtual factories, with much of their business being conducted on-line.

Much writing these days originates within the organizations being affected by these changes, but hardly any writers anywhere—even those laboring in the contemporary equivalents of garrets—will be immune to the impact. The change that electronic publishing makes on business has a dominant influence on all of us, so this topic must be examined in detail.

⇨ The comfort factor

The cost savings, increased efficiency, and logistical advantages of eliminating as much paper as possible are enormous, and already well-proven. Just before IBM embarked on its massive electronic

publishing project in 1986, it had to ship its European customers the manuals for a new release of midrange systems software. The paperwork crossed the Atlantic in seven Boeing Jumbo Jets at enormous expense and consumption of corporate and natural resources. Now a complete set of all those books can be contained on a single CD-ROM, and enough copies of that disk to meet the needs of IBM's European customers could be checked in on a passenger flight as accompanied baggage!

By transferring personnel documentation such as employee benefits packages, scholarships, and medical programs from paper to computerized formats, IBM saved over $63 million in a five-year period. The comparatively small conversion costs were recovered in just the first year, and from then on the savings have kept on escalating. By 1993, for a modest $105,000 expenditure on maintaining the electronic publishing program, Big Blue was recouping over $15 million each year in the benefits it could quantify. The intangible rewards were probably much higher, particularly at the most critical time for human resource issues as IBM went through a traumatic reorganization of its whole employee structure.

Difficult decisions

A company or other organization considering going to paperless documentation must make some difficult initial decisions and be prepared to exercise strong discipline on its people to make the change successful. Paper is such a familiar and comfortable medium that the problems for many organizations in trying to move from it to electronic media are as much emotional and psychological as they are practical. Trying to make this major change in an organization is almost certainly doomed to failure if the whole management team does not buy into it, and at least as much attention is given to the human issues raised as to the technology involved.

It is particularly important to reassure all those who must abandon their safe, familiar paper environments that they will personally be more successful in their work as a result of the new paperless systems. Managers at Aetna Life & Casualty did this successfully by

offering $20 bets to staff who could retrieve information faster
through the traditional editions of their manuals than they could in
the new electronic equivalents.

The law firm of Hunton & Williams holds annual Infobase Fairs in the
lawyers' dining room, at which employees can see new developments
in the internal electronic publishing system and make their own
suggestions. The type of questions asked at these events changed
quickly from "What is it?" to "What's new this year?" as enthusiasm
for the paperless environment grew.

Employee involvement at all levels was the key to Aetna's solution to
handling 87 million pieces of paper in one of the earliest and most
successful introductions of an internal corporate electronic publishing
system. Employees even got to suggest which charities should receive
the 10,000 manila file folders made redundant by the change over.

Prying them away from paper

"We're talking about a culture so steeped in paper and paper
processes, we thought we'd have to pry the paper out of their cold,
dead fingers," recalled Charlie Coon, Aetna's director of
Mechanization Strategies. Now nobody at the famous insurance
company would even think about reverting to their 150-year-old
paper tradition dating from the era of quill pens. The savings have
been enormous. Just eliminating the regular updating on paper of the
manuals used by underwriters saves nearly $3 million in lost time
each year. It would have cost nearly $4 million to print the 87 million
pages that were eliminated on the initial implementation alone of the
Folio VIEWS Infobase system that Aetna has adopted. The easily
quantified *hard cost savings*—the actual expenditure no longer
necessary—are estimated at $6 million a year, with the increases in
productivity and other soft benefits probably at least as much, if not
more.

As in many organizations, the paper crunch came for Aetna when
it was forced to find a better way of storing and accessing its
archival information. An old mainframe computer system was
costing Aetna $500,000 a year just to maintain inactive insurance

policies, and the possibility of converting them to the familiar paper would have generated a pile of 8½-x-11 sheets over a mile high, with another half-million dollars needed for the filing cabinets to contain them.

Many possibilities for handling this historical data were evaluated before the Aetna people found that their colleagues trying to cope with maintaining underwriting manuals were facing similar problems. Again, it is a common corporate situation that similar document-management difficulties exist in several departments, and that a corporate-wide solution needs to be applied, sooner or later. The moral is not to try to plow a lonely furrow when coping with information overload, but to get a company-wide policy coordinated right from the beginning. Even the new, more fragmented, IBM Corporation, with all its emphasis on smaller autonomous units, has made electronic publishing a global corporate strategy. You can benefit from all that corporate muscle by using IBM's excellent BookManager, which in 1994 was moving steadily from DOS and OS/2 to Windows and other business computing platforms.

Software support is critical

There are now many software offerings that, in theory, can cope with almost any business paperless publishing strategy. Aetna's crucial need for speed and reliability underlines the lesson that the service backing up the product must be assessed along with the more easily quantified results of the benchmark testing.

Aetna needed more than twelve million records—100 gigabytes—transferred within a year from its policy archives on the mainframe to CD-ROMs that could be handled on the desktop. The deadlines were beaten, with hundreds of mainframe tape cartridges being compressed by a ratio of 70% to fit onto CD-ROM discs. The payback has been impressive, but that is fairly typical when a move to a largely paperless environment has been implemented so carefully. It now costs Aetna only a dollar to make an inquiry on an expired policy, representing a 90% cost saving. The whole operation has paid back its initial investment in just nine months.

New perspectives on information

"Taking advantage of this new electronic medium means thinking differently about how information is communicated, used, shared, and distributed," emphasized Mike Judson, the Folio Corporation's director of corporate communications. "Emulating electronically the look and feel of the paper document should be secondary to helping people find what they need, when they need it."

He continued, "Information is dynamic. It changes, it gets pulled apart, and put back together for a myriad of different needs. That's why it makes no sense to carry over the static nature of paper into the electronic medium. A true electronic publishing solution doesn't mimic the static nature of paper, it removes that artificial limitation and lets people do what they need to do with the document because it is dynamic, like the information it bears."

Lotus Development Corporation founder Mitch Kapor has drawn a parallel between much initial implementation of electronic publishing and the early days of cinema. The early movies were dominated by theatrical conventions, and many were just filmed records of stage productions. Moviemaking quickly developed its own style and manner of communicating, however, just as electronic publishing is developing its own distinctive way of conveying information, free from the shackles of print.

Don't mimic paper

When making the change, try not to compromise by keeping so much of your document management and publishing strategies stuck in a paper-based mold that they hold you back from properly exploiting the new media. This is happening a lot with the use of document imaging systems that focus on trying to transform print on paper to print on the computer monitor, as if this was a microfiche, photographic process. At the very least, the change to digitized information must offer search features that enable the information within the documents to be located quickly and easily without a lot of intensive human indexing effort.

Hypertext features are vital to make the information dynamic, so that users can track through instinctively to explore the connections between items. The indexing and cross-referencing should be comprehensive, and preferably automatic, and the system should be selected by those knowledgeable about information who will not confuse digitized text libraries with databases.

The screen displays, particularly the typefaces, must make the most of the monitors, at which fonts and formatting that mimic paper often fail miserably. Trying to transfer a typeface directly from paper to screen with no better reason than that it worked well in print is complete nonsense. Some type designs just do not look good on screen, and so should be replaced by those that are easier to read and have aesthetic features appropriate to the electronic medium.

It is almost always necessary to have a larger sans serif font on a screen for ease of reading. Such print features as boldfacing, underlining, and italics that are used in print to give emphasis or distinguish from the main text might be better achieved on-screen by the use of color. The creative and practical use of "white space" is at least as important in a paperless document as it is for a hardcopy, but the techniques involved might be very different. One of the problems with plain ASCII text readers is that they rarely lay the type out on the screen to best effect, let alone provide an attractive readable typeface. For example, the margins required for a sheet of paper are not desirable for a screen that already has defining margins around it.

An important concept often overlooked is that paperless documents can become literally pageless, breaking out of the physical restraints of a sheet of paper. This might not always be an advantage, however, because the computer screen also has limitations and is not as competent as paper at some tasks, such as displaying a long list. Allow for the negative as well as the positive differences between paper and the screen.

A major strength of true electronic documents is that they overcome the problem of "text migration" often encountered in print, in which illustrations can become divorced from the section of text that they are supposed to make clearer. In electronic publications, the ability to resize text and illustrations in windows on the same screen, or switch quickly from text references to the relevant illustrations, can be a great help to comprehension *if* you have adopted a system that makes such actions possible. Add the flexibility to incorporate full-color images at little or no additional cost and multimedia features that let those images move and make sounds, and you can see that electronic publishing's communication ability is inherently far more powerful than the typical business document or publication.

Size, life, and use define your software needs

The size of your publications and how they will be used are major factors in evaluating their suitability for paper or electronic media, along with which software authoring tools to use. A short document with a limited lifespan that needs to be very portable to everyone in an organization, not just those using computers, is an obvious candidate for paper. As the size of the document increases, and the need to refer to it over a longer period becomes greater, electronic publishing becomes more attractive.

A large, complex reference work is far more portable and accessible in electronic form, even when you take into account the portable computing device necessary to read it. This stimulates the use of PDAs like the one in Fig. 3-1 by technicians, warehouse staff, and other employees not able to interface easily with desktop hardware. Where there is a need to publish to employees not having access to computers at all, some corporations are achieving significant successes with interactive kiosks, particularly for publications emanating from the human resources department.

Portability can be crucial

However large the organization, it cannot switch to digital documentation in isolation. It must consider the need for *publishing portability*—the ability to be an interactive reader of materials coming in from customers, suppliers, and local and national

Figure 3-1

Electronically published "smart manuals" give technicians access to technical information wherever they might be working. Some systems can learn the varying skill levels of different employees, and answer queries with repair or servicing instructions tailored to the individual's knowledge.
Sharp Electronics Corporation

government organizations, together with the requirement to publish back to them in formats compatible with external systems.

Publishing portability is happening almost by default. Electronic publishing will become almost instinctive as more personal computer users exploit the document portability that is actually being embedded in their operating systems and applications. DOS, Windows, Unix, the Macintosh platform, and OS/2 will steadily get better at enabling anyone using recent versions of these operating systems to exchange formatted documents. This will make feasible much electronic publishing without the need for any special reading programs. Windows users have long been able to exchange Rich Text Format documents between different word processing programs, almost with the same ease and consistency as plain ASCII texts move around different computing environments.

Microsoft's dominance among personal computer operating systems and its commitment to the increasingly popular TrueType font technology make it feasible for the world's largest personal computing software company to again establish a new standard, while WordPerfect also seeks to create a *lingua franca* for electronic publishing. By the mid-1990s, newer versions of both Windows and

MS-DOS will contain more proficient tools for making documents portable.

Unfortunately, uncertainty will prevail for several years about the viability of publishing with any of the various proprietary independent formats, none of which meet every need. Any electronic publishing software that stays in the game must become increasingly chameleon-like in mimicking the fonts and formatting created by the leading word processing and desktop publishing programs. One leading contender, actually called FontChameleon, can mimic most of the fonts in common usage. This ability is shared by such other programs as Infinifont, but it is an approach that solves one problem by posing others. Faking fonts can be heavy on system resources, particularly memory and disk space. That's where programs such as Acrobat and Replica score, with their ability to actually embed TrueType fonts in the documents they convert.

In this aspect of electronic publishing, much will depend on the importance both publishers and readers give to exactly preserving formats and typefaces. A side skirmish will be "The Battle of the Fonts" between PostScript, which in the past has dominated computerized print publishing, and TrueType, which is being driven by the popularity of Windows. One can only hope that common sense will prevail and paperless publishing reverts to the best traditions of print, in which clarity and classical simplicity represent quality in typography, not a plethora of typefaces that often detract rather than enhance the readability and aesthetic qualities of documents.

Multiple personalities aid portability

Making publications portable among platforms is becoming easier as computers acquire "multiple personalities." In the old days they used to be very distinctive, insular characters, with DOS systems not talking to Macs not talking to Amigas, and so on. Now there is ever-increasing cross-platform dialogue, an important element in the production and marketing strategies of many electronic publishers.

However, there is a battle going on among scores of competing electronic publishing software targeted primarily at the business

community to try to establish a standard. Some of this software is very insular, and unless it has the capacity to make your publications truly portable across platforms and document managing environments, you risk the corporate equivalent of ending up with a Betamax VCR in a VHS world.

Data and information as objects

Another factor to take into consideration when seeking portability for maximum publishing power is the trend for data in any form—texts, numbers, or graphics—to become independent of the application that created it. This opens the door to new forms of publishing. Alan Ashton, President of WordPerfect Corporation, envisages a future in which millions more people are linked by new developments in electronic mail services, so that they can exchange information in many formats. Version 6 of WordPerfect, the most popular of all word processors with over 11 million users around the world, incorporates more features to make this kind of universal publishing far more practical.

Everyone who uses Windows is already getting a foretaste of such new electronic publishing concepts. Its Clipboard saves data or graphics that you select in three formats that cover the requirements for them to be transferred to any other application running under Windows. Transfer the contents of the Clipboard to a floppy disk, or as a transmission by modem or over a network, and you effectively "publish" in a form that can be read by another Windows user anywhere, on any Windows system.

Clients and servers for dynamic data exchange

Dynamic data exchange (DDE) takes this concept a little further and brings us up against those much misunderstood buzzwords of network computing: client and server. A *server* is essentially an author—the provider of the data—while the *client* is the reader. In networking, the terms are usually applied to the computer systems playing these

roles; the server is the computer controlling the network, while the clients are the workstations.

There are also specific software applications, such as a word processor or spreadsheet, that play client and server roles. You might, as the server or publisher in an organization, establish a DDE link between your word processor and the spreadsheets running on hundreds of workstations around your organization. You might want certain spreadsheet reports to incorporate particular corporate information that is updated regularly. When a workstation client accesses the spreadsheet files that have been identified as requiring this DDE link, they can automatically be updated with the latest information from the relevant word processing file.

Olé for OLE

The next phase, *object linking and embedding* (OLE, pronounced "oh-lay"), goes farther by making far stronger links through a registry of all data or graphic objects that have been linked, so that the updating and transfer processes are far more efficient.

Embedding is making a copy of an object and placing it within a document or other form of electronic publication. When, as a client, you click on an embedded object, your computer makes all kinds of inquiries about how that object was created. If necessary, your computer sends a message to the server computer on the network to call up any functions that you, as the client, might need from the application software used to create the object. This adds a great deal of extra power and flexibility to publishing on a network.

The concept of OLE is continually being refined and expanded in its flexibility and capabilities. It is one of the driving forces transforming personal computers from their primary initial roles, as the creators of information, to their far more widespread destiny as primarily the retrievers of information that originated outside any particular individual system or workstation.

In other words, the personal computer moves from being primarily a publisher to being primarily a reader—which is just as it has to be,

since there will always be more readers than publishers. However, every reader has the potential to be able to publish back into the system, if allowed to do so. In some cases, authors will permit any, or selected, readers to make amendments. In other instances, documents will be published in forms that prevent them from being altered, although it may be possible to add notations and comments.

⇨ Exploit existing resources

Look closely also at what other applications are being used by your target readers (and by those publishing material to you that you might want to republish internally). For example, an organization already geared to Lotus spreadsheets, using Lotus Notes on a network, and perhaps with Ami Pro as the word processor of choice, has very good reasons to choose SmarText from Lotus for its internal publishing requirements.

Indeed, if the external audience is well-defined, SmarText can cover a lot of external publishing requirements also, despite the $99 charged for the Reader program at the time of this writing.

⇨ Is the reader truly portable?

The mention of a reader program brings up a major issue in electronic publishing. The best document-managing and publishing software might present you with additional complications and expense if you wish to use it outside its native environment, in a place where the ability to read it is severely restricted. Some of the leading applications to generate electronic publications do not have run-time reading modules that travel easily along with the files to enable your title to be read almost anywhere. Much of the electronic publishing software intended for business use is only fully effective on networked computers, or requires the licensing and installation of expensive and often large reader programs.

Even when you can attach a reader module that does not increase your publication's file size inordinately, the software company might impose considerable restrictions and stiff licensing fees if you publish externally, particularly for profit. Most of the shareware authoring programs have very few restrictions, if any, so you might want to consider, say, Writer's Dream, Dart, or Rexxcom Systems' XLPLUS for at least your external publishing requirements. They might not have all the power and features that you require to run a large and complex corporate internal system, but they could save you a lot of time, trouble, and money for external publishing.

Figure 3-2

This is the screen that readers see when they use the MiniViewer *that can be distributed along with* Common Ground *electronic publications. There is a pixel-by-pixel preservation of the original page that can be reproduced in either Windows or the Macintosh platforms.* No Hands Software, Inc.

Among the leading commercial software players, Common Ground (Fig. 3-2) was among the first to adopt the enlightened policy of placing very few restrictions on reader modules that a registered user of the authoring program could distribute. They encouraged you to distribute the reader without badgering you for additional contracts, permissions, and royalty payments—but only when you publish for noncommercial purposes.

Others, like Adobe with Acrobat (Fig. 3-3), and IBM with BookManager (Fig. 3-4), have been more restrictive, although market forces might compel them to loosen up. When choosing your authoring program, take very serious account of the usage policy and prices for the reader modules to ensure that they are as compatible as possible with your ultimate marketing and distribution objectives.

Figure 3-3

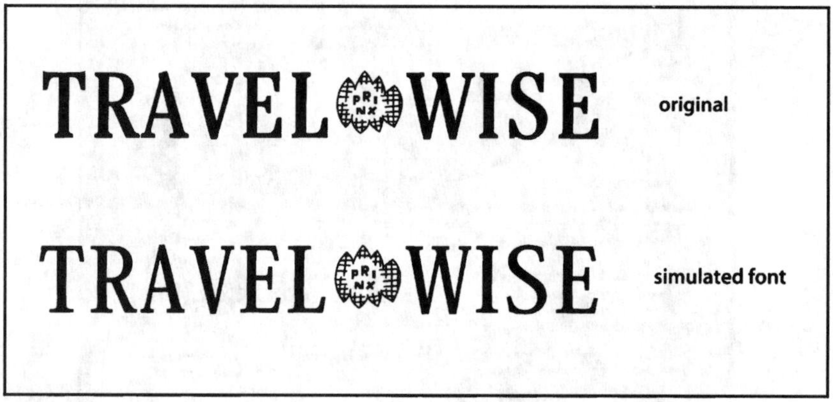

TRAVEL⊕WISE
original

TRAVEL⊕WISE
simulated font

Adobe Acrobat *tackles the problems of reproducing fonts that are not in the reader's system by special font-simulation technology.*
Adobe Systems, Inc.

Multimedia publications present particular problems, with the legal issues raised by Compton's NewMedia patents on search systems for multimedia CD-ROMs not clear at this time. It would be a sad thing for electronic publishing if such issues are not resolved quickly and drag on for years, as did the legal battles over "look and feel" graphical user interfaces.

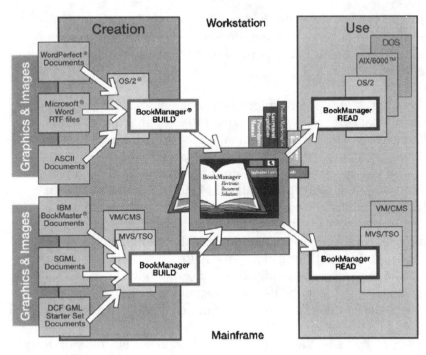

Figure 3-4

IBM's BookManager *system is a sophisticated family of software that enable e-books to be built from a wide variety of applications used in the business environment. They can be published for reading on most of the popular operating systems platforms, both mainframes and personal computers.* BookManager *is particularly proficient at "fuzzy logic" searches and multilingual publishing.*
© IBM Corporation, 1993

⇨ Simple solutions may be best for small operators

With those external publishing considerations in mind, some of the recommended shareware programs have added attractions for small organizations without SGML concerns. These shareware programs are particularly appropriate if you do not already have such facilities as computer networks and e-mail, so that your distribution will be largely on floppies. The best shareware programs have powerful hypertext and word-search capabilities, and because of their small

reader modules, the published pieces can be placed easily into a wide variety of electronic filing and document management systems, onto bulletin boards and network servers, or transmitted via modem or floppies.

Of course, larger organizations will probably prefer to go to advanced commercial software systems, such as Acrobat or Folio Views, but the shareware programs with minimal system requirements and complexity demonstrate for business users as well as individual authors that electronic publishing need not be highly complex, expensive, and difficult to achieve. Much that is written about electronic publishing focuses on commercial software that requires powerful hardware and steep learning curves for most of the staff who will use these programs. Much of the complexity arises from preoccupations with preserving formatting and other conventions from paper-based communications, or a perceived need to have very advanced search capabilities. Consequently, decisions to move away from paper are delayed because of the cost and disruption involved.

However, by using the appropriate programs, a business of any size can begin publishing and storing information electronically with minimal expense or trauma. Large text databases can be maintained and published with powerful search engines that take up minute memory or disk facilities. With askSam, for example, you can work fast and efficiently to search large text files on a basic PC with only a single floppy disk drive. I did that at one stage of researching this book, and as a result it would be a comparatively simple process to sort through those massive files, select material that could not be accommodated in the book, attach the little askSam reader search engine, and publish a self-contained expanded electronic version of this book with all my notes. XL2000 and Illustrated Reader are other examples of shareware programs that can create monitor screens with text formatted just as attractively as on the typical business paper document.

Consider such programs also for pilot projects in large organizations. Although a global corporate shift towards digitizing paper documentation is the preferred course in most cases, there might be situations in which it is more practical to initiate pilot programs involving a few individuals or departments. Here, you can experiment

with concepts before major commitments need to be made. The less complex, more compact, software with proficient readers that can easily be attached to text files offer practical publishing opportunities not feasible with the big guns in the business.

Coping with the flood

When going paperless, an organization must decide what to do with the inevitable continuing flood of hardcopy documentation on paper that you both receive and generate. It is not too difficult to ensure that what you create or receive electronically goes into your current and archival digital filing system, but incoming hardcopies also need to be scanned into digitized form.

Most document management systems use some form of scanning. This can range from scanning and filing every arriving document worth keeping to selectively scanning the most relevant information and maintaining cross-linked digital and hardcopy filing systems. The documents can be scanned to create graphic files that are facsimiles of the originals, or converted as they are scanned by optical character recognition (OCR) software to transform the words and numbers on paper into a format that the computer can understand.

Conversion makes it far easier to search for and find data, but no OCR programs are 100 percent reliable, so you can never be absolutely certain that OCR converted data is completely accurate. That might not always be important in the case of text, where the occasional literal mistake can be compensated for, but it could be vital when dealing with numbers, specifications, formulae, and other critical data, or when the originals are not ideal candidates for OCR because of the typefaces, formatting, color of the paper, or other practical limitations.

To cope with this, some organizations have dual systems, with documents scanned and converted for ease of reference, and the original paper sources also scanned graphically into bitmap images to provide a backup check for accuracy when required. Such a hybrid system can cope better with graphical material, such as charts, tables,

and diagrams. You can search through the digitized text quickly for the information that you need, then call up the bitmap graphical image of the original, complete with text and any graphics that it contained. With some software, both versions can be displayed side-by-side on the screen.

⇨ You might already have what you need

Even a small organization might already have familiar software in place that could form the basis for a painless move into electronic publishing on disk or over networks. Such software won't take you all the way and give you all the benefits, but as an easy interim phase, there is the potential to save a lot of time, money, and paper.

For example, integrated software packages have become far more sophisticated in recent years. One of these might be all you ever need to create sophisticated documents, complete with illustrations and search facilities. Microsoft Works (for DOS or Windows) and similar collections of word processors, spreadsheets, databases, and communications programs usually require quite modest system resources, so they work well on older hardware and particularly on portables, some of which even have these programs permanently installed in their ROM chips. Ease of use is also a prime feature of integrated software, so the learning curve is short and easy.

In a corporate environment in which such an integrated program is universally available, there might be no need to introduce new hardware or software, or provide additional training. Such an approach, in the appropriate circumstances, can prove to be a very painless first step to paperless publishing, with the prospect of significant cost savings. Management might, for example, request that monthly reports be distributed on floppies or over the network as Works files.

The later generations of full-featured word processing programs, such as WordPerfect, Ami Pro, and Microsoft Word also integrate

advanced drawing and other functions, so one of them might be the appropriate medium to adopt if the application is available to all your target readers.

The workgroup concept

Borland, famous for applications such as dBASE, Paradox, and Quattro Pro, has been developing an interesting internal publishing concept called Workgroup Desktop. As explained by chairman Philippe Kahn, it builds into applications the ability to function as part of a working group, thereby incorporating a publishing capability as a natural extension of the program.

The enabling technology is called OBEX, and it either comes with recent versions of Borland programs, or you can buy a Workgroup Enabling Kit to add what are called "publish and subscribe" facilities. In this sense, *publishing* involves supplying a data object—a file, document, or other piece of information—to the subscribers, who are other members of the workgroup. The subscribers can use a published data object wherever they are, either with the same application or in another application.

A key element of the concept is that the publishers can retain considerable control over who has access to their information. Many organizations find it easy to install OBEX because it can be used on any standard LAN, WAN, or e-mail system. By using it, you might be able to leverage an efficient paperless publishing system out of your existing familiar applications, without going through the trauma of having to move your information into a specialized document managing or publishing system.

Borland is one of a growing number of software publishers with active user group programs, so you might well be able to find people with similar needs and problems. It is always worth checking with manufacturers and on-line services for user groups or other special-interest groups when evaluating what systems to adopt. There is nothing to beat impartial, hands-on experience, and people in these groups are usually very generous in sharing what they have learned—including the mistakes they have made.

Creating search capabilities

The degree to which you have to index and create reference facilities for your paperless system depends on the kind of data in it, how you use that data, and the software and hardware systems in place. Some applications might require more work, at least initially, than maintaining traditional paper records.

Advantages of automatic hypertext

Hypertext, which involves creating links between related items of information, is a basic requirement, but programs vary enormously in how they forge these links. Some are very smart at doing it automatically according to various parameters, while others leave the author with the often very demanding task of deciding what section of texts should be linked, or if a graphic should be linked to other references.

It can take a lot of effort with some software to embed these *live cross-references* into text. After you have finished this daunting task, your document might have lost one of the main advantages of electronic publishing: its flexibility. The hypertext structure that you have created might make it more difficult to update or revise the document.

If, for example, you make changes to information that forms part of a chain of hypertext cross-references, you might have a snowball effect of new problems that need resolving. This can be a particular difficulty with those programs that, even if they do provide efficient hypertext links, try to imitate the formatting of hard copy documents.

SmarText from Lotus is a leading example of software that can reestablish hypertext links after changes have been made to text, a major requirement for electronic publications that will be revised frequently. SmarText achieves this by being independent of the hypertext framework embedded by the author in the source file. Unless you want tight control and are prepared to devote the time

required to do the job manually, look for automatic hypertext facilities in your authoring software.

Indexing can be automatic

Automatic indexing is a valuable feature also, but again, all authoring programs that do this job do not perform equally. There are many trade-offs. Some of the most sophisticated create powerful indices, but greatly increase the size of your publications—even doubling the file size.

A full-word index might also take up a lot of room and be slow to execute, particularly on an inherently slow medium like CDs or tape. Binary-tree structure indices can be very sophisticated in the way that they track through alphabetical relationships to pinpoint the word you see, but work far more slowly on many systems than the more primitive word-list type of index.

Also, as the software engineer tries to make an indexing capability smarter, there is the risk of introducing errors as well as slowing down the process. It is impossible to give generalized recommendations, because indexing and hypertext software programs keep leapfrogging each other in proficiency in this highly competitive market. It is a "horses for courses" situation; a program that performs well when the electronic publication is read from a fast hard drive might be an absolute dog when used to access a large database on a CD-ROM, or when running on a system with a comparatively slow CPU.

Good news for indexing professionals is that even an electronic publication offering full-text searching by word or phrase, or one with great hypertext links or keyword search parameters, probably still needs conceptual indexing. Even after centuries of print, the creative role of the indexer is still not properly understood, so we are still a long way from fully exploiting this skill in electronic publishing. Professional indexers might charge $40 an hour—or more—and take hundreds of hours to index a large book, so it is a task that can have significant timing and cost implications.

Software indexing programs can result in substantial savings, but at some stage with either hardcopy or electronic texts, skilled and sensitive human judgment must be applied to ensure that the index works from the viewpoint of the reader. Authors tend to want to put too much into an index and are so close to their subject that they might not be sensitive to how a typical reader will search. Very long indices are less of a problem with electronic than with printed texts, but authors should still seek a second opinion on whether their indexes really help to guide readers to the right places quickly. If you are self-publishing for the first time, or if indexing has always been left to your print publisher, you might find the American Society of Indexers', *A Guide to Indexing Software,* a good $15 investment. Helpful information is available from

American Society of Indexers
1700 18th Street NW
Washington, DC 20000

 # Full-word indexing

Once you get beyond the paper culture, you start to realize the flexibility in indexing and other search capabilities that are possible with electronic documents. Folio VIEWS, ZyIndex, Lotus Notes, and askSam are examples of full-text databases that do not require structures to be imposed on the data they contain. Every word is indexed, and the delays this could cause during search procedures are reduced by their efficiency, and, in some cases, data compression.

An important advantage of this kind of approach is that the information in the database tends to be far more dynamic. For example, a Folio "infobase" can develop as the changing information and the preferences of users mold it. With Acrobat, Replica, or Common Ground, or with the networked document managers, more rules need to be established up front.

Pick your software to fit the needs and style of the searching that will be conducted by your readers. A program with inherent flexibility is likely to be more forgiving if you don't identify all the needs and problems correctly up front. Look for features that make the system

easy to customize, by, for example, varying the degree to which various users are allowed to access or modify data.

The ability to search adds value

Once you add efficient searching to your organization's information resources, you might find that you have created a really tangible asset that now merits publishing more widely, either internally or externally. Folio VIEWS is an example of software that enables you to exploit such opportunities. It has some neat features for building a publication on disk to publish to people within an organization or externally to a wider audience. The Publish software necessary to view the document can be distributed with your publication for no extra cost, but there is a sliding scale of royalty fees if the publication is sold commercially.

VIEWS has various controls that the "owner" of a document (the originating author or publisher in control of the information) can impose on an end-user. There is considerable flexibility, going well beyond the file-control type of security. As well as regulating access to information, the owner can impose various restrictions on what the end-user can do with that information once able to read the file.

Over 100 publishers have put more than a thousand titles onto floppies and CD-ROMs using Folio VIEWS, so it is well up there among the leaders trying to establish an electronic publishing standard. In 1994, it was adding greater cross-platform capability, so information can readily be shared throughout the DOS, Windows, Macintosh, and Unix operating environments, making it suitable for mass-market publishing if you can strike a viable royalty deal with Folio to incorporate reading and search software that meets your needs.

Its flexibility and freeform structure make Folio VIEWS particularly appealing for both book and periodical publishers who have amassed a large backlist that can be tapped for additional revenues by releasing in electronic format. The weekly newspaper for lawyers, *Lawyers Weekly*, did this with excellent results.

Lawyers Weekly targets itself toward the small- and medium-sized legal practices, most of which do not have comprehensive or sophisticated research library facilities. Editorial staff were getting swamped with inquiries from readers seeking to know where in the back issues they could find reports of legal opinions and other useful information. Those inquiries added up to nearly 8,000 hours annually of expensive staff time, providing a prime motivation to put the back issues onto disk.

Within a year, five percent of the reader base was subscribing to *Lawyers Weekly on Disk*, which is updated quarterly on floppies and is generating significant revenue from both subscribers and advertisers. A clever touch is the way that editorial references are linked by hypertext to advertised products. This virtually eliminates the production problems that conventional print publications face in meeting advertiser demands for positioning.

An electronic advertisement can be as dynamic and mobile as editorial text, providing, of course, that the two can continue to be identified for what they are, and the linking does not become intrusive and arouse adverse reader reaction. This mobility and power have been used effectively in this case by advertisers with information services for attorneys. Just a click by the reader's mouse button can launch an animated demonstration of an on-line database or a CD-ROM title.

Where to start?

An existing e-mail internal network is often the starting point for launching an internal electronic publishing system because much of the corporate paper is already in computerized format. The next step in most cases is to computerize form-filling, and there is now a wide selection of excellent software to create electronic forms. The most appropriate one for your particular situation should blend well with your existing e-mail and database systems as the organization moves increasingly to paperless documentation.

If you want to start with a specific, largely self-contained activity, employee handbooks and technical manuals are obvious candidates. Computerize your employee handbook, and you might turn a nightmare into a powerful internal communications tool!

Electronic employee handbooks overcome many problems

One of the biggest pay-offs in business electronic publishing can be computerizing the documentation used to inform employees of their obligations and benefits. It is a job that tends to get put off, takes too long to complete, and is a persistent nightmare to keep updating. Putting this single most important internal document of any company, large or small, into electronic form can be very rewarding. The ease with which it can be updated also protects management in meeting its various legal needs to inform employees.

Smart manuals accommodate different skills levels

The varying skills levels within an organization have long bedeviled the authors of technical manuals striving to give comprehensive information to the inexperienced, without burdening more highly skilled staff with unnecessary details of familiar procedures and principles. Electronic publishing can overcome this human resources problem in several intriguing ways, particularly by giving end-users the ability to customize a manual to fit their needs and knowledge.

That customizing process can even become largely automatic, as illustrated in the combination of computer repair manuals turned into on-line electronic documents using FrameMaker. This authoring program was made to work together with a small data management application. The controlling management program monitors each technician's use of the electronic manuals and learns to customize its responses to individual requests. The responses given are those most appropriate to the knowledge level of each technician.

In adding such values, electronic publishing within the business environment goes much further than just saving money compared to paper. When your information goes electronic, it becomes more dynamic, and then it is possible to make it really work for you.

Marketing your electronic books

A UTHOR Henry Brooks Adams reaches out from before the time of electronic publishing to give us a fundamental truth about the marketing today of words in any medium, particularly in electronic formats. "The difference is slight, to the influence of an author," wrote Adams, "whether he is read by five hundred readers, or by five hundred thousand; if he can select the five hundred, he reaches the five hundred thousand."

Although he didn't know it then, Adams is writing about database marketing, the third most important development after electronic publishing and information highways to empower authors and entrepreneurs seeking to publish profitably, or to get their messages to their target audiences. Database marketing offers you previously undreamed of efficiency in targeting your titles directly to those most likely to be interested in them.

Except for purely creative or personal works, such as poetry and autobiography, identifying the right database of potential readers should be the first step in creating a successful title, rather than first writing and compiling an electronic publication, then looking around trying to identify the market for it. To be profitable, almost any work must be reader-driven, created to fit the needs of a defined database of readers who will be most interested in its subject matter and treatment. For example, if most of your target readers have sound systems on their computers (Fig. 4-1), make sure your publications exploit it.

It is virtually impossible to make money publishing today if your marketing depends on buying advertising space or engaging in direct mail to reach mass markets. The cost and wastage are simply prohibitive. Of course, if you have a really hot title or author, you might be able to generate enough sales to cover the cost of an effective mass-market publicity campaign. But such titles are the exceptions, and most of them are best handled by the big publishing houses.

The general rule for the small publisher and self-publishing author is to zero in on your prime prospects and concentrate your efforts on reaching them. There must be close coordination of the creative and marketing processes, with the inherent advantages of electronic publishing giving the self-publisher significant advantages.

Figure 4-1

Authors must keep informed of fast-changing patterns of consumer demand, which can greatly influence the style and content of marketable e-books. Sound, for example, has become very important to millions of users, who are investing heavily in sophisticated sound cards and speakers, such as this SoundWave 32 *package.*
Orchid Technology

Identify your market

The best starting point is usually to identify the professional organization, special-interest group, trade association, or specialist publication that caters specifically for the readers you are targeting. There might only be one, or perhaps several, such means of reaching them.

The next step is to verify that there are bulletin boards, newsletters, journals, conferences, or at least cost-effective mailing lists to provide vehicles through which to promote your title to potential readers. Rethink your project carefully if there are severe restrictions on using these resources. Some professional organizations will neither give you exposure in their journals, nor permit you to rent their lists of members. If you cannot see a cost-efficient way to reach your target readers, rethink the validity of your entire project—unless, of course, you just want to do it for fun, personal satisfaction, or some altruistic motive without an income-generating element.

 # The right marketing database can launch a creative project

When you identify a target market with a database and cost-efficient ways of using it, you have a good starting point from which to launch a project. The viability is enhanced greatly when you link that database to a closely matched source of information or expertise to tap into. Electronic publishing can be very efficient at linking hard-to-find information with the readers who have a need to know.

For example, I am involved in a multimedia title that will help owners of older air-cooled Volkswagen cars and vans prevent their vehicles from overheating. It became a viable project when we identified a technician with unique experience in this field, and two monthly magazines with affordable advertising rates and appropriate editorial opportunities to reach a large proportion of our target readers. Our testing of those comparatively low-cost media will influence whether to launch an enhanced CD-ROM version that might economically incorporate video clips from stock, and further sequences and searchable specification sheets and catalogs from manufacturers.

 # Commonsense essentials

So much has been written, so many seminars given, and so much nonsense spoken about the so-called secrets of successful marketing that any would-be electronic publishing entrepreneur would be well advised to get back to basic commonsense essentials. There are no miracle ways to market publishing's hardcopy or electronic products—although being able to load an entire electronic publication, or promotional material for it, to a few bulletin boards and see it spread quickly around the world comes close to being miraculous!

Your publication will not be distributed or even read if it does not meet a need for the end-users and is not competently put together. That maxim applies also to marketing over the new information highways. Do not expect them to be a cheap and easy way to make

money from writing and publishing mediocre material. What you write and publish must meet a need from readers who you can reach with your marketing to tell them what is available. Your publication must be written and presented to an acceptable standard, and released in a format appropriate to its markets.

Of course, there are exceptions, but they do tend to prove the basic rules. For example, a uniquely successful bookstore in Arizona sells only one book. It succeeds, not so much because of the subject matter or content of the book, but because of the novelty of a bookstore in which the colorful author sits and promotes his volume of homely anecdotes about Western life. It pulls in lots of tourist business, but I cannot see it working on the Internet. Nor, as several publishers and bookstores have already declared, is this book appropriate for conventional print publishing and distribution.

Nontraditional book marketing

Book publishers, distributors, wholesalers, and retailers are being challenged by a steadily increasing number of alternative ways of selling books. Electronic-book (e-book) retail outlets are not limited to computer stores or bookstores. Just as printed books have broken into many nontraditional retail categories, so can publications on disks, with specialty stores, hardware and home supply centers, drug stores, souvenir shops, and many others being potential sales outlets if they cater for the same consumer categories as your title.

Point-of-sale displays

The acceptability of your electronic publication by retailers could well be influenced very much by its packaging. You will find it much easier to get good selling positions and do some realistic test marketing if you package your titles in attractive and functional point-of-sale displays. These can be expensive to create in small quantities, but good results can be obtained by dressing up the plain cardboard display units sold by larger office suppliers, and printing and paper supply stores.

In these display-unit packages, you get a set of cut-out card sheets that fold and slot together into a display case suitable for counter display. There are various sizes available, with those used for displaying printed flyers suitable for compactly packaged disks. You can customize these display cases by sticking on desktop-published material containing the title, descriptions, price, and other essential information. Make this information bold, graphic, and easily read so that it attracts impulse purchasers. You can create the point-of-sale display material on your computer, print a color master out on a laser or inkjet printer, and then have color copies made at a printshop.

This is a good application also for silkscreen printing, so that you can have display material on all the visible faces of the display unit printed in one pass before the display is folded.

It is common wholesale practice to offer the display along with the product as a package for a minimum order of, say, 10 units. When the retailer reorders, you just supply the product to go into the display unit. These cardboard point-of-sale displays also lend themselves to racking operations, where the publisher visits the retail outlets and replenishes the inventory that has been sold to keep the rack full.

The world's largest cookbook

Some of these marketing concepts have been used with a remarkable electronic publication, the world's largest cookbook, CookBook USA from J&D Distributing in Orem, Utah (800-847-2890). Over a million different recipes are crammed onto a single CD-ROM. The exact number is 1,094,579, including 893 recipes for diabetics and 80,943 different ways of preparing brownies!

This remarkable compilation comes from over 4,000 different regional cookbooks that in print would cost $30,000, and take up a lot of shelf space—all strong marketing and publicity points to amplify the attention-grabbing title. A practical feature for readers is the option to print out individual recipes as 3-x-5-inch hardcopies, the size of cards often favored by recipe collectors for ease of reference.

J&D realized the potential for selling this kind of publication in nontraditional bookstore or software outlets, and has been offering retailers an imaginative multilevel marketing package. The $800 dealer kit comprises 20 CD-ROMs with a recommended selling price of $49.95 each, 40 floppies made up of five in each of eight categories of specific recipe selections, and a wooden display rack with signage. For smaller orders, or to restock the rack, wholesale discounts range from 40% for single CDs or floppies, to 50% in lots of 250.

Obviously, the key to the project was having ready access to the original print versions of the cookbooks, which have been published over many years. Many titles would be permanently out of print and just disappear from view, if it were not for this unusual electronic publishing project.

Organizations to help you market

Many of the marketing methods used by print publishers to sell through nontraditional outlets can be applied to electronic publishing, which is why you might benefit from joining local or national organizations that still focus almost exclusively on printed works. Those that offer cooperative marketing programs can greatly reduce the costs and risks, and increase the results, of your marketing program. Such organizations can be particularly cost-efficient in direct-mail promotions to target markets such as librarians and professional organizations.

Local self-publisher groups tend to be richer in creative diversity and high hopes than they are in marketing expertise. However, The Publishers Marketing Association and its associated state and regional publishers' associations bring together many professionals, and provides a range of cooperative marketing activities. The PMA is a nonprofit association of book, audio, and video publishers which can be a very cost-effective route into exhibiting at national and international book fairs. In 1994 it launched a mentoring program that Executive Director Jan Nathan says will "assist fledgling

publishers in getting started and hopefully avoiding catastrophic mistakes." Contact this organization at

PMA
2401 Pacific Coast Highway, Suite 102
Hermosa Beach, CA 90254
310-372-2732

Particularly interesting for many small publishers are the PMA's cooperative mailings to libraries. Throughout the year, it targets various categories of acquisition librarians, and the cost to participate is very reasonable. For only $145 and 3,300 copies of your letter-size flyers (which can be printed on both sides) you can reach the college, junior college, and university libraries who are becoming far more electronic-publishing conscious.

There are also PMA mailings to independent bookstore buyers and to genre-specific reviewers, which enable you to participate in effective, well-targeted cooperative catalogs. This can be by far the safest and cheapest way to get details of your title into the hands of reviewers. Each catalog is in a newsletter format, with a typical cost being $145 to feature in an issue sent to nearly 4,000 daily and weekly newspaper reviewers across the U.S.

Your front cover and 100 words of description introduce your title to these reviewers, and they can order review copies easily by sending back an included request card.

Competing for shelf space

Before getting involved in any existing book-marketing efforts, always remember the inherent advantages and disadvantages of the electronic media. Your floppies might get lost among the hardcopies competing for shelf or table space in a cooperative stand at a book fair, or if the pitch is being made to distributors and bookstores who are not really interested in electronic editions.

You might do better with local, regional, national, and highly specialized works targeted at niche markets, if you direct your marketing efforts along the information highways as well as the local routes. Used efficiently, they might be the best way to hit your targets. These are among the exciting prospects opened up by the Clinton Administration's policy for open cable, telephone, and data transmission networks that reach into virtually every home and can be used by all information providers. For writers and other creative artists, this is far more significant than concepts like public-access television in providing real electronic muscle to disseminate and market your works.

Begin with research

Unless you already have a clearly defined market, know what that market requires and, equally important, know how to alert it that your product is available, then you must start with some basic research. Fortunately, there are excellent ways to tap into the necessary expertise, much of it developed in the shareware arena where electronic publishing is becoming a major player.

Authors as marketers and publishers

Steve Hudgik, one of the pioneers of electronic publishing in the shareware environment, emphasizes that authors seeking profits "must remember that 80% of what they must do is not related to writing. They must have business skills and, in particular, marketing skills."

"The electronic book," says Steve, "must be more than written—it must be *designed* in all respects for its target market. This includes software design and the packaging, which does not necessarily refer to the box that something is packed in, but includes aspects such as the opening and closing screens. Also, the distribution channel must be carefully evaluated, courted, sold to, and supplied with product." Steve has lots of marketing and distribution ideas about how authors can be remunerated for their works—and remember that he speaks from experience as, so far, one of comparatively few financially successful electronic self-publishers.

"Having updates to a book available via modem can be very important," Steve emphasizes, and his HomeCraft business moved quickly into providing on-line services because of his conviction that this will be a major growth area for marketing electronic publications.

When planning your marketing strategy to include on-line facilities, consider carefully if you are targeting readers who will be attracted by the speed and convenience of using a modem. If you have an appropriate concept for such a market sector, you could be on to a real winner.

Easy ways to keep informed

A basic requirement in any marketing is to be well-informed about what is happening in your markets. Without good intelligence, the odds of succeeding decrease greatly. Fortunately, there are many easy and low-cost ways to keep informed about what is happening in electronic publishing so that your own publications stand the best chance for success or you can identify best where to market your work.

The marketing intelligence you require is very different from that provided in the typical computer magazines. Despite all the new-product hype in the computer magazines, you really don't need, as a self-publishing author, to keep well informed about cutting-edge advances in the technology. If you become part of the obsession to keep up with hardware and software development, you risk wasting time and money and, even worse, losing touch with your markets.

As an electronic publisher, you must never forget that most of your potential readers have systems that are two, three, four, or more years behind the current generation of hardware being touted by the computer industry. While the latest technology might therefore be largely irrelevant to you, you must keep up to date with what people are actually doing with personal computing resources, particularly in the field of shareware distribution and marketing.

Some of the best and hottest information about shareware marketing has been coming in recent years from Jim Hood on Mercer Island in

Washington, who uses a humble PC-AT with most modest memory and speed capabilities that won't come close to running Windows! Jim has been using comparatively basic hardware to produce sophisticated intelligence about electronic publishing and the shareware industry. It's not the machine that counts, but the human intellect telling it what to do.

The shareware market that Jim monitors so well for electronic authors and publishers ranges from millionaires with substantial corporations to large numbers of entrepreneurs and creative software programmers working from home. These independent software authors established the environment in which electronic self-publishing became possible, and their enterprise and the enormous range of programs they generate continues to fuel the disk libraries, distribution companies, and thousands of bulletin boards that offer you so many opportunities to market your works.

There is no single print publication, or even a combination of books and magazines, that really keep you up-to-date with what is happening in the shareware field. But, at very little cost, you can have ready access to a superb source of continuing informed comment and potentially valuable information through The Electronic Publishing Forum from John Galuszka's Serendipity Systems. Combine this on-disk information services with Bob Schenot's, *The Shareware Book*, Steve Hudgik's, *Writing & Marketing Shareware*, and the traffic on the Digital Publishing Association's bulletin board and other on-line services, and you have access to exceptional expertise about the marketing of shareware programs and electronic publications at minimal cost.

You might also want to join the Association of Shareware Professionals (ASP), a very valuable source of information relevant to the marketing and distribution of electronic publications, even if they are not marketed as shareware. ASP members are branching out into such fields as rack vending in supermarkets and department stores, and participating in on-disk catalog collections.

There is a camaraderie and spirit of cooperation in the shareware business that enables these experts to report fully on the bad as well as the good results that electronic authors and publishing

entrepreneurs experience when they test the enormous range of marketing opportunities available. Remember, however, that most electronic publications are not targeted at computer users per se, but at people in special-interest groups who also have access to personal computers. The medium itself is not necessarily the best way to get your marketing message out.

If you are writing about computing, you probably need to target computer users and can use the shareware distribution and marketing environment to particularly good effect. Everyone venturing into electronic publishing through shareware should read Robert Schenot's, *The Shareware Book*. It is available electronically through shareware channels and packed with practical information that can be applied to the creation, distribution, and marketing of publications in electronic formats.

This book could save you hundreds—perhaps thousands—of dollars just with Robert's tips about discount postage opportunities. Not only is the content of Robert's book valuable, he also provides an object lesson in practical electronic and hardcopy publishing. An evaluation shareware copy of his book is distributed with very few restrictions for anyone to copy, generating sales for the printed paperback version and a package of useful software programs.

Join the club for marketing help and information

To narrow your focus and link up with a group specifically concerned with marketing electronic publications, consider joining the Digital Publishing Association (DPA). When the history of electronic publishing comes to be written, there will be a special place in it for DPA's founder, Dr. Ronald Albright. Ron is a specialist in internal medicine who found the experience of publishing electronically so fascinating that he wrote one of the first electronic books about it, and established the first association of enthusiasts for this new medium.

Even when Ron underwent a heart-bypass operation in 1993, he continued his commitment to nurturing the infant Digital Publishing Association that he had founded a little more than a year earlier. Continuing as president of the DPA, he has done a great deal to bring together writers, software authors, and entrepreneurs who share his belief in the future of electronic publishing.

"I started the DPA to try to help organize a new band of talented but disorganized artists into an effective group," Ron recalls. "I hope that we will continue to gather momentum in establishing electronic publishing as a legitimate medium for authors and publishers."

Ron provides an interesting marketing case history. He self-published three computer books in conventional print form before discovering the benefits of releasing his work on disk. He sold out the 1,500 copies of the first edition of his book, *The Communicating Computer*, but although the sales had been brisk, he doubted if a viable market remained for a reprint costing $2,000. Then he came across the shareware Hyperwriter program, which enables text files to be compiled into attractive screen displays with hypertext reference facilities. This, one of the first shareware book-authoring programs, made it possible for Ron to issue an electronic edition of his book.

"Thousands more readers have now seen my work, and the cost to publish the book in this form is negligible," Ron reports. "I had discovered paperless publishing and am now convinced that it will be the wave of the future. I foresee the day when electronic publishing will become more common than printed materials."

Soon after Ron established the DPA and set up its bulletin board in 1991, the word spread that here was a source of quality information about a totally new way of publishing. Often the lines to the board have been jammed with authors, programmers, and even curious print publishers trying to get on-line to find out more.

In addition to being able to go on-line for discussions with other writers and publishers, the DPA's bulletin board is a unique source of

information that could pay off handsomely in the way you produce and market your publications. The board reflects DPA's vision, as expressed in Ron Albright's forecast that "it will be the norm for most books to be available from modem-accessible electronic publishing houses. Readers will be billed for downloading. The authors will get royalties based on electronic sales. You will get updates quickly and easily. Bookshelves will be replaced by disk cabinets."

By investing the modest $25 annual membership fee to join the Digital Publishing Association, you become part of a very diverse group of writers, publishers, and programmers with a shared objective to promote electronic publishing as an alternative to traditional, paper-based publishing. The primary goals of the DPA are

➤ To inform the general public and the writing community about the economic and creative advantages of digital publishing over paper-based publishing.

➤ To encourage broader distribution of disk-based reading materials through libraries, computer user groups, and booksellers.

➤ To assist members in marketing and distributing their publications.

➤ To provide a forum through which DPA members may communicate, share ideas, and learn from each other.

➤ To foster a high degree of professionalism among authors, publishers, and programmers working in the digital publishing marketplace.

The DPA and its members, who now range across the United States, Canada, and Europe, use the world's expanding bulletin board systems, commercial communications systems (such as CompuServe and GEnie), and computer user groups to increase awareness among computer users of the quality of reading material available through electronic publications. As a member, you have direct access to a unique source of expertise and will be pleasantly surprised by the generosity with which members share their knowledge.

The DPA bulletin board number in the U.S. is 205-854-1660. It has an expanding list of electronic books that you can download.

 # Marketing to the world

You can market to the world with disks and files transmitted by modem in ways denied to traditional book publishing. The Internet, discussed in a later chapter, is helpful, but has some built-in problems when actually trying to sell products. However, it and other on-line services and organizations offer valuable marketing intelligence and promotional resources.

 # Foreign language editions get easier

The international market really opens up with the much-improved translation software now available. Even the major problems of moving from the Arabic alphabets of most Western languages into the graphical and symbolical elements of written Asian languages are being bridged more effectively. You now have a choice of creating at least draft translations in the main European and Central and South American languages for an outlay of under $100 for programs such as the surprisingly competent Spanish Assistant and its French, German, and Italian stablemates.

Trying to create a Japanese translation using the over 6,000 possible combinations of Kanji, Hiragana, and Katakana will set you back more in initial cost because the task becomes much more complex and difficult, but the returns can be very attractive if you make available fast treatments of subjects otherwise only covered in English. The Japanese market promises to become very important for electronic publishers and, because so many readers there are quite proficient in English as a second language, it is practical to format English originals and computer-generated translations side-by-side for release in situations where there is not the time or the budget to generate a professionally translated and edited Japanese version.

The program with which to generate this type of electronic publication is EZ Japanese Writer (Fig. 4-2). Writers can start using it at the initial marketing planning phase, well ahead of the publishing process, to start good things happening sooner. It took some two years after the original North American publication for the first of my books to be released in Japan, by which time I was already deep into an update. Now I can use my computer to turn my original proposal in English for a new book into comprehensible Japanese that can either help in negotiations with a prospective American publisher or be sent directly to a possible Japanese publishing partner.

Figure 4-2

An example of fax message translated by EZ Japanese Writer and printed by HP laser printer.

FAX MESSAGE*
ファックス・メッセージ

January 2nd, 1993, 3:00 p.m.
１９９３年１月２日、午後の３：００．

TO*, Mr. Tanaka, Tokyo Electric
宛名（様）、Mr.タナカ、東京エレクトリック

FROM*, Mr. Brend Bellmar
発信者、Mr.ブレンド　ベルマー

SUBJECT*, your product inquiry
件名、あなたの製品の引合い

Dear Mr. Tanaka.
親愛なるMr.タナカ．

Thank you for your interest in our products.
あなたの私たちの商品に関する興味にありがとう．

I mailed the catalogs.
私はカタログを郵便で出しました．

In 1960, we started the electronics business.
１９６０年に、私たちはエレクトロニクスの事業を始めました．

Then, we have diversified into many industries.
そして、私たちは多くの産業に多様化しました．

We have been manufacturing these products for 5 years.
私たちは５年の間にこれらの商品を製造していました．

As the next step, we recommend you to buy our sample products.
次のステップとして、私たちはあなたに私たちの見本の商品を買うように勧めます．

You can buy samples at 40% discount off suggested retail price.
あなたは希望小売価格から見本を４０％の割引で買うことができます．

Currently, we do not have distribution in Japan.
現在、私たちは日本において販売を持ちません．

We look forward to receiving your proposal in this matter.
私たちはこの内容でのあなたの提案を受け取ることを期待します．

Sincerely yours.
敬具．   (rpyprdiq.for)

Writers are empowered to crash through linguistic barriers and exploit global markets with radically new software such as EZ Japanese Writer. Having the original language and the translation formatted to run together makes fast and economical machine translation feasible.
E.J. Bilingual, Inc.

I+t is still essential to have any machine translation edited by a native speaker of the language before commercial publication. However, in the case of an initial proposal, it is acceptable in most cases to submit both language versions, with an explanation that the translation is only a machine-generated draft.

Many of the translation programs enable you to do a printout with the original and the translation running side-by-side, or with each line of the original language above the equivalent line of the translation. This is going to become a very common way of communicating internationally in business correspondence, and so particularly appropriate to many business, technical, and scientific research publications. It is a real boon to a reader in, say, Japan, for whom English is a second language with which he or she still battles for fluency, to receive a technical document or book in both the original English and a reasonable literal Japanese translation.

Software translators

Other new aids to international electronic publishing are programs that actually translate the menus and help screens for software programs, not just text. (The Help menus and texts in Windows are fast becoming a viable publishing medium in their own rights, particularly to accompany published databases. Programs such as RoboHelp enable you to create these Help documents directly from a word processor.)

CyberMedia of Los Angeles (310-843-0800) recently released its Multitalk Ambassador to enable an English-language version of a Windows program to function with the menus, and other user-interface elements of most of the world's major languages. This could be very important if you are shipping your electronic texts with run-time reader modules with which your end-users are not familiar. CyberMedia also produces diagnostic and repair software for Windows called First Aid, which I suspect will become essential for many people coping with the system conflicts created by multimedia hardware.

Europeans have their own group also

Despite NAFTA, Europe remains effectively the world's largest publishing market, so if you have an international strategy, it must be included. There is no electronic publishing group in Europe equivalent to the DPA in the U.S., but if you want to market in

Europe and keep abreast of what is happening there, consider joining the Author-Publisher Enterprise (A-PE). Its satellite enterprise, New Meridian Limited, provides products and services for authors. Together they are a rich source of practical marketing information for self-published works.

Although the A-PE has been given an initial impetus by the venerable Society of Authors, it is completely independent and spearheads efforts in Europe to enable writers of all kinds to exercise their rights to be published without being fleeced by the vanity presses. The A-PE evolved from a visit to England in 1985 by Dan Poynter, who has done so much to stimulate self-publishing in print in the U.S. British authors interested in self-publishing began networking informally after Dan's presentation at a Society conference, and then set up as a separate organization.

"Within three months—without any promotion on our part—we had received several thousand inquiries from aspiring writers," founding chairman John Dawes recalls. "No wonder vanity publishers are flourishing!"

That remarkable response reflects the universal urge to write and be published. British authors express the same frustration with their print publishing establishment as their counterparts in the U.S. British involvement in electronic publishing is very important, because Britain is still the intellectual gateway into much of the English-speaking world, particularly the developing nations in Africa and Asia.

The A-PE offers networking, marketing, and information facilities that tend to be print-oriented, but usually can be just as applicable to electronic publications. The members are predominantly experienced authors, very practical, and passionate about maintaining standards in author-publishing in any format. Membership costs only 25 pounds annually. For more information, write to A-PE's secretary, Trevor Lockwood, at

7 Kingsland Road
West Mersea
Colchester, Essex CO5 8RB
England, U.K.

Foreign marketing sources

For evaluating international as well as North American trends and prospects, *Publishers Weekly* keeps its finger on the pulse of both hardcopy and electronic book publishing. Subscriptions are expensive, but most local librarians subscribe. You might have to ask specifically, as librarians tend to keep it tucked away in their offices and are reluctant to allow it to be checked out. The same goes for another useful resource for marketing information, the American Library Association's *American Libraries*.

If you need specific information on foreign markets, go directly to consulates and such sources as the annual U.S. book export and import figures compiled by the Department of Commerce's Bureau of the Census. In recent years, these have been showing massive increases in exports of books to Mexico and some South American countries, with Japan and some European markets buoyant also. With CompuServe and other on-line services expanding into Mexico, the opportunities for electronic publishing might increase there significantly.

UNESCO (the United Nations Educational, Scientific, and Cultural Organization) in Paris provides lots of valuable market research pointers in its annual Statistical Yearbook and various special reports. By matching up international patterns of computer availability and usage with the UNESCO figures for printed books, you can predict where potential markets might exist. Although the U.S. tends to be viewed as the world's most attractive market for almost any product, in fact Germany and the United Kingdom each release more book titles annually, with France, Italy, and Japan being among other significant publishing territories.

China publishes far more titles every year—over 70,000—than any other single country, but poses particular problems for electronic book exports because of the few computers per capita and widespread piracy. Expect those Chinese with computers and access to on-line services to get hold of an increasing number of English texts available electronically, then pirate those copies on disk and on paper. The same situation prevails in the former Soviet Union. It is

becoming easier to get distributed in the world's largest reading markets, but even more difficult to get paid!

Keep in touch—
and don't forget to list your works

Another great way for electronic authors and publishers around the world to keep in touch with what is happening in this young medium is through Serendipity Systems' bulletin board. This organization also offers you the facility to list your electronic publications just as books in print are listed in directories and reference works. If you do not like spending time on-line, you can get a lot of valuable information mailed to you regularly as an electronic publication on disk.

Serendipity Systems releases an on-disk magazine called The Electronic Publishing Forum quarterly. It includes evaluation copies of new or updated shareware, as well as news and technical and marketing information. The subscription is $12 a year.

It also publishes the annual Electronic Books in Print, which costs $6 on disk in the U.S. and $8 (in U.S. funds) for overseas orders. If you are publishing on-disk or on-line, make sure that your titles are listed in the next edition. It is compiled in the final quarter of the year, and there is no charge to have your book listed. Information on a new publication is usually first briefly listed in the New Electronic Publications section of its forum, then added to Electronic Books in Print at the end of the year.

To be listed by Serendipity Systems, you will need to supply comprehensive information about your work on disk as an ASCII text file. Here is the information that you must provide to get a listing in Electronic Books in Print:

➤ *Author*: the name(s) of the author(s) or editor(s), as appropriate

➤ *Title*: the title by which your work is identified

➤ *Category*: the nature of your book or program, e.g., fiction or nonfiction, poetry, novel, self-help, technical, etc.

➤ *Subject*: a summary of the topics covered

➤ *Interface*: the program used to compile and display your work, such as DART

➤ *Systems supported*: IBM-PC, Macintosh, etc.

➤ *System requirements*: exactly what hardware and operating system end-users require to run your publication—the RAM; hard disk size, high-density floppy, or CD-ROM; the type of monitor; Windows and operating system needs; and so on

➤ *Publisher*: the name and address of the publisher or distributor (you, for self-publishers)

➤ *Price*: the price of a single copy, multiple copies, and site licenses if appropriate, plus any surcharges for different disk sizes and formats, shipping in the U.S. or to foreign destinations, sales taxes, etc.

➤ *Available from*: the specific address where copies can be obtained, including a mailing address, plus bulletin board details if you supply on-line

➤ *Notes*: any special features, such as whether you are distributing as shareware

➤ *Descriptive blurb*: a brief description of the work—not a duplication of information you have given already, but such details as the target readership categories, any unique features, and the qualifications of the author

➤ *Excerpt*: a representative sample of the contents so that potential readers can evaluate your book. (There is no formal limit to the size of the extract, but don't provide so much that the potential reader will not need the whole work!)

The requirements are listed here because they constitute a very useful exercise to bring together the basic information you must have about your publication for marketing and other purposes. For example, compiling your listing for Electronic Books in Print can be a big help in creating the media releases you distribute and the background briefing to accompany review copies of your work.

Address your listing, or write for more information, to

John Galuszka, Editor
Electronic Books in Print
Serendipity Systems
P.O. Box 140
San Simeon, CA 93452

(That address, near fantastic Big Sur on the Pacific Coast, illustrates the footloose geographic flexibility of locating an electronic publishing enterprise!)

How to get an ISBN number

It might be vital for your publication to carry an ISBN (International Standard Book Number). The ISBN system applies to books, software, and mixed media. It is used throughout the publishing industry as a reference for ordering and tracking publications. Although you are not required to put this ten-digit number on your title, it can be crucial in making sales.

In the U.S., the agency for this international system is

R.R. Bowker
121 Chanlon Road
New Providence, NJ 07984

They will send the forms that get you started. This is a service available only to publishers, not authors, so put on your publishing hat when applying for an allocation of ISBN numbers.

Every title has its own unique ISBN that can never be reassigned, even if the work goes out of print. That number should appear in the book, on the packaging, and in all promotional materials. You would be amazed how quickly it can find its way into various databases and references that could lead to sales for you. When you reprint a title, it must keep the same ISBN, but when you change formats or revise a work, you need a new ISBN. If you are transferring a book from print to electronic media, it will require a new ISBN, even if you make no changes to the content.

Different ISBNs are required for different disk formats, so if you publish on floppies and on CD-ROM, make sure to give each its own number from the list allocated to you as a publisher. When packaging several components, such as a book with disks, one ISBN number covers everything in the package. For example, this book, which includes a disk, has only one ISBN because the disk is not available separately. However, if you have a print version and a disk available separately, each requires an ISBN.

Software publishers do not give new ISBNs to new versions of their programs because these revisions and enhancements usually make the previous version of the program obsolete and not readily available to purchase. However, you need to think carefully about a new issue of an electronic publication to assess whether it ranks as a revised edition of a book and justifies a new ISBN.

If you are really serious about marketing your work through trade channels, you will probably also want to use the ISBN/BOOKLAND EAN barcode, which enables your ISBN to be printed in a worldwide compatible barcode format. Although you can generate barcodes from a laser printer, you might find it more cost-effective to get a barcode master film from one of the suppliers on the list that Bowker will provide with your ISBN allocations.

Even if you do not plan to sell to libraries or through the book trade, still consider getting an ISBN. It might enhance the credibility of your work to the particularly important marketing medium considered next: the journalists who might write about your book, or review it.

Editorial publicity

Editorial publicity, contrary to what many do-it-yourself marketing books tell you, is not free. It requires an investment of time and money, both of which are expensive. If you are prepared to use your own time, the actual cash outlay can be very modest and limited mainly to creating and mailing hardcopy and on-disk information to carefully selected media people.

As a former public-relations consultant to several major companies, you might expect me to suggest that you get professional help from the experts. Not so, unless it is very important to use someone with the right media contacts. If you are able to create an electronic publication that merits attention by the media, then you are probably the best-qualified person to create the editorial material to promote it. Thousands of press releases from PR professionals all over the world have crossed my desk, and I can tell you that it's not difficult to do as well, or better, than most of them.

For a start, most media releases are boring. They lack human interest and genuine news angles. Presumably, to write a book you feel some enthusiasm about the subject, perhaps even a passion. If you're passionate about your book, so much the better. Try in your publicity to communicate that passion to the media, and give journalists topical news angles and human-interest stories about you, your book, or the subjects covered in it.

Don't expect journalists plowing through piles of PR mail every day to see the stories unless you hit them right between the eyes with attention-grabbing illustrations and strong informative first paragraphs. Customize your approach to the special interests of the targeted journalists and their publications. For example, your electronic book on model railways featuring long-forgotten sounds of steam engines as audio clips has one angle for the popular, general-interest media, and probably something quite different for the magazines catering to model railway enthusiasts.

Don't hesitate to back up your printed media release with a copy of it on a floppy packed with other relevant information, including a complete review copy of your title, if that is possible. Get a jump on others who haven't woken up to the fact that almost every journalist now writes on a computer and so is receptive to well-compiled promotional material on disk. Journalists appreciate being able to search efficiently through text files, and abstract quotes, excerpts, and illustrations without needing to retype the text or make time-consuming telephone calls.

Don't expect the *New York Times* to carry word-for-word the story you submit about your work, but there are hundreds of other

publications that might do so with minimum editing if you present it to them in universal forms such as ASCII and RTF that they can dump straight into their electronic editing systems. Some of those smaller publications might actually be more effective in reaching your target markets than the big guns.

A well-planned mail shot of promotional material and review copies to the media might be all you need to do to kick-start the direct selling of your electronic publication. This will only work, though, if you have a really hot title or can provide unique information that will appeal to the specific target markets covered by the publications in which you seek exposure, whose readers have a definite "need to know" what you are offering.

For example, if you have compiled on-disk the most comprehensive and up-to-date information on stamp forgeries and counterfeits, editorial publicity about your product in *Linn's Stamp News* and a few other specialist philatelic publications would reach a large proportion of your target market very cost-effectively. To get such editorial coverage, however, you must prepare an effective media release.

Media release tips

Keep your media releases tight and written in the editorial style of the publication(s) or broadcasting organizations in which you hope to get them used. Double-space them on one side of standard, white, letter-size bond paper, with your name, address, and telephone number prominently at the top, as well as at the foot of the last page, if there is more than one.

The ideal release is a single page answering the basic *how, where, what, when*, and *why* questions that comprise a publishable story, then describe your book and why it is worthy of editorial mention. There is a myth perpetuated in marketing and publicity courses that journalists will only read one page of anything that lands on their desks. Don't confine yourself to a single page if your message is strong, and particularly if you are pitching to feature editors who are more likely to run longer stories than in the news pages.

An effective compromise to overcome the printing and mailing costs of long releases is to have such a strong message on one or two pages that you get the journalist to explore the full-text version on disk. Start with a heading in uppercase that is crisp, descriptive, and eye-catching. Make your first paragraph topical, hard-hitting, and appropriate to the publication. Make your second paragraph informative and comprehensive. If possible, try to achieve your publicity objectives in those first two paragraphs, so that you get your point across if that is all that the newspaper or magazine uses.

Try to construct your release in the traditional inverted pyramid structure, with the strong essential details at the top, and the less important information below. Then the editor (or the compositor, at the stage when stories are being patched into page layouts) can more easily cut the story to fit the available space by trimming complete sentences or paragraphs from the bottom.

Again, don't forget to include or offer to supply a longer, more comprehensive text on disk so that the editorial staff can download it into their electronic editing systems without retyping. In some publications with low budgets and few staff, such a labor-saving offer could get you far more space. It is always worthwhile putting the full text of your media release in a separate file (or directory, if necessary) on the disk containing your electronic publication. Draw the editors' attention to it in a covering letter or note on the summarized hardcopy of the release, and include simple instructions on how to access it on the disk label, also.

In the text of your release, don't try to sell too hard. Write a feature or news piece about the subject matter contained in your book, in which you quote the book or yourself as the author so that you discreetly bring in the publisher's name, price, and address or telephone number as the source.

Don't be stingy with review copies

You might be tempted, particularly when doing a large mailing, to be stingy in providing journalists with free review copies. Or you might compromise by including a postcard (preferably postage-paid) to make

it easier for them to request a review copy. Such measures can be a false economy in times when journalists are spoon-fed by publishers seeking publicity, and when disks—even CD-ROMs—are so cheap.

Unless your release is very strong, you will get a very low return rate of requests for review copies. If you have chosen your media mailing list carefully, try to make the small additional outlay required to deliver the review copy at the same time as you pitch the editorial story. The ease with which you can provide books for review compared to the costs incurred by print publishers gives you an edge that you should exploit.

Mailing to the media

However good your release, it won't get published unless you deliver it to the right person at the right place. To achieve that, you need reliable and up-to-date mailing lists. The *Writer's Market* directory is one familiar to most writers, and likely to be on your desk already. It is full of useful contacts and tips, but is not a comprehensive listing. To track down publications that are more obscure but still important, go to the library and examine the listings in such directories as the *Literary Marketplace* and those covering organizations likely to have newsletters. There might well be an industry, trade, or volunteer group with thousands of members interested in your subject, who you can reach at virtually no cost through the organization's journal.

Another source of lists for electronic publishers seeking publicity is *International Features*, the organization that publishes the *Bates Directories* of different media, as well as listings of public libraries throughout the U.S. The shareware version of the *Bates Directory of U.S. Daily Newspapers* provides information about all of the 1,600 daily newspapers in print in the U.S. When you register, you get the latest version, plus worthwhile editing and mail-merge features that make the $45 fee a bargain—you could spend more renting an inferior list for just one-time use.

Note that this list does not include names and titles. You can add these, as necessary. If you are doing a large mailing to the media, you might prefer to rent a list that includes, for example, the name

and official title of the editorial staffer or freelancer responsible for book reviews or the computer column. However, while newspapers rarely move addresses, I have found that many media lists that give names and titles become outdated so quickly that they can be expensively wasteful. Journalists change jobs more often than almost any other occupation, so use the telephone numbers in the Bates directories to call a carefully selected list of prime review prospects, and find out the names of the members of the editorial team to whom you should address your media release and review copy.

For larger mailings where making many telephone calls is not practical, customize the listing to produce address labels by editorial title alone. Although media offices get swamped by mail, most are fairly efficient at skimming through everything to sort out what might potentially be important, so letters addressed to, say, "The Drama Critic" should at least reach the correct desk and be opened.

Depending on the nature of your electronic publication, there are other Bates media directories that might be useful for you. The *Bates Directory of Selected Weekly Newspapers* lists 2,000 weeklies in the U.S. with circulations over 5,000. If you have a product of specific interest to the business community, then $10 is a remarkably cheap way to get the Bates listing of over 100 city and regional business journals.

If your product lends itself to radio or television coverage, then get the *Bates Directory of Selected TV and Radio Stations* for $35. I know from my own experience how radio phone-in chat shows can generate sales if listeners have an immediate way of making a purchase. Offer radio contacts the opportunity to do live interviews and phone-in shows, and be ready to respond immediately in filling telephoned orders.

Coordinating fulfillment with publicity is often difficult with conventional publishing. I once did an hour-long syndicated radio show that got tremendous listener response, but my publisher, which set up the publicity opportunity, did not have my book available in stores at the time the show aired. Many other writers have had similar frustrating experiences. If you are self-publishing an electronic book,

you should be able to give a telephone number over the air at which orders can be taken, and arrange for copies to be duplicated and shipped immediately to meet the demand.

Consider also the *Bates Media Hitlist*, which zeroes in on over 300 of the leading news organizations in radio, television, and print. For $45, it provides contact addresses for television talk shows and the radio and television syndicates. However, it is only worth chasing such media if you have a really hot product on a subject that is genuinely newsworthy. The competition to get the attention of the media on the hit list is very intense, and often important, serious subjects are of no interest at all to the mass-market television shows. Don't try to get Oprah Winfrey's attention with a learned work on archaeology, but you might well score if you have profiled transvestites as an underprivileged minority.

Likewise, if your title is very specialized, the mass-market media are probably of little interest to you. You might not generate as good a response from publicity reaching millions of viewers of a top television talk show as you would get from a carefully targeted effort reaching only a few thousand people.

Don't worry too much about negative comments in reviews. Use valid criticisms to try to improve your product, but almost any exposure will help the marketing effort. Dr. Samuel Johnson's message to fellow authors was, "Sir, if they cease to talk of me, I must starve." The famous lexicographer frankly admitted, "I would rather be attacked than unnoticed, for the worst thing you can do to an author is to be silent as to his works."

⇨ Promoting to libraries

If you want to mail to libraries, a good starting point is the *Bates Directory of U.S. Public Libraries*, which has 9,000 listings and the ability to generate mailing labels for all, or a selection, of them. There are directories also for colleges, universities, trade and technical schools, and public high schools.

For more information on the Bates directories, contact

International Features
P.O. Box 1349
Lake Worth, FL 33460
ph: 407-582-8320

In Australia, the contact is

Southern Media Services
P.O. Box 529
Kiama, NSW 2533
ph: 042-331-773

 # Television to sell books

Local or national television shopping channels have proven excellent vehicles for hardcopy book marketing, particularly for self-help, lifestyle nonfiction, and children's books. Sales of 10,000 copies an hour have been achieved, and authors who have appeared on television to promote their books generally seem to have found it a worthwhile—even enjoyable—experience. The QVC home shopping network, plus its Q2 service being launched in 1994, are the leaders in this field.

The shopping programs are live, and authors go to the studios at specific times for broadcasts of, perhaps, 20 minutes duration. A good hook to get purchases during this situation is to offer signed copies; you can sign a well-packaged electronic book just as easily as the fly-leaf of a printed volume. If the promotion works, be prepared to sign several thousand copies to be shipped directly from the warehouses.

To sell by television, you must have a title that is appropriate for the audience at the time of day the program is scheduled, which for many electronic books might be around the slots devoted to selling computers and other electronic products. A shopping channel also gives you an opportunity to show video clips and other visuals, or to demonstrate something, if that is appropriate to your title.

When selling on television, try to have attractive packaging, even if there is essentially only a floppy disk as the product. The exposure could help with any retail, direct mail, or other selling activities in which you are engaged.

Market through seminars

Electronic books make ideal back-of-the-room products for sale at seminars, adding greatly to the profitability of such events. Business seminars, in particular, are likely to attract a high proportion of computer users with low resistance levels to paying premium prices for information on disk that they need.

If your publication is information-rich, incorporate hypertext or other sophisticated search facilities and call it a database, which should enhance its image and the price at which you can offer it.

If you can create such a product that would fit well with the many seminars now run on financial management for retirement, establishing a home-based business, investing in real estate, or similar popular topics, you might have the ideal distribution route for direct sales, particularly if the organizers do not have a good selection of their own back-of-the-room merchandise.

Getting your disks and files safely to the right place

Once you have adopted the concept of paperless publishing, you can save time and money and increase your efficiency by trying to extend the use of your personal computer into other aspects of your creative work and its subsequent marketing.

Jim Hood's ventures into electronic publishing include a really comprehensive work on backache relief, his Professor P.C. Laptop tutorial on the use of portable systems, and his very successful PC-Learn title, which takes beginners through the history of computers to selecting and using a system appropriate to their particular needs.

"Not only do I now publish electronically, but I also market many of my products electronically via CompuServe classified ads, and other methods," Jim Hood says. "Many of the functions of my home-based business—marketing, publishing, research, customer service—now take place electronically, and paper is never used.

"This method of operating continues to 'collapse' into a smoother and more rapid way of working," he continues. "It does not need high-level technology, just a simple 286 computer, 2400-baud modem, and an ample supply of recycled diskettes costing only 15 cents each. This rather low-tech 'trailing edge' technology produces stunning results."

Jim's use of on-line services such as CompuServe has become an attractive proposition for nearly all electronic publishers. It is possible to upload your files to the services, which provide the medium by which thousands of people can download them for evaluation, and the services then process registrations for you, collecting credit card payments on-line and passing them on to you with a reasonable percentage deduction.

"The shareware industry is now organizing itself into very efficient publishing-marketing-distribution channels which can be remarkably profitable for the new SOHO [small office, home office]," says Jim.

This shareware expert is now also finding an increasing number of registrations for his products coming via the low-cost shareware collections on CD-ROM. These are becoming a major means of distribution, some even circulating as promotional "freebies" to support direct-marketing campaigns.

How to get published on CD-ROM for nothing!

Having got your attention with the heading, there's some bad news and good news about marketing your titles on CD-ROM. First, the bad news is that you won't get published profitably anywhere for nothing unless your work is worth publishing by the distributor's

definitions of editorial quality and marketing. If your electronic publication is not written and compiled competently, and does not meet a need in viable target markets to entertain or inform, you will have to keep on throwing effort and money at it to try to motivate anyone to even look at your work.

Now for the good news. If you do have a suitable publication that can be distributed in electronic form, there is a first-rate way of getting it to the market on CD-ROM at no direct cost to you as part of the JCSM Shareware Collection. This CD-ROM is one of the best collections of shareware software available, so it is a prestigious place to be, and one that should get your work to a large and growing market.

Not only that, the publisher, Bud Jay, encourages you to construct an edition of your work that will generate all-important "second sales" for you. Use your CD-ROM release to entice readers to place further orders directly with you for expanded editions of the same work, or for other products and services that you offer. This concept is probably the most cost-effective form of marketing available for most electronic books, whether you distribute via bulletin boards, floppies, or in CD-ROM collections.

The good news is not complete yet. When you become an author with work accepted for this CD-ROM shareware collection, you get a free copy of the latest edition when it is issued at intervals of four months. That alone is worth nearly $50 a year.

Bud Jay, the brains behind this unique venture, is an expert in small computer systems from Lakeville, Minnesota. He explains, "The collection was born when I became frustrated by the high price and low quality of currently available shareware CD-ROMs. We set two objectives for ourselves: to be the first choice for authors, offering the creators of shareware and electronic publications the medium that they would most want their work to feature in. And to make our collection the first choice for the computer end-users because of the quality of the programs that we feature and the attractive pricing of our disks."

Unlike many shareware distributors, Bud and his colleagues at JCS seem to be building their business by going out of their way to consult with and nurture their authors. They want to know what you are

doing and thinking, so they survey their authors at least six times a year. If you have any experience with either conventional publishing or the shareware distribution business, you know only too well how refreshing this is.

JCS does more than just stroke the egos of its author-suppliers, however. According to reports from several authors, JCS is generating increasing sales by its aggressive and well-planned marketing. The collection has been promoted heavily in magazine advertisements and in direct mailings. As I write, there are plans to get the collection into thousands of retail computer outlets, as well as on the shelves of the large discount office supply stores in North America and overseas.

With over 3,900 programs on the latest disk edition, and a retail price of around $23 (a twentieth of a cent per program!) this product just has to be attractive as an impulse purchase for a large proportion of CD-ROM users. If the subscription base continues to grow also, the JCS operation could become a major factor in the development of electronic publishing.

"Shareware is a rapidly growing—even exploding—industry," Bud Jay maintains. "The vast majority of computer users are only now seeing and appreciating their first shareware programs. CD-ROMs are 'exploding' also, and they offer one of the most efficient delivery systems for shareware and electronic publications. When many of these CD-ROM owners start getting bored with their encyclopedia and atlas discs, they will seek other software creating a demand that we and our authors will meet because we offer high quality at a very attractive price."

Contact Bud Jay directly if you have a program or publication to offer him. JCS could be a useful source also if you want to self-publish on CD-ROM, since they can do the technical and production work required to convert material on floppies into the CD-ROM format. The address is

P.O. Box 1216
Lakeville, MN 55044
612-469-5898

Kiosks and catalogs

Consider whether kiosks and catalogs on disk or on bulletin boards should be elements of your marketing strategy. Several people got burned with interactive kiosk terminals, but now that automatic teller machines have become so familiar, users are much more comfortable interfacing with a screen, and kiosks will be cropping up everywhere. The next chapter details a case history of an electronic publishing project that would be particularly suited for kiosks.

If you do multimedia authoring, a new market is opening up to compile interactive catalogs for retail stores. Where these in-store kiosk catalogs have been tested, they have generated over 15% of sales revenues—and as much as 40% in the Christmas peak selling periods.

Electronic catalogs for marketing electronic books

When marketing through electronic catalogs, either on-line or on disc, you can afford to be generous in providing detailed contents lists and extracts. Use the flexibility of the electronic media to give a comprehensive overview of your work, including information in extracts that readers might immediately be able to put to good use.

It is almost always counterproductive to be stingy with the samples you make freely available in such cases. In almost all cases, it is advisable to go out there, "beat the drum," and show the best of what you've got. I found this principle proven time and again when I was in the movie distribution business. We would often joke after seeing a preview of a movie that crammed most of its visual and dramatic highlights into a high-impact trailer that, once you'd seen the trailer, you didn't need to sit through 90 minutes of the full movie. In fact, a strong trailer was nearly always the most cost-effective way of generating good opening business for a movie, and very few patrons who liked the trailer asked for their money back when they "bought" the movie.

Another movie business marketing tactic that you can use over bulletin boards is the electronic equivalent of advance teasers and advertisements. If your title is appropriate, disseminate as widely as possible advance tidbits that are likely to develop interest ahead of your publication or release date. This can be particularly useful if your title covers an event or trend of particular topical interest.

⇨ Prepublication offers for positive cash flow

A perennial problem for writers and small publishers is cash flow. Just how do you fund the creative work, and then the production and marketing costs, to keep the project alive until revenues start flowing in? The usual way for any business enterprise is a loan or some form of investment financing. However, another interesting option in publishing involves *prepublication offers*, a form of marketing that can be very effective and a financial life-saver. To find out how well it can work, I talked to a self-publishing author who has been very successful in the kind of niche market that lends itself well to e-books. His experience reinforces many of the key points in this chapter about commonsense marketing and promotional activities.

Ron Barlow of El Cajon, California demonstrates the potential of pre-publication offers with his self-published hardcopy books. The success he achieves could be obtained far more cost-efficiently by publishing electronically, but don't try to emulate him unless you have real confidence in the viability of your publication and are prepared to do all the other work involved in bringing it successfully to its market.

"I raised the cash to publish both of my books with pre-publication offers of a $12.95 book for $9.95 postpaid" Ron recalls. He suggests as a proven formula discounts to distributors of 60% off orders of five or more copies, and 40% off single orders, both plus shipping, for cash up front, and with specific time limits.

"These discounts might seem excessive if you have never purchased a print run of the optimum 3,500 to 10,000 copies," Ron comments. "Small print runs will cost you almost the retail price."

Ron used this discounting prepublication strategy for his books describing antique woodworking tools and listing current collector values for them. He kept a self-publishing snowball gathering momentum in this niche market until it quickly developed into a successful business that, in the late 1980s, netted him $50,000 a year for three years in a row.

Ron's latest book has an even tighter target market: barbers and hair stylists. His *Vanishing American Barbershop* was initially promoted with a target mailing to 20,000 barber shops and their suppliers.

"We only got a five percent response, but some of the nation's biggest barber supply houses have reordered every 30 days since," he explains. "Five percent is considered a successful response by the big mail-order houses, so it is obvious that you must really control your costs when doing bulk mailing."

Ron, from his extensive experience, provides two examples of what can happen to an author of a book that is viable for either conventional commercial publication or for self-publishing.

In Scenario #1, the author signs with a commercial publisher. The author might get a $3,000 to $5,000 advance, plus, if sales exceed 5,000 copies, a few royalty checks. The book is likely to be out of print in 24 months, however, so the author's total returns over two years (not counting the time needed to research and write the book) might be $4,000 to $6,000.

That's a pretty miserable return, but statistics from Europe and North America show that the great majority of published authors do even worse. That's why self-publishing appears so attractive—providing you don't compound your problems by adding heavy expenditures to low income!

Here is Scenario #2, the way that Ron Barlow self-published so profitably:

❶ Author sends manuscript to a typesetter, and takes a pair of scissors to his or her galley proofs.

❷ Author commissions suitable illustrations and photos, or uses clip art, to make the book visually attractive.

❸ Author commissions a striking cover design. (Don't pinch pennies here. Expect to pay from $300 to $500 from a local commercial artist for a sales motivating cover.)

❹ Author has a paste-up person combine the type and illustrations for camera-ready art. (Ron did that task himself, but it's not as easy as it might appear.)

❺ Author gets three bids for a 4,000-copy press run (which could work out to about $2 each for a typical paperbound book of about 200 pages, with no color illustrations). Multiplying the print cost five or six times to cover other costs and show a profit, you get a retail price of $9.95 per copy.

❻ Author places a quarter-page advertisement in the two best tabloid newspapers or magazines to reach his or her target market.

"If the cost of sales does not exceed $3 per copy, the author can double his or her money in a few months," says Ron. "The author can net $8,000 in six months, with the potential to roll out advertisements on a nationwide basis and so net $50,000 a year—which I did three years in a row on my tool book. If you can find 40 or 50 magazines which would produce 50 orders each per month, you would have 2,000 orders a month coming in, each earning you $4 net, or $8,000 a month net, with no need for employees."

Sound like a dream concept? Well, Ron did it, and he started the ball rolling with very little money up-front by generating positive early cash flow from prepublication offers before he had to pay his print bill. With electronic publishing, positive cash flow should be much easier to achieve because the print bill is not a big expense. You can duplicate disks as the responses come in, but do budget enough for printing to package your product attractively.

"In our self-publishing, we found that bookstores and distributors are only a small—and troublesome!—portion of your market," Ron cautions. The same might be said for a book on a disk if you try to move it through the channels catering specifically for computer users.

You won't make many sales, and have lots of hassles, if you try to sell through retail computing outlets, unless, of course, your publication is

targeted specifically at computer users. Instead, go directly to places where your target market is accessible to your pitch. In the case of Ron's book about tools, collectors who needed his information could be found at fairs and shows. However, often you cannot isolate your potential market effectively, and might need to get your product in front of the general public in the hope that it is seen coincidentally by as many of your potential buyers as possible.

"We have found that libraries, catalog houses, and specialty stores—from health foods to hardware and hospital gift shops—are the real 'wholesale' markets," Ron says. "We have concentrated on direct-mail sales first, then waited for small merchants to respond as they saw our retail ads.

"We also insert a wholesale discount schedule in with every book sold," he continues. "Unimagined customers will materialize: church groups, little league parents, historical societies, anyone who feels that they can make a profit on your book will respond if you make it simple to place a cash wholesale order, and guarantee to give them their money back on unsold copies returned in good condition."

Ron found that, using magazine advertising, crucial early flow of cash hinged on the quality and placement of his advertising. The same principles apply to creating a direct mail piece and sending it to an effective address list.

"Since mail-order responses are generated only by the ad, not by viewing your product first-hand, 90 percent of your early success could be directly connected to writing and illustrating a very motivating space ad, and placing it in a tried-and-true magazine," Ron advises.

⇨ Don't promise what you can't deliver

Remember that many publications, as well as the U.S. Postal Service, do not permit soliciting business for mythical products or services. Be responsible in making prepublication offers by ensuring that you can be ready to ship the finished product within three weeks of your offer reaching potential customers. Some magazines and newspapers might

insist on seeing a sample before they will accept your advertisement, while the USPS will retrospectively clobber you if it gets complaints.

If you are visited by postal inspectors, you need to convince them that you had the capability to complete your product and ship it in adequate quantities to customers within about three weeks of the first orders coming in. You can't use the mails to promote a prepublication offer that is really just a test to see if a concept will fly.

Certainly don't put any customer checks in the bank or process credit card orders until you are actually shipping. If there is going to be a delay, notify customers and offer refunds within eight days of receiving their orders. State a new publishing date (and add two weeks to it for shipping).

If you try to generate prepublication revenue by means of editorial coverage, you must have acceptable prototype samples to send to writers and editors who are attracted by your media release. There is hardly a journalist alive—particularly in the computer press—who at some time has not been embarrassed by writing about a product that never ships, or is horribly late.

Catering for long lead times

Try to work with publications that have long lead times. Many magazines need four to six months, so must have information well in advance to ensure that publication of a report or a review will coincide as closely as possible with your release date.

If your title is likely to appeal to a particular issue of a publication that is important to your marketing strategy, try to get into a dialogue with the appropriate editorial staffer as early as possible. For example, your guide to computer security procedures would stand little chance of coverage in most issues of a magazine for lawyers, but could be just what an editor is looking for in an annual supplement dedicated to security in the legal profession.

Most newspapers and magazines release details of any special supplements or seasonal issues up to a year in advance. This gives

advertisers an opportunity to plan their budgets and schedules, and also alerts editorial contributors. You will usually find such a listing available just for the asking, and it could be the best place to start developing your pre-publication offers and positive cash-flow strategies.

If you want details of a particular publication, call the advertising department and ask for a *media kit*, which contains advertising costs, a demographic breakdown of the readership, and a listing of forthcoming special subject issues or supplements.

Beware the digitized versions of vanity publishing

Self-promotion and marketing are alien to many authors, so those who do not want to get involved directly in these tasks and have sufficient funds are inevitably tempted to pay for someone else to do them. In such situations, beware the growth of electronic vanity publishing, carrying over into the new media most of the deplorable practices of irresponsible operators who have exploited the burning desire of authors to get into print.

The vast scope for the production and distribution of electronic manuscripts will attract many entrepreneurs, and some will undoubtedly offer worthy services by providing professional expertise in the editing and compiling of titles, and their effective marketing and distribution. Others will offer much and deliver little, just like their print counterparts at vanity presses.

As you will see in the coming chapters, it really is much easier and cheaper to prepare, duplicate, and distribute an electronic publication yourself than a printed book, so the financial risk can be much less.

Use some of the marketing options discussed in this chapter, and your *expenses need not be significant.* You can afford to experiment and learn as you go because you need not be exposed to the heavy losses possible for a self-published traditional book. Of course, there are still valid grounds for seeking professional expertise about

different aspects of the marketing process if you lack the knowledge or time to do it yourself. Marketing expertise, research, and extensive testing are essential if the project represents a substantial up-front investment, as could be the case with a complex multimedia work.

Distributing your works

AUTHORS and other artists who publish only in print and other traditional media can divorce themselves to a large degree from the distribution function. That is not the case with electronic publishing, where the method of distribution of the finished work has a direct impact on the creative and marketing processes.

Virtual publications need have no physical existence

If you are used to working in traditional media, it might require a considerable adjustment to accept the new concept of a virtual publication not needing a physical presence. The products created in electronic publishing just do not have the shape, form, weight, and substance of familiar books, magazines, and cassettes. E-books cast no shadow, take up no space in the conventional sense, and can fly invisibly in seconds from one side of the world to the other with negligible cost or consumption of energy and physical resources. They can be compressed, expanded, copied, and manipulated dynamically almost without restraint. Their geographical location is largely irrelevant.

Only if you appreciate this totally new concept of a printed book, newspaper, magazine, or taped production, can you tune in fully to the opportunities for distributing, and therefore creating and marketing, these virtual publications. All the dimensions with which you relate to physical publications are changed, including time.

When authors write books for printing, they research and complete a manuscript that, after a long process, comes back to them from the publisher as edited page proofs for the author to make final corrections. Then, more months later, the book is published as a complete physical entity and the author can do no more with it until, if he or she is lucky, the publisher calls a couple of years later and offers another edition.

Print publishing and distribution comprise an inherently slow, stop-and-start process that locks the information in the manuscript into a

series of rigid physical and time structures. Deadlines must be met as the book is edited and typeset, illustrations processed, pages made up, and the cover designed and printed. These activities involve much physical activity and consumption of resources in different locations, some perhaps on the other side of the world.

Other deadlines, changes in physical location, and consumption of materials occur as the pages are assembled into forms, printed, the paper cut and trimmed, and the cover added and binding completed. Then the finished book imposes further physical demands and costs because it must be warehoused, inventoried, ordered, protectively packaged, and physically distributed as a complete unit. This is all great for Federal Express, the timber and paper industries, and printers. For authors and their publishers it is, literally, a big drag.

Electronic publishing need not be like that at all—and the degree to which it differs is dictated largely by the distribution method being used. In much author-publishing, the entire process can take place from the author's desktop.

 # The single sale becomes more profitable

There is a particular benefit for e-books that will be sold and distributed in small quantities or single units to different addresses. Fulfillment of single orders for printed books often represents a loss to publishers, a factor that, along with high warehousing costs, contributes to premature remaindering. But authors, and even large publishers, can distribute single e-books very profitably.

A major work, such as an encyclopedia on a CD-ROM, might have very similar creative, production, and marketing methods to those established for printed books. If it is distributed, perhaps piecemeal, along the information highways, however, it can still become virtual, dynamic, and very flexible. It moves more freely, and is probably used very differently, than a traditional book.

 # Rent a book—bit by bit!

Readers might not even purchase a large electronic reference work as a complete package. Because it has few physical restrictions, it can be rented piece by piece.

Imagine going into a reference library, taking one of their most prized volumes from the shelves, ripping out the pages you need, and offering to pay a few cents for what you have abstracted while mutilating a book that might cost $80 to replace! You can do just that in an electronic library, and nobody will protest because the valuable reference book from which you have taken the pages is not damaged; it is on disk or CD, as shown in Fig. 5-1. All, or any part of it, can be cloned indefinitely.

Figure 5-1

Concepts of the physical substance of books change drastically when they are published electronically. Whole libraries are being transferred to CD-ROM disks like this. Just one disk can be used to publish—or keep in print—a million recipes, or over 2,000 books and other literary works, with minimal consumption of materials and distribution costs.
Maxell Corporation

The author of such a book being distributed on-line is unlikely to be able to sit back and relax as he or she would after an edited manuscript has gone to the printers. Virtual books need not have clearly defined moments when no more changes can be made. The author can be involved in a continual evolutionary updating process, even having to process sections of the text that have been altered and returned by readers, or constantly incorporating and then distributing new additions or amendments.

Wireless distribution

The potential for distributing virtual books becomes apparent when you consider how they can travel around the world by radio. Although we are being bombarded by the significance of the information highways flowing along optical and wired cables over our heads and under our streets, electronic documents do not need these physical transport systems. They can fly through the ether in a type of "beam-me-a-book" technology, as shown in Fig. 5-2.

Figure 5-2

Publishing by radio is already a reality, and will grow with the development of services via satellite relays to portable hand-held units such as this AT&T EO 440, shown with its optional cellular phone module. AT&T

Some of the most impressive medium and long-term technological changes in communications are taking place in radio. The dream of vast electronic bookstores and libraries that authors and readers can use from anywhere in the world without even needing a telephone is moving quickly towards reality. Planning is already well advanced to create a digital library in the U.S. with ten million volumes. There is mounting academic and political opinion that such projects here and in other countries should be treated as national priorities. Some

people are concerned that if access and distribution of such libraries is available only through commercial on-line services, fundamental freedoms of information will be compromised. If for no other reason, radio must be nurtured as an important medium for distributing electronic publications. Radio has always been an effective medium to challenge political control and commercial exploitation.

A product that does not need physical form is ideal for distribution by radio, and there is a vast global wireless infrastructure hungry for new products that has already demonstrated its unique ability to deliver publications. Radio is expanding by leaps and bounds, with development being enhanced by a remarkable degree of international cooperation. As a result, the coverage gets greater and the rates, for services where payment must be made, should come down to make e-book distribution by radio viable. Electronic publications distributed on the Internet and other on-line services are already accessible from hand-held, untethered personal computing devices, as well as via cable connections.

 # New satellites connect the world cheaply

In addition to the major developments taking place in person-to-person radio communication in the U.S. and Europe, international links are being forged that will have a great impact on how information is distributed around the world.

The Immarsat international satellite network, linked to ground services all over the world, has ambitious plans for both high-speed and low-cost data services to be introduced during the middle and late 1990s. These services could be very important for international publishing by radio.

Cellular radio services will never cover all of the U.S., but radio communications anywhere in the country should become practical and affordable from an American Mobile Satellite Corporation service due to begin in 1995 with rates of about $1.50 a minute. A Telestat

satellite will bring similar benefits to Canada. Globalstar satellites due to start providing international services in 1997 might cut transmission charges to well under a dollar a minute.

New life from an old technology

One of the keys to the future is radio teletype technology. It is not new at all, but the applications for it created by electronic publishing are both novel and exciting.

Over 20 years ago, when I was a foreign correspondent broadcasting for the BBC, syndicated radio services in the U.S., and other agencies, radio teletype enabled me to get stories in and out of the most difficult places. The technology's enormous potential first became apparent to me when I used it to outwit the censors to disseminate the first reports of starvation and atrocities in Nigeria.

Two decades ago, I was publishing thousands of words daily to a radio receiver feeding a teleprinter, both independent of electric or cable services, located in a remote part of Africa. It is immensely satisfying to be able to grab texts out of the air, or transmit them, in defiance of official attempts to blindfold and gag you. This becomes far easier now that you can transmit or process radio-teletyped words and pictures in your personal computer, just as you would handle files by modem with an on-line service or bulletin board. The radio process works well in both directions, to transmit or receive words and pictures around the world with no restrictions—and no telephone or other charges!

Easy and affordable

Fax messages can be exchanged in the same way, as Chinese protesters for democracy have demonstrated, but it is the use of radio to send and receive electronic books, magazines, newspapers, and other publications that has such fascinating potential. The equipment required is surprisingly affordable and not that difficult to learn to use.

At present, radio teletype communications are limited mainly to specialist activities, such as diplomatic traffic between embassies and their home offices, weather services, intelligence agencies such as the CIA, shipping, and the international news services. Although the radio waves are the most open of all the media, radio teletype has been a relatively closed medium, restricted to these special types of activities not so readily catered for by telephone links.

That is changing slowly, but the rate of change is likely to accelerate rapidly with the explosion in electronic publishing. The die has been cast already with the proliferation of domestic satellite dishes to capture television transmissions beamed via satellites. Those same satellites are already carrying a variety of publications in electronic format. The *USA Today* newspaper is printed at locations in the United States, Europe, and the Far East from computer text and graphic files transmitted by radio. There are similar operations by *The Wall Street Journal* and *International Herald Tribune*.

On a personal, self-publishing, scale, that extraordinary nomadic American writer Steven Roberts transmits and receives literary files via the solar-powered radio satellite transceiver mounted on his bicycle. But his newsletter and articles only travel part of the way to their readers by radio, and, like *USA Today* and other newspapers, the transmissions are in closed systems not accessible to the general public.

The radio newspaper

The first electronic publication by radio readily available to the general public was the daily newspaper broadcast by Swiss Radio International in French, German, and English. With a personal computer, a good shortwave radio, and about $200 worth of additional hardware, you could download such an electronic publication in your own home or office virtually anywhere in the world, then print out all or part of it on your printer.

This Swiss radio enterprise was short-lived, but it was the first substantial application of the concept of truly electronic home deliveries of newspapers, something that has been possible for years,

but never effectively applied by either the telephone or cable television services. Now this whole field is being re-examined, fueled by the competitive scramble to exploit the hard-wired cable information highways in our homes and offices. Radio offers attractive entrepreneurial alternatives for those not blessed with cable facilities.

New software is constantly becoming available to expand wired and wireless publishing opportunities, and it can be quick and easy to get up and running. Living in southern Arizona, I have a 100-mile drive to the nearest bookstore selling European newspapers. Using Journalist from PED Software Corporation, my PC can tap into CompuServe's various news services and assembly a daily—or even hourly—newspaper customized entirely to the European topics that I define. I look forward to the day not far off when my shortwave radio linked to my PC will enable me to do the same with broadcasts from London, Moscow, and other world centers.

In all the hype about cable-based services, radio's vast potential is being overlooked because, the air waves being free, it does not appear to offer the same big profit. As an international medium, however, radio will play an important role in the chain of delivering electronic products and services. Radio must always continue to have an edge over the more rigid cable media because it is universal, free, and virtually immune to interference from commercial or political interests.

The possibilities for books to be published by radio are mind-boggling, and it would be particularly appropriate if a lead is taken by the venerable British Broadcasting Corporation. The BBC is the leading broadcasting service to combine traditional loyalty to the importance of the spoken and written word with the entrepreneurial commercial flair that makes its programs and its publications so successful around the world.

The BBC has long had a unique relationship with authors quite unlike that of any other broadcasting organization. As a reflection of this, about one-sixth of the Society of Authors' 5,500 members in Britain belong to The Broadcasting Group, and radio is regarded by many of them as the prime medium for their fiction and nonfiction work. That

relationship between authors and broadcasters is no small factor in the BBC being a major supplier of programming to the PBS radio and television services in North America, the Arts & Entertainment cable channel, and similar broadcasting services in other parts of the world.

Publishing by shortwave—the fax of the future?

If you want to explore more thoroughly than is possible here the vast potential of radio for electronic publishing, turn first to *Passport to World Band Radio*, the best introductory sourcebook on the subject, with lively articles on every aspect of the shortwave universe. (The 24-hour line for orders worldwide is 215-794-8252.)

Publisher and editor-in-chief Lawrence Magne forecasts the future of electronic publishing by radio as offering opportunities similar to those achieved by the now-ubiquitous faxing of documents.

"Shortwave radio, unlike other international media, disseminates news direct and uncut by gatekeepers," he explains. "Shortwave-delivered news comes primarily in audio form—world band radio broadcasts. But its nonsequential form—book, magazine, or newspaper creation via RTTY [radio teletype] and fax—is potentially so cost-effective for organizations to transmit and individuals to receive that it recalls where office faxing stood ten years ago. It is poised to take off, providing savvy marketing and distribution are put into place."

How do you start publishing by radio?

If you want to prepare for viable publishing by shortwave radio, you can set up a receiving and transmitting (publisher and reader) system at remarkably low cost. First, you need hardware from an expert supplier. Some are featured in *Passport*, while local sources can be tracked down through the Yellow Pages and local ham radio clubs.

You can get into this publishing environment for as little as $200 for a good portable shortwave receiver, plus about the same amount for a decoder to convert the signals into a format that your computer can recognize. However, it is more practical—and might be essential in some cases—to have a powerful desktop receiver. They start from about $400. If you want to transmit electronic publications by radio, shortwave radio transmitters of the types used by ham radio operators start at about the same price, and it is much easier now to get a license to operate these transmitters.

The total capital outlay (excluding the computer) for such a system can be under $1,000 in the U.S. Expect to pay more, however, for all electronic equipment in Europe and many other countries.

For free, hands-on, technical advice anywhere, tap into the friendly, cooperative spirit of local radio hams. A good starting point is to link up with your nearest amateur radio club. The American Radio Relay League is the umbrella organization for amateur radio in the United States. It can be reached at

225 Main Street
Newington, CT 06111
203-666-1541

There are similar organizations in many countries—the Radio Society of Britain, for example.

Snags and opportunities

Of course, radio electronic publishing is not perfect. Two major snags are that radio transmitting is a real-time medium, and the audience able to receive your texts is at present comparatively small. Your target markets must be alerted to the times and wavelengths when transmissions will take place, and, if you want payment for your works, you must build in similar incentives to those for distributing through on-line and shareware channels. The small size of the direct market is inhibiting, but electronic publishing via radio could become significant very quickly if it is picked up by major broadcasting organizations and other institutions.

Perhaps The Monitor's World Service, the BBC, or Voice of America will come to regard radio publishing as part of their services to developing countries to disseminate out-of-copyright works, and to pay contemporary authors acceptable royalties for regular transmissions of copyrighted publications in electronic form. Although the audience among individuals might be small, the attractions for educational and research institutions and the business community are considerable, so those first books by radio broadcasts could be just the seeds from which large information trees grow.

For example, Monitor Radio could open each transmission period to Latin America with Spanish translations and original English texts from its own weekly and daily newspapers appropriate to high-school current affairs studies, followed by works on Christian Science for use in college courses on religious topics. The transmission times for compressed computer text files is very small, and the facilities to receive and process those signals could be available in virtually every major town throughout Latin America, where reception of the Monitor is good.

The BBC could beam into the English-language markets of Africa, Asia, and the Caribbean, where it enjoys excellent reception, texts relevant to Open University correspondence courses, and supplementary documentation for its famous English by Radio programming. The Monitor's corporate supporters would identify many opportunities to be associated with the dissemination of texts to global or specific regional targets. British companies could pick up the tab to augment the exposure they get on the World Service's weekly documentary on innovative products.

Other radio services could use text transmissions to meet a wide variety of their needs. Radio France International, for example, has as part of its mission to promote the French language, which is under threat in many areas by the greater availability at lower cost of texts in English. Radio Japan/NHK is keen to enhance global understanding of Japanese culture, much of which is written and visual, and so can be communicated more effectively via computerized text and graphics files than in radio broadcasts.

Charitable objectives

Foundations and similar institutions would be attracted to such electronic publishing by radio. New opportunities would be created for them to meet myriad charitable objectives, from making classical texts more readily available to millions of blind people to tackling glaucoma in the Third World by promulgating new information about treatments.

So, although the primary audience for books and other publications by radio may seem very small, it could be extended through receiving and duplication/distribution facilities around the world. The benefits would be felt particularly in the areas worst served by conventional print publishing. In many countries books are ridiculously expensive and in limited supply, but personal computers can become steadily cheaper and more readily accessible. That could motivate many universities to become involved in publishing by radio as they and their students are the prime victims of the negative aspects of the print textbook publishing industry.

Broadcast your book to 20 million people

Shortwave is far from being the only radio medium that will fuel the demand for electronic publications. Spectrum Information Technologies, Inc. of New York estimates that by 1997 there will be some 20 million Americans using various types of wireless devices able to receive and transmit at least text files. Many of these mobile computers and personal communications tools will also be able to handle graphics and multimedia publications.

Spectrum claimed to control, through its patents, significant aspects of the technology that enables an electronic publication—or any data file, for that matter—to be transmitted or received via the cellular telephone network and other radio links. The company's patent for Direct Connect devices puts much of the hardware needed for wireless communications onto a single chip. This technology will,

during the mid-1990s, enable personal communication devices to become ever smaller and more functional. So, when you have finished reading a new novel on a radio/computer device smaller than a conventional paperback book, it will be technologically feasible to download another title from the *New York Times*' bestseller list without leaving your beach chair.

 # Soon there will be a billion potential readers

AT&T, one of Spectrum's major clients, is forecasting a billion personal computer users by the end of the century, with an accelerating proportion of them regularly receiving electronic documents by radio. This could stimulate reading rather than threaten this important aspect of our cultural traditions. The opportunities and motivations for reading must increase as the new technologies enable so many people to have a pocketable wireless device that they can use to access an electronic publication virtually anytime or place.

If you are out on a lake in your bass boat and the fishing is slow, you will be able to download a book of poetry, a Zane Grey story, or the latest edition of *The Economist* into your personal communicator in between changing lures. You could even download a talking book; audio files of voice interviews are already being distributed successfully on the Internet. In less relaxed situations, when the need for information more quickly is paramount, developments in pager information services offer undreamed of possibilities.

 # Database publishing through pagers

For example, the research for my two books on fakes, forgeries, and counterfeits has resulted in a large database of information about all kinds of deceptions which I will publish electronically. It might pay me not to disseminate all the information I have, but to offer it selectively at different times and at different prices.

With a hypertext search engine, information can be extracted from this database quickly and easily. Before hot new information goes into the latest edition of the major work, I can provide it as a premium service to registered readers or subscribers who need quick updates or references. For example, suppose an art or antique dealer at an auction in New York wants immediate, unbiased, expert information about the counterfeiting of a particular Dali print. There is such a print coming up for bidding in a few minutes, but the dealer suspects it might be from the same source as a similar limited-edition copy unmasked as a counterfeit in Chicago the previous week. Without leaving his seat in the sales room, he could use his cellular phone or other personal communicator to radio his query to my database, and receive information back to influence his bidding decision before the questionable print comes under the auctioneer's hammer.

The hardware capable of receiving such information anytime and virtually anywhere is already commonplace. It is called the radio pager, carried in the pockets of 15 million people in the U.S. alone—and as many again in other developed nations. The total could reach 100 million by the end of the century, with a rapidly increasing proportion of them alphanumeric pagers capable of receiving and storing short text messages for display on a small LCD screen.

Pager information services are still mainly confined to hot news of financial importance, such as stock prices and currency fluctuations, but the range of information being published this way is expanding. Also growing is the capacity of pocketable pagers to store increasing amounts of data transmitted by radio. Even if the pager's memory runs short, there can be enough in a radioed summary to indicate to the user whether it is worth downloading more details by computer or fax/modem through a line or radio link to the database. In such applications, an electronically published work could be the core product to attract business for the other specialist services linked to it.

 # Fast-changing information

These trends are important to those who publish electronically, opening up all kinds of possibilities for projects that would never be viable in print. They are particular relevant if you deal in fast-changing information. Fairly timeless works that give overviews of a topic, such as my titles on counterfeiting, could be given away with no restraints as freeware on floppies or bulletin boards if they are the marketing "loss leader" to bring in paying subscribers for updates provided on-line or by radio.

You do not need to be an information provider in a national or international high-stakes area to take advantage of publishing by radio. Paging and other radio services are structured largely as local entities and may be able to set up facilities at a reasonable cost that will target a particular local special-interest group or event. Even short-term, niche-market projects can become viable with the flexibility and comparatively low cost of paging services that exploit users' "need to know." What great opportunities this technology offers for the authors about subjects such as philately, gemstones, or trading-card collecting, where prices fluctuate constantly and there are large events where buyers concentrate in thousands to shop!

The subscribers to your publications whether they be in print or on disk could have access to rented pagers on a localized radio transmission frequency covering the show. You transmit the changing details of inventories, prices, and where to find items in short supply. You use your expertise and contacts to gather the information, and then publish it for profit or to generate sales opportunities for your main publishing ventures.

 # Pager publishing power and pizzazz

There are many sporting and other types of events where such radio services can add power and pizzazz to the largely unexplored potential of electronic publishing. What a boon such a service would be at the giant Comdex computer convention, for example. We need to rethink conventional concepts of communicating in general, and

publishing in particular, to take advantage of these opportunities. You might profit greatly by mixing media, perhaps only infrequently using radio's flexibility and speed to augment other ventures in print, on-line, and on disk.

Again, consider my fakes and forgeries publishing ventures as an example of what might be done. There are many major antiques fairs with hundreds of sellers and a bewildering selection of items on offer. Collectors and dealers who buy my books or subscribe to my newsletters would have the edge with a radio paging service tapping the expert sources I could line up on the good and the bad deals to be found. I could charge premium prices for such a service that alerted buyers to reproductions and outright counterfeits; you could do something similar in your specialty.

Maximize profitability by recycling your information

With residents of big cities in North America having access to 500 or more communication channels in the foreseeable future, there is obviously going to be a large demand for material that only a rapid increase in many forms of electronic publishing will be able to fill.

When evaluating these new, and sometimes seemingly odd, distribution methods for electronic publishing, always bear in mind that publishing information several times over maximizes its profitability. I remember well sitting in the San Francisco garden of a millionaire publisher, listening in awe as he revealed how his success was built on clever distribution tactics and repeat sales of important facts.

When his reporters and editors got hot new information, they would generate immediate revenue from it by sales to a small circle of subscribers paying very high premium prices for customized, immediate reports on topics that really interested them.

That same information would go out again in less expensive, but still premium-priced, weekly newsletters to wider target groups with a

well-defined need-to-know. Then the facts would be recycled again in a range of monthly magazines with large readerships and low cover prices because most of their profit came from advertising. Much of the same information would continue generating revenue for months, sometimes years, by being incorporated into detailed reports of a particular sector of technology or business activity, or into conventional books that this publisher also produces in large numbers.

The same principle of recycling your information can be applied to many small publishing enterprises, and becomes far more practical if you fully exploit the increasing distribution and marketing opportunities offered by electronic media of all kinds.

Distributing and selling on-line

The proliferation of independent and commercial on-line services accessible by any computer linked by modem appears to solve all the problems of electronic book distribution. Unfortunately, this is not the case. Only a minority of the services, albeit some of the biggest, offer effective methods for selling, delivering, and collecting the receipts for individual electronic books. Many titles are not appropriate for this method of distribution because a large proportion of their target markets is not using on-line services frequently enough, or at all.

Also, book-length texts can be inordinately time-consuming and expensive to download, particularly if they have any multimedia elements. That will change as cable television companies provide special boxes to enable your PC to connect to the Internet via fiber-optic lines, increasing the data transfer rate dramatically. Although 40 million homes in the U.S. are expected to be connected in a fiber-optic cable network of some kind by the year 2000, it is by no means clear just how many of them will be generating a serious demand for the electronic products and services being touted.

By 1994 nearly 30 million American households had computer systems of some kind, but many of them were not being used very much. Even among recent purchasers, surveys indicated that nearly one in five of the home systems was being used less than five hours a

week. Multimedia will increase home computer usage, but it remains a big step for the majority of home users to go from playing games, word processing, or doing accounts on a computer, to hooking up and going on-line, particularly trying to navigate the complexities of the Internet.

With these facts in mind, you might do better to focus your on-line efforts to promoting your works and promulgating the information about where and how to buy them. The actual distribution could be as physical entities on disk that you mail to customers, as encrypted or otherwise protected files on-line or in catalog and shareware CD collections, or as files that you transmit directly to customers by modem, or which they can download from your own bulletin board.

⇨ The Internet

Defining the Internet is rather like trying to describe a rapidly morphing image. It just keeps changing and evolving all the time, so what is not possible this week might be readily achievable the next. Also, as the network gets larger and more complex, other on-line facilities for marketing or distributing electronic publications become available—and perhaps more profitable.

The Internet began as several small, virtual academic and scientific communities that the U.S. government fostered during the 1970s and 1980s to help communications between widely scattered researchers. Now it just keeps on growing under its own momentum and comprises over 10,000 individual networks. It has shot past being a virtual village, to become a virtual city, and now a virtual nation with somewhere between 15 and 30 million users (see Fig. 5-3).

By the end of the decade, there might be more people interacting with each other over "the Net," as it is popularly known, than live in either the European Economic Community or North America. Consequently, it is expanding as the largest identifiable market and distribution channel for book publishers, as shown by Infonet booths appearing for the first time in 1993 at the American Booksellers annual convention and the Frankfurt Book Fair.

Figure 5-3

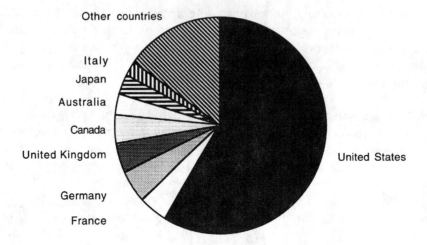

The demographics of the Internet are making it a powerful international marketing medium for book publishing. Here is how Internet usage breaks down by nation. © 1993, Infotronics, Inc.

Membership of a university or some other institution used to be necessary to pass through a gateway into the Net, but now that facility is available to anyone through commercial on-line services. They vary in the costs imposed and the ease of the interface they provide. Also, in making your choice, select a gateway that caters best for your particular interests. You are no longer visiting a virtual village community where you can explore and meet nearly everybody quickly.

Think of it instead as coming to the U.S. for the first time, and needing to be specific in setting up an itinerary. Having your own personal guide would help, and that becomes possible with the new "agent" search software becoming available. With coding similar in some respects to the virus and worm programs that roam around networks, these agent applications can be briefed with the categories of information you need, or the contacts you want to make, and then let loose to roam on your behalf.

Each gateway to the Net has distinctive characteristics and caters to a particular type of user. For example, the BIX gateway to Internet is an extension of the virtual community where thousands of computing

professionals make their on-line homes. Any technical problems that you might have or any research you are doing on computing-related issues can be directed easily at the appropriate experts through BIX's special interest group conferences, including one devoted to Internet matters.

As with most services, BIX now has a Windows interface to make things easier. You can get onto BIX with any communications program by dialing 800-695-4882 and entering BIX.BYTE39 at the *name?* prompt. There is also a toll-free voice line for queries (800-695-4775) and various free time introductory offers.

America Online also has a graphical interface for entering the Internet universe through its gateway. Called the Internet Center, you can even access it through some of the PDAs (personal digital assistants) that run special editions of America Online. For more details, call 800-827-6364.

For general information about the Net, call the Network Information Center at 800-444-4345, or read magazines such as *Internet World* (800-632-5537, or 071-976-0405 in London). There are a number of useful books also, with good ones for beginners including *The PC Internet Tour Guide* by Michael Fraase from Ventura Press, and Daniel P. Dern's, *The Internet Guide for New Users*, from McGraw-Hill.

Daniel demonstrated how to use the Internet for promotional purposes by uploading his book's introduction and table of contents, together with ordering information, onto the Net. This is now becoming routine for significant numbers of authors and publishers.

Even the biggest names in fiction are finding it worthwhile to get involved increasingly with the on-line promotion and distribution for their print books. Stephen King's 50-page short story, "Umney's Last Case," was released as a text file on the Net three weeks before the *Nightmare and Dreamscape* collection in which it's featured was released by Viking as a paperback.

 # Interacting with readers

On-line services are bringing readers and authors directly together, as well as disseminating information about books—not just information to help the marketing, but discussion, criticism, and general debates on a wide variety of topics. Authors of both fiction and nonfiction can expect that going on-line to participate in authors' forums, in which they interact with readers, will become more frequent than the traditional author tours.

Some authors will find it worthwhile to establish their own on-line forums or meeting rooms with readers. You could do this with your own bulletin board, but will probably find it easier to work through one of the on-line services. Their staffs can be very helpful if your proposition seems likely to generate significant traffic.

Going on-line can be a very effective way of gathering research for a future book, as well as gauging reader reaction and sales for one already completed. It certainly need not be as expensive or time-consuming as having to travel to do interviews or make personal appearances. A big advantage is that you can time-shift, working at times of your own convenience to call in and examine messages left for you, then go off-line to compose replies.

Real-time conferences or meetings on-line can be built into actuality events with the potential for greater participation and impact. They can also be used to launch a more sustained bulletin board or e-mail interactivity with readers.

 # Your own bulletin board

Very few of the over 50,000 public bulletin board services (BBSs) in the United States actually make a profit. Probably fewer than one in five even covers its costs. But that's hardly surprising, as only a minority seriously set out to be profitable, and an even smaller proportion use their boards primarily as a means of marketing published material in either electronic or print form, or both.

Just as using modems and going on-line become much more routine, so the bulletin board has the capacity to develop rapidly as a marketing and distribution medium. It provides a remarkably cost-efficient way to establish an electronic bookstore either as a major commercial venture, or as a way for an author or small publisher to keep in touch with readers.

⇨ On-line book clubs

There seems to be particular interest in services that are the virtual equivalent of book clubs. Once they have identified their clientele, such bulletin boards can establish long-term relationships by running special reader discount programs and fulfilling orders placed on-line over the Net or commercial services.

The PaperLess Readers Club launched in 1991 by Jay Phillips of Advantage International in Houston, Texas, is probably the first of what promises to be many electronic book clubs. Although the club started with mainly out-of-copyright classical works, some interesting contemporary writings are now also appearing on this publisher's list. A notable achievement was Josef Newman's *Family Values*, being first published by The PaperLess Readers Club in 1992, then becoming part of the Library of Congress permanent exhibit on The Holocaust, a nominee for the 1993 Pulitzer prize for literature, and contender for the National Jewish Book Award for Fiction.

Advantage pays no advances, but compensates authors with royalties at rates agreed before publication and linked directly to the numbers of copies sold either on disk or through the various bulletin boards and on-line services used to distribute paperless books. These services include Advantage's own BBS, The PaperLess Book Shoppe (713-977-9505, 300 to 9600 bps, 8-N-1), and CompuServe.

Copies on floppy disk are available through leading shareware distributors, but if you are an author don't expect this method of distribution to generate many royalties directly. Few readers will pay more than the charge imposed by the disk distributor, unless the work has a strong incentive to purchase an update or more comprehensive

version. But using shareware distribution channels provides valuable publicity for the club, and the prospect of making second and subsequent direct sales from which its authors can derive royalties.

Club membership costs readers a one-time charge of $24.95. For this, they get the latest version of the Advantage Reader software, plus the ROL (Read Out Loud) version of the Reader, and their choice of four from a list of popular classic titles, such as *The Adventures of Tom Sawyer*, *The Time Machine* by H.G. Wells, *The Adventures of Sherlock Holmes* and other works by Sir Arthur Conan Doyle, and *Alice's Adventures in Wonderland*.

Unlike most conventional book clubs, members have no obligation to buy additional books. By using their credit cards, they can go on-line to download additional titles at any time. Members are allowed to use the BBS without charge for 40 minutes per day, with the price of club publications that they successfully download being charged to their Visa or MasterCard. Also, floppy disk copies can be ordered on-line or by mail and paid for by check or money order as well as by credit cards for an additional $1 per title.

The Read Out Loud version of the Advantage Reader supplied to members is a boon for the visually handicapped, and could be used also for children or to create audio tapes for those who like to listen to books while traveling or exercising. This software should prove compatible with most speech synthesizers. Of course, you should not create audio versions or make copies for other than your own personal use without written permission from the publishers.

If you have a manuscript that you want to submit for release by Advantage International and The PaperLess Book Club, you must do so in the normal way. Write a preliminary query letter; they will not evaluate unsolicited manuscripts unless submitted through an established literary agent. Nor are they electronic vanity or subsidy publishers. Your manuscript must be viable and to a high standard.

The ability to create virtual book clubs on bulletin boards extends the tradition in the print business for book lovers to open outlets as second careers or retirement enterprises. This development in

electronic publishing might, in the long-term, help to compensate for the fact that conventional book retailing is becoming ever more dominated by a few major chains, thereby reducing opportunities for authors and small imprints with works not suited to mass merchandising.

⇨ Virtual bookstores

Independent owner-operated bookstores are often labors of love. The publishing world really needs those with a genuine interest in literature for its own sake, as well as the potential profits, to get into electronic book retailing. There are many attractions, not the least that all the problems associated with geographically constrained retailing are resolved. Make a good job of setting up and stocking your bookstore electronically as a on-line bulletin board service, and it can sell to the world with comparatively low overhead and few of the inventory and staffing problems that plague conventional independent bookstores.

One of the first such virtual bookstores not to be spun off from an existing shareware enterprise was established early in 1994 by two California book lovers, Grant Hoel and Michael Todd of Capistrano Beach. It is interesting how much of their effort to establish their Author's Showcase electronic bookstore has been focused, like any good traditional bookstore, on making it a welcoming place for browsers.

They even preserve the visual metaphor of a typical book store. When you enter it electronically via your modem, you see titles stacked up on shelves, fiction on one side, nonfiction on the other. You can browse, select a volume that looks interesting, and click with your mouse button to open up a 100-word synopsis that helps you decide whether to make a purchase.

"Michael and I love books, and are fascinated by the opportunities that the new technology is providing," Grant explains. At 72, he came out of retirement to launch his bookstore, and his passion for the project is motivated more by a love of books than by the new technologies.

"I became very frustrated when doing volunteer work for my local library, and trying to build my own collection, to discover how many worthy books are just going out of print because of the economic forces operating in commercial book publishing," Grant recalls. "So I want Author's Showcase particularly to help authors keep their titles in print and available to readers, even if the market for them is relatively small. We want to offer authors opportunities also to publish manuscripts that deserve publishing, but for various reasons could not get into print. We hope to encourage authors to open their filing cabinets and give new opportunities for such manuscripts."

Grant's partner, Michael Todd, is particularly interested in servicing the business traveler market.

"So often I used to find myself in a hotel wanting a book when the hotel gift shop was closed, the weather outside was awful, and I had no idea where the nearest bookstore was located, or if it would be open," Michael says. "With the increased popularity of portable computers, there is an obvious demand among business travelers for a bookstore that they can buy from at any time, wherever they are."

These are both experienced businessmen. Grant spent most of his working life in banking and insurance, while Michael was a contractor and consultant who has been involved in establishing shopping malls around the U.S. It is illuminating to see how, with the hard business background that so many self-publishing writers lack, they modified their business plan and bookstore concept for good business reasons as they got deeper into the project. There are many lessons to be learned here for those going into similar ventures, including self-publishing enterprises.

"We soon found that it was impractical to have an 800 toll-free number by which potential readers could access Author's Showcase, browse through our titles, and make their selection," Grant reports. "We could have incurred telephone charges of $5 or $6 before a potential customer even decided on a purchase, and in the case of those just browsing and not buying, this would be a straight loss. Even if the decision was made to purchase, downloading a large work on our dime, using a slow modem, could quickly eliminate any returns that we or our authors could expect.

"So we had no choice but to move away from a toll-free service, and to encourage readers to become subscribers at a monthly fee," he continues. "We found that, like any bookstore, we need to be very selective in the books that we carry. We must make it attractive for authors to supply us with good titles, so now we treat each submission individually on its merits, and our costings are geared more towards higher royalties for works by published writers with titles that are viable for us to carry with little or no initial cost for the author."

Author's Showcase is doing most of its promotional work by using bulletin board services to reach a significant proportion of the estimated ten million customers that Grant and Michael believe are available on-line. Authors receive regular detailed reports on how often the synopsis of their title is being read, and the numbers of actual purchases being made. The Showcase also downloads, without charge to the author, any work that a commercial book publisher browsing the shelves finds interesting.

For further information on Author's Showcase, write or call Grant or Michael at

26866 Calle Hermosa
Capistrano Beach, CA 92624
800-503-3434

Running a bulletin board for profit

Unless you are knowledgeable about running both a small business and a bulletin board, read as much as you can about both before setting up a bulletin board as a business enterprise. You must be prepared to invest a lot of time, and possibly money, into the venture, and market it aggressively just to get the number across, let alone attract customers.

There are several shareware programs as well as commercial software that lets you run a bulletin board from your PC. Some include helpful documentation on generating revenue, as well. For an overview, consider *How to Successfully Run a BBS for Profit*, by S. Carol

Allen and Carcy C. Harwin from InfoLink. It is expensive at $49.95, but includes a disk of software to help you reach the right decisions.

 # Specialist boards as publishing services

Many academics and researchers are creating their own bulletin boards that focus on very specific subject areas and professional specialties. Theoretical physicist Paul Ginsparg's board for physicists is but one example of this development. If you are establishing a scientific or academic bulletin board or on-line publishing service, it could be worth adapting the concept developed by the American Association for the Advancement of Science for its annual meetings.

Delegates are invited to submit proposals for Poster Papers, which the Association describes as "an informal, visually oriented way for you to present contributed papers to a multidisciplinary assembly of your peers." Those submitting abstracts that are accepted are assigned a physical bulletin board measuring four feet square on which they present their poster paper in their chosen montage of hardcopy texts and graphics.

This is an enterprising way for students and first-time authors to get their work published—if only in the form of one hardcopy available for a short time to a limited audience. It is easy to extend the concept to an electronic bulletin board or on-line service, with that four-foot square board replaced by a limited number of screens, or a file of a particular size. Authors would be given the opportunity to communicate to a much wider audience internationally over a longer period than could gather for any physical scientific conference. Of course, the files should be presented in a universal format, either incorporating a run-time module or able to be used in most popular computing platforms. This kind of application is well-suited to the Multimedia Workshop on the enclosed disk, or the new Lotus ScreenCam multimedia authoring tool, which does not require any special software other than Windows 3.1 to play back publications.

Distributing through on-line and disk catalogs

If you have several titles or a range of related products and services, you can create your own e-book catalog, and distribute it on-line or on disk. If you do not have the resources to do it yourself, you can try to get listed in a commercial catalog created by a direct-selling operation or compiled as a cooperative venture.

Catalogs as e-books are becoming popular because there is no easier or more cost-effective way to create, distribute, and update a list of products or services for sale than to put the details on a disk or upload them to an on-line service patronized by your target market.

How to create catalogs

As multimedia files become smaller, electronic catalogs with illustrations of the products will play an important role. No glossy still picture in a printed catalog can compete for impact with an animated, full-color presentation showing the product's main features and how it is used. You can produce catalogs with virtually any text or multimedia authoring program, and there is also specialist software designed just for the task.

For example, the Electronic Catalog Construction Kit creates a catalog similar to a simple spreadsheet of items, and is suitable for distribution on floppies. Customers press a single key to get more information about items that interest them, then make their choices by completing the spreadsheet on their computers. The catalog builds the order and invoice, automatically generating a subtotal and calculating any tax due.

The Catalog Construction Kit creates catalogs with up to 12 categories of products or services, which form the basic structure. You list the individual items under their relevant categories, and also build customized order forms and invoices. The program was written

by Mark A. Garber of Cerebral Software and is distributed as shareware. The address is

1815 Wynfair Way
Marietta, GA 30062
CIS 71571,2006
MCI Mail: Cerebral Software

The Internet Catalog

The enthusiasm with which some scientists are adopting the electronic media was illustrated by the speed with which the American Chemical Society seized the opportunity provided by The Internet Catalog to list the Society's titles (Fig. 5-4). The Internet Catalog illustrates how to build a sales and distribution bridge between the hardcopy and on-line environments, offering publishers an opportunity to upload into an electronic "shop window" more comprehensive sales catalogs than the physical and cost limitations of print permit. The speed with which a listing can be updated is a major advantage, enabling publishers' catalogs to become truly dynamic.

For example, a pre-publication listing can be updated as reviews start to come in, and sales figures, awards, bestseller listings, and other relevant information can be added easily and quickly. If this concept develops, it could transform the way that a significant proportion of librarians and booksellers evaluate and order titles, especially as more of them start using on-line services.

Already, about 20,000 librarians are believed to be using Internet and so could be exposed to these catalogs. There are other areas of Internet and other on-line services where publishers and authors are posting details of their works. For information about the Internet Catalog itself, call or write

Inforonics, Inc.
550 Newton Road, P.O. Box 458
Littleton, MA 01460
508-486-8976

Their e-mail contact is Gopher.infor.com.

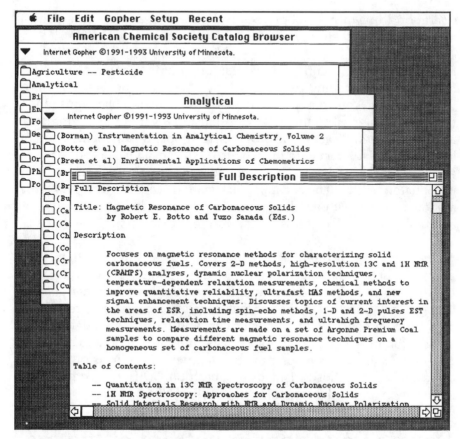

Figure 5-4

The American Chemical Society was one of the first publishers to list its titles in the Internet Catalog. This screen, from a Macintosh running the Gopher search system, illustrates the extensive amount of information about a title that can be given, and the powerful search features.
© 1993, Infotronics, Inc.

Catalogs with locks

Combining catalogs with various encrypting and locking devices, and the ability of disks to hold many compressed e-book files opens further distribution options. The declining cost of CD-ROMs makes instant telephone delivery of any title from a publisher's entire list a practical proposition. The basic concepts can be adapted to small

operations, in which small presses and individual authors can make all or a selection of their works available on floppies or CD-ROMs.

Font and typeface companies were among the first to use this method, now spreading to other fields. It has many attractive features for publishing. You compile the files for the actual publications, and they are transferred to the catalog disc using a variety of compression and access-control techniques. Demonstrations, title screens, contents lists, and book extracts are loaded also, but these files do not have electronic locks, and readers are encouraged to browse from an introductory menu. These catalog disks are distributed to prime target markets, usually without charge. You might already be receiving some and realize how difficult it is to ignore these disks, unlike "junk mail."

If sales prospects are sufficiently stimulated by a demo or other promotional file, they need only make a telephone call to order a title, pay for it by credit card, and be given the key code that unlocks it to give them instant access. Impulse-buying inclinations are converted immediately into actual sales, and there are no delays, distribution problems, or shipping costs. Rainbow Technologies Inc. of Irvine, California is among the most experienced firms offering these services for those wishing to publish on CD-ROM. To get more information (and a demo disk), call 800-852-8569.

Dangle your dongle in front of buyers

Rainbow also deals in *dongles*, hardware devices that plug into the ports at the back of your computer and control access to software. Primarily developed as data security and anti-pirating software keys, they can also have electronic publications hard-wired into them, so that your book or collection of books is marketed as what looks like a slightly enlarged version of the plug on the end of your modem or printer cable. Publishing by dongle might seem a bit weird, but it could make sense for some applications, particularly those involving large files but for which CD-ROMs are not appropriate.

Dongles and controlled-access discs are particularly effective distribution media when you are offering a large number of individual items and a buyer wants instant delivery at realistic unit prices, rather

than paying a lot up-front for an entire collection. Art, editorial, and video clips are some examples. David Dukes, the chief operating officer of Ingram Micro Inc., is one of a growing number of enthusiasts for electronic distribution this way, and thinks it might account for one in five software sales by 1995.

⇨ Financial success from free distribution

It is possible to be financially successful if you distribute on-line or on disk through the shareware and other routes without charging readers anything. Extend into cyberspace the concepts of sponsored and entirely advertiser-financed virtual publications that are appropriate to these media. An excellent example of this is Lynn Hildre's Vacation Alaska.

Lynn compiled a travel guide to Alaska containing editorial items high in reader interest, added practical data that a visitor to the state really needs, then found advertisers to generate revenue in return for the opportunity to promote their products and services. They also provided additional information of benefit to the end user. The whole package was assembled onto disks for shareware distributors, and in compressed files sent to bulletin boards so that it soon spread around the world.

As long as the ratio of advertising content to editorial is acceptable to the reader, an electronic guide can be expanded to almost any size to accommodate the number of advertisers wanting to participate. You eliminate many of the problems that print publications face of having to balance advertising revenue with increased print and distribution costs. You could have a thousand advertisements on a CD-ROM disk, if the demand was there, without significantly increasing your production or distribution costs.

Lynn set the price of an advertisement in the first edition of her Vacation Alaska at only $250. It was such an attractive deal that hundreds of businesses wanted to get into the next edition. The rates could easily be much higher for a guide devoted to a state with a larger tourist business than Alaska enjoys. In fact, the cost-per-exposure ratio

that print advertisers use to measure the cost-efficiency of a publication could justify rates two or three times higher.

The Orpheus software package was used to compile Vacation Alaska. The program's creator, Rod Willmot, describes Lynn Hildre's venture as "a brilliant demonstration of how to make digital publishing work for everyone: the advertiser gets much better coverage than in print or on TV, the end-user gets an entertaining and useful infobase, and the author gets an attractive income with the guarantee of repeat business every year."

A consortium of writers and publishers was formed to produce similar state guides in Texas, Washington, DC, and Georgia. There is plenty of scope for an author to create a unique guide appropriate to the needs and character of his or her state. Orpheus also has the flexibility to include graphics and other features, and guidelines to develop CD-ROM editions if that proves viable. For details on Orpheus, write or call

Rod Willmot
535 Duvernay
Sherbrooke, QC Canada J1L 1Y8
819-566-6296

This is just one example of the many topics ideal for electronic publishing on disk and targeted at business travelers and vacationers, who increasingly plan trips on their desktops and use portable computers when traveling. Any such group that uses computers to process information is a prime target for an electronic publication that provides them with information that they need.

Of course, when distributing to such markets, remember to gear for a very high proportion of 3.5-inch floppies, the type used most in portables. However, *flash cards* are moving towards portable platforms in a big way.

Flash memory cards are sealed and very tough electronic devices about the size of a typical business card that are undergoing intensive

development for use in portable computing devices. Despite their small size, they can hold an amazing amount of data—20 megabytes is becoming common, which not so long ago was an acceptable amount of storage capacity for the hard disk in a desktop computer.

PC cards, or flash memory, or smart cards, as they are variously called, are actually PCMCIA cards, meeting the standard set by the Personal Computer Memory Card International Association. The dimensions vary somewhat between types of cards, but in Version 2.0 of this standard, which is the same as the Japanese Electronic Industry Development Association release 4.1, the card can be up to 10.5mm thick and may contain a miniaturized hard disk capable of holding over 100MB of data.

Indeed, flash cards operate like fast hard disks, but consume a minute amount of power, so they can be used continuously for hours on the smallest of hand-held computing devices. Their costs continues to fall rapidly, and their efficiency and capacity steadily increase, so they have a great future for publishing large amounts of material in a very flexible format.

For example, you can include on a flash card an enormous amount of data and still have room for sophisticated applications programs to process that data faster and with less processing power than is achievable with CD-ROM. What's more, some flash cards can be written to, providing many opportunities for users to interact constructively with databases and other forms of publication. Updating becomes easier and more economical also, and there is greater scope for incorporating various security procedures.

Think about compressing your hard disk down to the size of your business card, and you can start to see this medium's enormous potential. These cards might not seem significant for volume electronic publishing at present, but they will become so, with portable computers likely to comprise at least half of all computer sales by about 1996.

Physical distribution on disks and cards

Some industry pundits believe that CD-ROMs, floppies, and even flash cards might be only interim media for a few years, until viable systems are established for most electronic publications to be distributed directly on-line over information highways from virtual bookstores and libraries, as well as directly from publishers and authors.

However, that forecast might prove as unreliable as the expectations at the start of the decade for the paperless office. I believe that there will always be significant numbers of people who do not want to go on-line often, or at all. These people prefer to build up their own collections of electronic publications, just as they have racks of magazines and shelves of books and videos.

Floppies, CD-ROMs, and perhaps smart cards and portable hard drives should therefore figure in your distribution strategy, particularly in situations where your title goes before the potential buyer and there is a touch-and-feel selling situation. This packaging can be vital for commercial reasons to give an e-book physical reality, even if this flies against so many of the strong arguments for virtual publishing. Packaging is discussed in detail in a later chapter.

Distribute by renting, and establish long-term relationships

There is a possible trend towards renting, rather than owning, computer software that could hold the key to making electronic publishing more viable for publishing houses and individual authors alike. This will only be appropriate for certain types of publications, with e-books having the enormous advantage over other rental operations that you do not need to get the actual volume that you rent back in good condition, or at all. Disks costs very little, while titles distributed on-line are only files that have no physical substance.

It is possible to build into rental e-books restrictions on how long they can be used. The end-user would just telephone in and make a further credit card payment to get another code that extends the rental period.

Low-cost rentals might be the best way to build up long-term sales relationships. Visionaries such as Borland's Phillipe Kahn and Microsoft's Bill Gates have become increasingly frank about marketing tactics that involve establishing direct relationships with end-users of their products at almost any price. The aim is to establish an installed base of users who become corporate assets that you nurture and try to keep selling to many times for small amounts on each occasion. Receipts could far exceed within a year or two the previous marketing strategies of charging high one-time costs to make the first sale of a software product.

The practice of high initial prices was based on the need to quickly recover the enormous start-up and product-development costs incurred by many software companies. Now there is a tendency to see the cash-flow patterns needing to be very different, with the income from a customer flowing in drip-by-drip over a sustained period, rather than in a flood at first, then an arid period until—hopefully—an upgrade causes the next flood of money.

With the controls now available for marketing software on-line or via CD-ROM and securing direct payments by credit card, the previously contrasting philosophies behind marketing shareware and commercial programs is blurring. There is much more "try before you buy" of commercial software, and then the decision might well not be to buy, but to rent according to use, becoming a registered user of a full-featured program for a certain payment each month.

As networking and the ability to cost-efficiently collect small sums increases, we might get to the point where, for example, every time you use one of the major spell-checkers, you make a payment of a cent or two to the owner of the copyright of the dictionary or encyclopedia involved. That might sound far-fetched, but it is really only an extension of the already well-established methods by which charges are made for accessing on-line databases.

 # Cutting mailing costs

Very important to book distribution in the United States is the attractively priced 4th-class book rate postal service. In principle, this same rate applies to videotapes, electronic publications, and hybrid hardcopy and electronic books. Regulations might change, so check with your local postmaster. I have recently been shipping significant quantities of printed books and videos by 4th class, and the savings have proved significant, although there is an element of inconsistency. Deliveries can be surprisingly quick, only a day or two behind first class mail for some destinations, and abysmally slow to others.

I have also had some consignments badly handled, so secure packaging is important. With this in mind, and as most electronic publications are much lighter than their print equivalents, you might prefer to use first class.

Overseas, in Europe for example, book rates (where they exist) tend not be anywhere near as attractive as in the U.S., giving electronic publications a further advantage in these markets. International airmail rates are high everywhere, often prohibitively expensive as a way of speedily distributing hardcopy books. Floppies and CD-ROMs, with their smaller bulk and lighter weight than paper, can make international publishing ventures more viable.

The small 3.5-inch disks travel safely with very little protection, as long as the outer envelope or packaging is reasonably strong. The larger floppies and CDs need stiffeners and very clear notices on the outside that the package should not be bent. In all mailings, identify the contents as magnetic or optical media needing careful handling and protection from electrical fields, excess heat, and so on.

If you distribute regularly to readers in countries where high duties are imposed, or where clearing packages through Customs and import controls can be difficult, expensive, and pose long delays, there are arguments for keeping the packaging and labeling of disks as simple and low in perceived value as possible, sending any invoicing or other

monetary information by letter under separate cover. Often, disks can be shipped by letter mail along with documents and pass across frontiers with few hassles.

Of course, when your e-books are zapped over national borders by radio or telephone, it becomes almost impossible for import duties and other restrictions to be imposed upon them. E-books will make an important contribution if they result in the ending of taxation on information. A particularly intriguing situation arises over the great variety in the levying of state and city sales taxes in the United States. It is not yet clear how a product that has no physical substance or geographical location should be taxed, if at all.

Capturing the look and feel

O NE of the main handicaps preventing electronic publishing from taking off is that it does not convey the touch, the feel, the character of distinctive printed publications, maintains Llewellyn King, a leading newsletter publisher based in Washington, DC. "It took me a long time to accept *The Economist* just going from newsprint to glossy paper. Imagine the reactions of many longtime readers if their favorite publications go from paper to disk!"

If you are serious about publishing profitably, you must listen to such experts in the newsletter game. They keep on demonstrating that these are times when small enterprises can flourish while large ones founder. Even more important for wordsmiths, there is no group in the publishing business closer to its readers and more sensitive to the way those reader reactions influence a publisher's bottom line.

Newsletter publishers constantly test and sample their markets. It is a revelation to attend one of their conferences and learn of their extensive knowledge of reader reactions to subtle differences in the selection of fonts, paper colors, and other details.

In so many other areas of publishing, readers seem to be treated casually, but in successful newsletter publishing, readers are wooed assiduously. The relationship with them is nurtured carefully because real profitability comes only with the second and subsequent subscription renewals. Experienced newsletter publishers do not risk alienating their readers by, for example, using those dreadful slabs of hard-to-read reversed type that feature in many magazines purely for design purposes—unless their readers tell them they want it.

Although, at first glance, newsletters might appear naive in layout and typography, some of the seemingly most primitive newsletters reflect the most sophisticated research and production resources. When one leading publisher installed cutting-edge computer technology, he continued to direct his final editorial output to an aging typewriter to generate the unjustified text and slightly misaligned letters that his many readers had grown to love!

"It adds that sense of intimacy and immediacy," he explains.

The trusted and familiar

"We get attached to things that have meaning for us, and this applies in particular to trusted and familiar publications," emphasizes Llewellyn King, who distributes a stable of both trusted and influential newsletters. "To switch from print to electronic media means losing that established format, with the familiar visual and tactile features, that you have worked so hard to establish.

"Of course, electronic publications are more acceptable to younger generations for whom the computer is becoming the prime medium, one that is even more important than print," he continues. "I found one of my young staff members working late at her computer recently, and she explained that she was learning a new program as much to help her social life as her career. One of the frequent opening gambits in the singles bar she frequents is the question 'what software do you work in,' much as my generation would have asked 'what's your tipple' to help size up a new acquaintance in a bar."

It seems that now you can be characterized as much by your preferred software as by your favorite drink! There certainly are computing social strata symbolized by the software equivalents to beer or cocktails, but the majority of the potential readers for most publications are not yet attuned to the subtleties of the electronic environment. Large numbers of them are becoming comfortable in the Windows or Macintosh environments, with familiar screen displays that make it far easier to interface with a computer, but the majority of readers still prefer paper. Author-publishers will have to live with that reality for a long time, however much they might want to publish with economy, speed, and convenience of digital media.

There is, therefore, a substantial body of publishing opinion believing that the best way to wean readers from print is to provide them with screen displays that simulate familiar printed formats. However great your hypertext and search facilities, and the sophistication of your graphics or other multimedia features, you should offer also the option of generating a hardcopy that is faithful to the print original, not a dull, characterless ASCII text print-out bereft of attractive typography.

Crossing the media frontiers

Until recently, that kind of electronic publishing has been very difficult. Moving between hardcopy print and softcopy digital has meant crossing formidable media frontiers, with the problems greatly aggravated if you want your works to move freely between the DOS and Macintosh platforms, as well as around the IBM-compatible world.

However, new solutions are arriving, largely as a result of the increasing popularity of Windows, which creates a greater commonality among computer systems. Because there are now so many computers running Windows with compatible features, it has been possible to develop software that enables documents formatted for print to be converted into portable files that can travel electronically on floppies, or by modem or network transmissions. When they reach their destinations, readers have the option of opening those publications and viewing them on screen, or printing them out with all the typefaces and other formatting features of the original retained.

This can be very important for a wide variety of works in which the format is an important element of the overall communications objective. The applications range from business documents to poetry, and are particularly applicable to nonfiction works such as scientific and academic papers that must still conform to rigid formatting conventions, or for texts which incorporate tables, charts, and other embedded graphics.

To exploit these opportunities fully, we must turn from the shareware authors who have done so much pioneering work in electronic publishing and look to the greater research and development resources of commercial software publishers. They have been able to come up with the means to make the design and formatting aspects of printed documents fully portable into the electronic publishing domain.

Attracting the most attention have been the desktop-publishing corporate heavyweight Adobe Systems, and a comparative newcomer, No Hands Software, which has a lot of venture-capital muscle. They compete fiercely to establish an accepted standard for electronic publishing by bridging the gap between electronic and print media. The best of this category of software might meet all your electronic publishing needs if you are confident that your readers all have higher-end systems in either the Macintosh or IBM environments, notably hardware capable of running Windows.

If the market to which you are distributing comprises significant numbers of customers with lower-end computers, however, produce electronic editions of your works using one of the shareware programs designed to handle ASCII text with limited formatting options. You might also require one of these shareware solutions if you need very compact files, although this is becoming less of a factor as file-compression techniques improve.

 # Powerful multimedia Windows publishing

If you want to publish electronically with multimedia features, there is a new category of software emerging. Led by the Lotus ScreenCam released in 1994, this class of authoring software offers a great deal of portability within the Windows platform. It is a valiant attempt to create a multimedia Windows equivalent to the portability of ASCII text.

ScreenCam does not require special hardware, such as a CD-ROM drive or video capture card, to create or run multimedia publications. You can capture anything happening on the screen, including full-motion video, and add sound by speaking into a microphone or patching in an audio feed at the appropriate places. The resulting files are compact and can be saved separately or embedded in your publication for distribution on disk or by modem. When they reach readers, the ScreenCam movies, as they are called, run under Windows without needing any of the applications that were used to create them.

DEMOquick has more features than ScreenCam for authoring demonstrations and tutorials in Windows. The simple procedures for creating distribution floppies and linking to multimedia systems are particularly useful for electronic publishing. Details from 508-263-3030.

 # Multiple approaches for universal e-books

In the case of e-books composed mainly of text that need to reach the widest possible markets, ASCII still rules. Despite all the advances made in hardware and software, and the natural urge to feel up-to-date with information highway and computing technology, this is the basic truth not be forgotten about electronic publishing. If you want to publish what you have to say to the widest possible audience, it has to be as a plain ASCII file that can be uploaded to any bulletin board, copied onto any floppy disk, transmitted by any modem, and read on any personal computer.

The more that you refine your publication from this plainest of all formats, the more you restrict your audience. Many shareware authors have confirmed that principle—it is astounding how many registrations they still receive from owners of basic 8088 PCs or early Macs. If the content of your message is important, and you express it well and distribute it efficiently, it can be heard without fancy formatting, embedded graphics, or other features. Sometimes a plain appearance can actually enhance the impact—which is why some of the most successful direct marketers spend a lot of money on high-tech processes to produce pieces in monospaced Courier typewriter fonts!

Progress is constantly being made by the creators of the shareware authoring programs recommended in the appendix to enhance ASCII texts with better typefaces, spacing, and margins without compromising cross-platform portability. These should not be regarded as inferior authoring products; they just set out to do a different task from the more expensive commercial authoring programs in fancy boxes.

In view of this, in many cases it makes sense to publish your work in two versions. One might use, say, Acrobat or Common Ground to

cater for readers with higher-end systems for whom you need to preserve familiar paper formats, regrettable as that may be in the long term. The other would be created using Dart, Writer's Dream, or other e-book compilers and released for low-end PCs.

If you have an existing formatted publication that looks great and works well in hardcopy form, you have additional reasons for releasing it in Acrobat or Common Ground because of the ease of converting it to the electronic medium while preserving its print qualities. Make sure that it really does work well on screen, however, and would not look much better if you changed the layout and typefaces. Often the author or originator is the last person able to make these judgments.

Another choice that fits in with some of the marketing options reviewed elsewhere in this book is to release an abridged or other appropriate version of your publication as freeware or shareware in a universal electronic publishing format based on ASCII. Use this as a promotional tool to market the fully formatted and printable edition. You could embed graphics files in your promotional edition to show those readers with the necessary hardware and software the superior appearance of the pages in the revenue-generating formatted edition.

Eventually, as old PCs and Macs get scrapped and your readers move on to greater processing power with the capacity to run Windows and VGA screens, you might well be able to go exclusively with either Acrobat or Common Ground for publishing electronic versions of formatted print magazines and e-books. This might be feasible already in much business and professional publishing where the target audiences are clearly defined.

Don't be seduced up blind alleys

One basic method of creating electronic documents that preserve familiar print appearance might be to use a graphics program that, in effect, takes snapshots of your screen and displays them on screen as graphic images. Do not be seduced into this dead end of electronic publishing! The graphics files that are generated are large, and the true merits of publishing electronically are not achieved because the

texts can only be viewed like the printed page. They do not allow for efficient searches, extracting, attaching of notes, and all the other benefits of true digital documents.

Even as an interim measure, computerized graphical copies of publications are not acceptable, and will hinder rather than help the development of the new medium. It is seductively appealing, if you already have a printed publication that you want to make electronic, just to run its pages through a scanner to create a stack of bitmap files that you can distribute for reading by any one of a number of graphics programs. Some early CD-ROM titles tried this route, but it just doesn't work for a number of reasons.

To create a viable electronic publication, you must add a step similar to optical character recognition (OCR), which turns those printed pages into digitized text. Using OCR alone to digitize print is prone to reading errors and turns attractively designed printed pages into plain ASCII text without formatting or fonts.

A document created on a computer already has its text in a form that can be processed electronically. The hurdle still to be overcome is to make that text portable without losing the formatting and any accompanying graphical elements in the pages. The need, then, is to incorporate aspects of graphic imaging into software that creates fully featured electronic documents with true portability across platforms. Acrobat, Common Ground, and a few other contenders tackle this task in a variety of ways. Such software has cost a great deal of money and resources to develop, and you can expect the sales push behind them to be very powerful in the scramble for the potentially big returns available if one emerges as a standard. Their main value, however, will prove to be for the distribution of business documentation, not general electronic publishing.

Choosing a publishing program

How do these print-mimicking document publishing programs work? And which is the one to choose? Acrobat and Common Ground both create their portable electronic documents using the printer-driver

software already running in whatever system you are using. In fact, for an author to convert a word-processed or desktop-published document to a portable electronic file is very similar to instructing your system to generate a hardcopy from the printer.

Although these products are seductively easy and logical to use, publishers and authors must be careful not to make unwise choices that, because of the preoccupation with preserving elements of the printed page, seriously hobble the electronic version. A wrong choice might not be serious when converting documents into electronic format within a confined and controllable situation, such as a large corporation or an academic institution. If you are publishing for profit in the larger world, however, selecting inappropriate software can spell disaster.

Here are some key points to consider:

> Are there any inherent restraints in the programs that seriously inhibit easy access to your publications by your target readers? If so, eliminate them from consideration. For example, do they create files that are excessively large? Are these files as easily handled on a typical Mac as on a PC, if it is important for you to reach Macintosh as well as IBM-compatible users? Are the files you create sufficiently compact and reliable for you to distribute them cost-efficiently by modem or on floppies. Are there any copyright or licensing problems?

> Will the software you are considering generate files that can be read on computer systems with the hardware and software facilities that your target readers are using already? Don't expect your readers to buy extra memory, upgrade their displays, or add different disk drives just to access your publications. If the software requires Windows, you eliminate sales to readers who have systems only capable of running DOS. This might not be important for your particular publishing venture, but you should bear such limiting factors in mind.

> It could also be important to use publishing software that will work on the small hand-held computers that are becoming a dominant factor in electronic publishing markets. In general,

the less the demands the software makes on your readers' systems, the more likely it is to be portable into these hand-held devices with their limited processing capabilities. Try for maximum computability in these situations; it is just not enough to achieve portability for your publications to move between desktop Macintosh and PCs.

➤ When run by the end users, will the software reproduce the design of your pages attractively, and enable your readers to process your text with at least the basic options that make electronic publishing so attractive? If the answer is no, then trying to preserve the look and feel of your original printed pages is a waste of time. You would be better off forgetting print and thinking exclusively electronic.

➤ Can you include with your publication the executable software program essential for your work to be read easily? If you cannot, you might be crippling your publication to the point where it cannot succeed. Your book or periodical would be rather like a diary, or one of the early Bibles, incorporating a lock, with the contents inaccessible to anyone who does not have the right key. However—and this could be important for some high-value or confidential publications such as premium newsletters—the ability to restrict access to your publication might be an advantage.

⇨ Avoid limiting factors

Before committing yourself, use these considerations, plus others specific to you, to ensure that the authoring or document-imaging software you are considering does not have any limiting factors that might make it a poor choice for you in the long run. For example, some leading computer companies have been advocating the concept of embedding outline fonts as a basic method to make formatted documents portable. This involves taking some of the program coding by which the fonts in these documents are created, and then incorporating this programming into the portable digital document conversion software.

In addition to the practical disadvantage of increasing the size of the portable files, this approach has potential legal pitfalls arising from the use of copyrighted program code. There is a real risk of running into intellectual property rights problems if your publication promotes the unlicensed use of outline fonts on systems not legally running them already. It could take years to sort out this legal complexity.

 # Acrobat and Common Ground compared

Businesses going through this selection process might well finish up with Acrobat or Common Ground as their favored alternatives for preserving paper print formats. Acrobat is very powerful, and comes from a proven, established source with which many businesses feel comfortable. But Common Ground gained an early edge when its compact MiniViewer program was effectively released into the public domain. In contrast, Adobe charged $50 for every computer running its Reader program, which is necessary to view Acrobat documents if your system does not have Acrobat already. This is a bit like selling a car with the wheels only available as an expensive option.

No Hands Software also stopped enforcing the limitation on registered users releasing Common Ground documents to more than 100 users. So even if you have an early Macintosh version with this restriction, you can now publish as many copies as you wish, and attach MiniViewer to all of them. When you read this, there might have been changes in Adobe's licensing policies also, so it pays to check the latest situation.

Acrobat is naturally very good at being able to handle any of Adobe's own PostScript fonts that appear in the original document. Indeed, Acrobat actually incorporates Adobe Type Manager software. When Acrobat encounters other fonts not from its own stable—of which there are an increasing number—it substitutes its own nearest equivalent. This substitution is often very well done, but might not always be satisfactory, particularly with special fonts that are an

important element of a design. Readability might suffer also. Consequently, if you are a commercial publisher, you can never be absolutely sure just how your publication will appear when run on the many different systems used by your readers.

Common Ground tackles the font problem by replicating the typefaces and formatting of the original page pixel-by-pixel for subsequent display or printing. This avoids the copyright problems of using proprietary font outlines, and produces files that are smaller than those with embedded outline fonts included. The reproduction is also more faithful to the original and predictable than when fonts are substituted. These are not just aesthetic considerations, but could affect the accuracy of your text if you are publishing internationally and need to preserve special foreign character sets, such as the accents over letters, or the distinctive characters in Arabic, Greek, or Kanji alphabets.

While Acrobat makes use of its own proprietary PostScript typographic technology to convert both text and graphics into portable documents, Common Ground converts documents into a portable format called DigitalPaper, which takes advantage of the ability of Windows and the Mac's QuickDraw software to enable the graphics embedded in documents to go along for the ride.

In theory, the output quality generated by Acrobat is limited only by the resolution of your readers' hardware. On the other hand, Common Ground is restricted to 300 dots per inch for printing and 100 dpi for its screen display, as of this writing.

Both Acrobat and Common Ground have advantages and disadvantages in their text-search capabilities, with Common Ground having probably more intuitive word and phrase searches, but Acrobat the more sophisticated hypertext linking. Your readers can place bookmarks and add notes to an Acrobat document, while Common Ground for Windows was first released late in 1993 without these features, but was due to acquire them within a year.

You cannot edit text directly in either program, but can copy and paste in and out of your word processor. Common Ground has the edge in requiring fewer system resources and probably generating

portable electronic publications faster, but Acrobat is better at compressing files, which could be vital if your documents include more elaborate formatting and use PostScript fonts.

Compare strengths in real-world situations

You will probably use computer magazine reviews to make further comparisons, but bear in mind that the computing magazines tend to make their comparisons and rate features in an unreal world biased towards higher-end technology. *Byte* magazine, for example, compared the two programs in October 1993 on systems described as "minimum configuration." That was perceived to be a 486SX with 4MB of RAM, and a Mac SE/30 with 5MB of RAM.

These might be the minimum configurations for most of *Byte's* computing-oriented readers, who like to keep on or near the cutting edge of the technology. There are over 70 million personal computer users still a long way from that "minimum," however, and most publishers will have substantial potential for sales in this sector.

Pause before rushing into digital publication

Many authors who already have their texts in digital form as word-processed files will get so fired up by the attractions of electronic publishing that they will want to focus entirely on the new medium without bothering with paper formatting and print-oriented typographic design. Remember, however, that the most important element in any publishing enterprise is the reader. Pause to consider how this improving technology will enable you to deliver your publications so that they become significantly more attractive to readers.

Rather than creating hypertext links and adding multimedia features to an already digitized text, it might be easier in some cases to add values from the results of the effort and expense already invested for

print. There are particular situations where preserving print formatting's appeal requires the minimum of extra work. Obviously, if you already have periodicals, newsletters, magazines, or books that have special visual appeal, it could be beneficial to try to preserve these production values when they go digital.

For example, in the small print of the typical author's contract is a clause that, when your book goes out of print because the publisher sees no more profit potential in it, the rights revert to you. Often the publisher will release not just the rights to the text and illustrations, but to the whole print production, including the design and layout. In such cases, you usually have the option to acquire the lithographic film from which plates can be made for a nominal sum, giving you the opportunity to reprint at your own expense.

You don't need the film to go electronic, but can scan the laid out pages into a document-imaging or authoring program. In future, if electronic publishing develops as it should, you might want to revise author's contracts to give you the rights also to the computer files from which those litho films and the original sets of plates are made. Then, when your book goes out of print, you could go even more quickly and economically into the electronic medium with an edition that preserves the print design.

 # Paperless magazines can survive where print versions fail

E-mags (paperless magazines) are an exciting new field because they can be produced and distributed to large potential audiences for little more than the time invested by their creators in the editorial process. As a result, the CIVNet academic network by 1993 had nearly 400 e-journals available, covering almost every conceivable magazine publishing category.

Some of the most unlikely journals that could never be launched, let alone survive, in print have been attracting large niche audiences. The *Unplastic News*, for example, is an eccentric, amusing publication that can exercise such publishing indulgences as devoting

an entire issue to bald people. *Unplastic News* editor Todd Tibbetts says in *Byte* (September 1993) that "we have thousands of readers—and we don't pollute the world with paper."

Steve Hudgik has no doubts that "for anyone who has a message to get out to a computer literate audience, electronic publishing is the way to go." Switching his own newsletter for registered users from print to disk enabled him greatly to increase the size, and so promote his expanding product line, yet reduce publishing costs significantly. Quality was enhanced also by publishing in full color, which would not be cost-effective on paper for most small publishing ventures. Adding color to an electronic publication need not increase the cost at all!

The XLPLUS authoring programs, also available as shareware, can do a particularly good job for magazines and newsletters because they enable an editor to add those visual elements which are so important for the success of magazines in print (Fig. 6-1). A magazine on disk should reach out to its readers also, not by trying to mimic print, but by expressing a unique, welcoming personality exploiting the strengths of the electronic media.

Figure 6-1

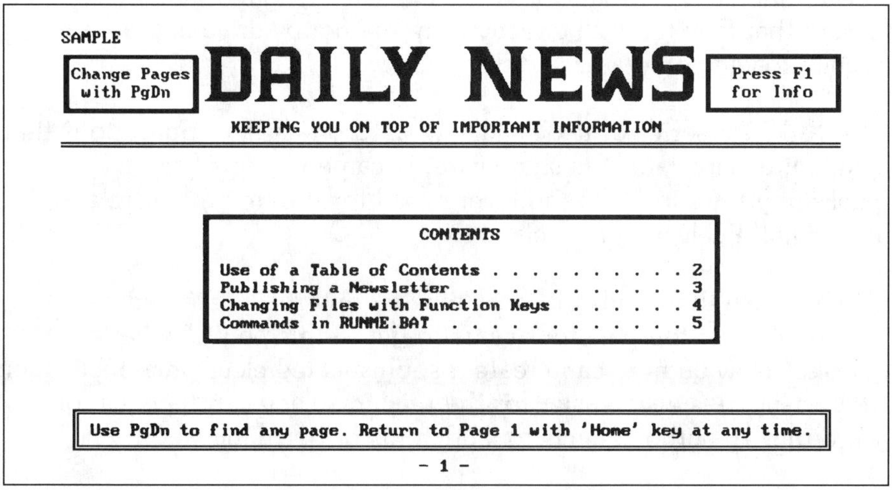

```
SAMPLE
┌──────────────┐ ┌──────────────┐
│ Change Pages │  DAILY NEWS  │  Press F1    │
│ with PgDn    │              │  for Info    │
└──────────────┘ └──────────────┘
        KEEPING YOU ON TOP OF IMPORTANT INFORMATION
───────────────────────────────────────────────────────

        ┌─────────────────────────────────────┐
        │              CONTENTS               │
        │ Use of a Table of Contents . . . . . . . . . . 2 │
        │ Publishing a Newsletter  . . . . . . . . . . 3 │
        │ Changing Files with Function Keys  . . . . . . 4 │
        │ Commands in RUNME.BAT  . . . . . . . . . . . 5 │
        └─────────────────────────────────────┘

┌─────────────────────────────────────────────────────────┐
│ Use PgDn to find any page. Return to Page 1 with 'Home' key at any time. │
└─────────────────────────────────────────────────────────┘
                        - 1 -
```

Software that can capture on-screen the familiar appearance of print need not require powerful, expensive computers. This document was created and read on a basic PC using XLPLUS software. Rexxcom Systems

⇨ The XLPLUS story

"An on-screen document can—and should—be vastly superior to its ink and paper cousin," maintains one of the pioneers of electronic publishing, Charles L. Wiedemann, president of Rexxcom Systems, P.O. Box 111, Schooleys Mountain, NJ 07870.

Charles has been working since 1989 to create software that he dubs "displayware" to transform plain text into really impressive screen displays. His XLPLUS family of programs turns ASCII text into fully formatted electronic publications with graphical borders, special fonts, and other display features. The displays make text colorful, giving authors opportunities to add visual emphasis to words or phrases. The navigation through texts is intuitive and fast; your readers will still be able to enjoy great effects even if they have to run your publications directly from a floppy disk.

This is important, because many hard disks are overcrowded already, and so there is a reluctance to load software that might be needed only temporarily. It is a particular advantage when releasing e-magazines, which inherently have a shorter life expectancy than e-books, to ensure that they run well directly from the floppy drive and do not require loading onto a hard disk.

The XLPLUS series of text readers, based on earlier applications that had limited circulation as shareware, became very proficient publishing tools in 1993, and were used for the first major release by the Digital Publishing Association.

"It has taken thousands of hours of work and really talented teamwork over the past four years to get to this point," Charles recalls. "Now authors can create a sophisticated electronic publication very easily. It is even easier for the readers. They can type just one word that an author selects to launch his or her publication.

"The Decor-Edge Scenes are an exciting feature that we added after the main programming was completed," he continues. "It was one of those times when everything clicked into place, and it worked perfectly. These scenes are what we call 'Text in Graphics,' which we

provide as TIG modules to enable authors to display their scrollable text files on a scene of mountains and waterfalls, or within the speech balloon of a cartoon character, or even as antique-style writing on a parchment scroll."

The basic concept of the XLPLUS family of software is simple. There are essentially three files. One, a COM or EXE file, manages how the electronic publication functions by controlling a file with a DEB extension containing the graphic Border, and another with a DET extension containing the Text. The managing executable files grab the DET and DEB files, and make them work together to display your publication with all the scrolling and other graphic display features. The facilities available to readers are displayed in a menu that appears when the F1 function key is pressed. All the instructions that readers need are on the screen and very intuitive.

Create batch files to make things easy

It is vital for e-magazines to make things as easy as possible for the readers by creating a *batch file* (a file with the BAT extension) that will set the whole process in motion automatically. You can name this file with a shortened form of the title of your publication, or some other appropriate identification, and put this name on the disk label. For example, if you call your publication *mystory*, write a batch file like this to get it up and running in XLPLUS:

```
echo off
hqsw
XL2000 MYSTORY
ega
vga
```

Save it as a plain ASCII text file to the same disk and directory as your DET, DEB and XL2000.EXE files. Call this batch file MYSTORY.BAT.

On the disk label, write "To start, type MYSTORY." When your readers type MYSTORY, they set off an automatic sequence in which the BAT file is activated and starts up the XL2000 program, which in

turn loads the files containing your publication. Your publication then appears on screen, ready to go.

Newsletter Clip Services

Many newsletters are not sold, but produced to circulate within organizations to keep employees or members informed, and distributed externally to potential clients. These types of newsletter publishing are beginning to feature in electronic media, offering increased opportunities for writers and photographers.

Newsletter publishers can also obtain low-cost, high-quality editorial to flow easily into softcopy and hardcopy editions in a new form of syndication. Dartnell Corporation's ClipEdit service (800-468-3038) out of Chicago supplies 35 professionally researched and written editorial articles on a floppy disk ready to patch into either a print or an electronic newsletter.

The articles are tailored for various categories so that if, for example, you are a CPA who produces a regular newsletter for clients, you can pick articles on business and financial topics to add production values. A health center would select features on nutrition and exercise for the newsletter to its clients and prospects.

This is essentially the clip art concept extended to words, using electronic publishing techniques to reduce costs and add speed and convenience in distribution. No keyboarding is required by the client; the selected texts just flow off the disk into any word processor or publishing program. ClipEdit Operations Manager Judy Wolffer expects the service to grow as electronic publishing of newsletters expands, and she has plans to make good use of on-line services for her marketing efforts.

Customized newspapers

"Some day, all news will come this way" says the text on one side of the masthead of *The ClariNews*. "All the news before it's printed" proclaims the other side. "The electronic newspaper you read on your

own computer—published 24 hours a day" declares the copy right under the title.

ClariNet Communications Corporation has been profitably delivering electronic newspapers via Internet for several years and has accumulated 40,000 readers. The cost can be as little as $1 a month for an individual user on a network, or around $11 for an individual subscription, still making it competitive with a printed newspaper delivered to your door.

"You get the speed of broadcast news along with the in-depth coverage of newspapers," says founder and publisher Brad Templeton. This virtual newspaper also is fully keyword searchable, and features over 30 new computing-related stories every business day in the accompanying Newsbytes magazine, which won the Computer Press Association award for Best On-line Publication.

There are various ways now available to build your own newspaper or magazine from on-line sources. The minimal time and effort involved make it practical as an individual project, particularly if you need selected information to further your business or career. The attractions are even greater for creating an electronic newspaper that can be published widely within an organization or externally to a special-interest group.

The information is readily available if you know how to get to it, which is now a task that can be left largely to software, without the need for expensive expertise in on-line searching. There are now over 4,000 on-line databases, and probably the best reference to them is the six-monthly Gale Directory of Databases (800-877-GALE). As journalists become more adept at making good use of these databases, the quality of coverage in commercial media should improve, while giving the editor of the smallest newsletter access to an international team of experienced correspondents.

For example, the Agence France-Presse, for whom I was an editor and bureau chief, can be accessed for news reports and backgrounders in English on parts of the world where the other wire services and news organizations have coverage gaps, notably French-speaking African and Asian countries. Some of these news sources,

together with various electronic clippings services, are available to e-mail subscribers, including those getting their e-mail by radio on small hand-held computers.

A particularly interesting approach offered by PED Software Corporation's Journalist for Windows (Fig. 6-2) is the virtually automatic creation of a properly laid-out newspaper on your desktop. You tell Journalist what topics interest you or your organization, and it goes out and finds them through your CompuServe account. It even updates the information automatically at predetermined times, offering one-person editorial staffs the ability to knock off early and let the computer produce the evening edition. The layout can mimic a newspaper, which is particularly useful for printouts, and there is a sensibly wide two-column format that works as well on screen as in print.

This could be the basic tool on which to launch a publishing business, making it much easier for a small enterprise to create newsletters, magazines, and newspapers catering for niche markets inadequately served by print. Motor industry executives and managers, for example, are always hungry for news about their industry. Every manufacturer operates a daily clippings service for internal distribution. Not only can that task now be carried out more efficiently in-house, it can also be extended in terms of coverage, assembled into a professional-looking publication, and delivered rapidly to staff in a company's offices and plants all over the world. Or an external publisher could compile an e-line newspaper from on-line sources that covers general industry topics, with separate editions of specific interest to individual corporate subscribers.

I have been conducting a feasibility study for just such a publishing venture in South Africa, Korea, and Australia, which have very active motor manufacturing industries where managers have a real need for a daily or weekly electronic publication to keep them informed of what is happening on the international scene. Of course, copyright and reproduction rights issues loom as soon as you consider doing something like this for profit, because you are reselling original material. Each on-line service states clearly what forms of reproduction are covered by the basic fees, and where further clearances and payments are necessary.

Figure 6-2

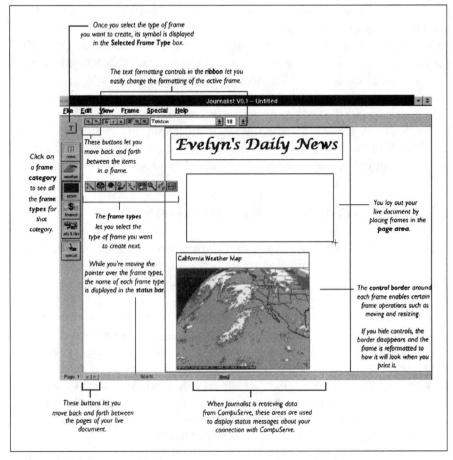

Once you select the type of frame you want to create, its symbol is displayed in the **Selected Frame Type** box.

The text formatting controls in the **ribbon** let you easily change the formatting of the active frame.

Click on a frame **category** to see all the **frame types** for that category.

These buttons let you move back and forth between the items in a frame.

The frame types let you select the type of frame you want to create next.

While you're moving the pointer over the frame types, the name of each frame type is displayed in the **status bar**.

You lay out your live document by placing frames in the **page area**.

The **control border** around each frame enables certain frame operations such as moving and resizing.

If you hide controls, the border disappears and the frame is reformatted to how it will look when you print it.

These buttons let you move back and forth between the pages of your live document.

When Journalist is retrieving data from CompuServe, these areas are used to display status messages about your connection with CompuServe.

This diagram illustrates how the Journalist *software builds a newspaper to meet individual needs by the use of frames within live documents.* Journalist *automatically finds the required information from CompuServe information resources, and downloads them directly into the layout.*
PED Software Corporation

⇒ **Serving the home office**

There is particular scope to develop customized on-line newsletters for the nearly eight million Americans doing a significant amount of work at home. As a high proportion of them are telecommuters, linked to their main offices by modem, they are fueling the need for paperless publishing within the business community.

E-newsletters are a great way for an organization to keep in touch with these distant employees, and help deal with the problem of isolation that is experienced by many of them. E-newsletters become far more powerful corporate communications tools because they can be distributed quickly and economically through existing e-mail facilities, increasing the likelihood that they will be read.

Lotus Notes is also an effective way of internally publishing to a workforce, including those who might not be permanently tied into a network but make only periodic contact via modem.

On-line in-flight magazines

The developments in electronic newsletters and magazines might soon greatly affect in-flight magazines, and even airport and rail station bookstores.

Large investments are being made to bring interactive multimedia, including electronic publications, to airline seats (coach as well as first class). Research indicates that, given the chance, passengers will spend a lot of money in-flight because they are receptive to all kinds of advertising messages when strapped into their seats. They won't just watch advertisements, however. The screens in front of them carrying electronic versions of in-flight magazines will need also to have quality editorial, yielding new opportunities for writers.

Travelers with portable computers are targets for e-books on floppies retailed through airport and rail station bookstores, or cheap enough to give away to business class passengers. It might become routine for in-flight magazines to have floppy editions that travelers are invited to take with them. The perceived value of such magazines is higher, but they actually cost less than the printed versions, with all their expensive color and paper stock.

Multimedia is spreading also into hotel rooms and onto cruise ships to compete with print for the business and vacationer traveler's time and money. The opportunities for such entrepreneurial publishing are much greater than with print, because the funding requirements are so much less.

⇨ Keep security in proportion

Llewellyn King emphasizes the concern among his fellow newsletter publishers about the ease with which electronic publications can be duplicated. Newsletter publishers have battled for years to try to control photocopying of their high-cost products, and met with little success. Their fears that publishing electronically just makes copying easier are well-founded. However, some publishing programs already incorporate a form of access or copy protection, such as password and encryption features, and these promise to become more sophisticated.

If it is important to you, make sure that these security and copy protection factors are included when selecting your electronic publishing software. Becoming too concerned with protecting your rights can be counterproductive, however. You don't want to be in the position of a store with such strong physical security that potential customers can't get through the door to inspect the goods! You might gain more readers and generate higher revenues if you accept that easy access will add more sales than are lost because of illicit copying. Factor in an acceptable loss level, just as supermarkets budget for shoplifting.

Many software publishers have found out that an illicit copy is not necessarily a lost sale. Distributing samples is a well-proven method to generate sales, and in electronic publishing your samples are manufactured and distributed at no cost to you. Piracy might actually create more legitimate sales for you in the long run than if your product had not been illegally tried by those who would otherwise not be exposed to it. This is the basic principle of shareware publishing, in which the most successful programs encourage, rather than try to inhibit, copying.

Experience in shareware has proved conclusively that allowing *crippled versions*—those inferior to the original—to circulate is nearly always counterproductive.

The impact of electronic publishing on your career

IN the beginning was the word, and the good news for wordsmiths is that words will continue to be culture's basic building blocks, whether they are there to see and touch on the printed page, or flying off in virtual forms into cyberspace.

"Words are the only things that last forever," said William Hazlitt, the 19th century English essayist. However, the fact that words now exist in such dramatically different digitized forms affects most professions, but particularly writers, academics, scientific researchers, managers, and librarians. All of these professionals are wordsmiths with varying levels of skills and degrees of involvement in authoring and publishing. For some, the advent of the e-book and e-journal offers great opportunities, for others very serious challenges to career prospects.

Information is power in almost every occupation. The changes in the on-line creation and dissemination of information pose major social and economic issues for the community at large, and lots of personal considerations at individual career levels. By looking at some of the occupations most directly affected, you can see how these changes might affect your own situation, and how best to accommodate them.

Footloose wordsmiths

Of particular interest are the new freelance opportunities being created, particularly with the growth of footloose information industries that do not need to be located in traditional business centers, nor be concerned about where their staff or the freelance specialists they use choose to live. For example, authors and publishers located in North Carolina have the potential to compete in e-books on a level playing field with those living and working in New York.

North Carolina's information highway is regarded by its governor as giving the state "a dramatic new chance to educate our children, provide medical services, create jobs, streamline our criminal justice system, and increase the efficiency of our government." This state highway for data is claimed to be the fastest wide-area multimedia communications network of its kind in the world. Building it enables

North Carolina to become a major international center for many activities that depend only on access to the information superhighway network, just as the smokestack industries of the past located close to strategically important waterways and rail systems.

Librarians: essential or redundant?

While many librarians see themselves as being attacked by the new media, others are embracing the technology that makes e-books possible. Some identify career opportunities where others see a bleak future. The pioneers of the Information Age and those being dragged into it are often working alongside each other.

A good librarian's mind is too precious an asset to waste on such mundane tasks as humping books around, stamping dates on little bits of cardboard, or any of the many other comparatively menial tasks that over 100,000 of these professionals in the U.S. alone perform every day. Fortunately, electronic paperless publishing offers librarians exciting opportunities to cut back on the physical drudgery and to increase the intellectual creativity of their jobs. It is sad that so many view the changes as threats rather than opportunities.

In paying tribute in this book to Lisa, Michael, and Virginia at the Copper Queen library in Bisbee, Arizona, as well as to the many other librarians around the world who have been of such help to me in a long writing career, I have been very conscious that theirs is the profession that potentially has both the most to lose and to gain from the new ways of disseminating reading materials.

Contrasts in libraryland

The way that different libraries are coping with the new technologies is rife with contrasts. The ultra-traditional British Library, with holdings going back over 500 years to before Shakespeare, has created an electronic bibliographic database of over four million

records. Charles Harmon, Headquarters Librarian at the American Library Association, draws attention to the thousands of instances of librarians offering their communities a wealth of electronic information, leading their patrons into the Information Age.

"We were using vast national networks when other professions in the education realm were mostly unaware of the role telecommunications could play in transferring information," he says.

We must blame politicians, not librarians, for the fact that hundreds of libraries in and near California's Silicon Valley, where the cutting edge of information-processing technology is slicing forward, are battling with inadequate technical facilities and budgets. It has reached the point where the services they provide to the law-abiding adults and children in their local communities are significantly inferior to those available to prisoners in nearby jails. Massive funds are being allocated to the most ambitious prison-building program the world has ever seen, but the nation that already finds it necessary to confine a higher proportion of its citizens in jail than any other is slashing the library services so essential to the functioning of successful societies— including the library schools and colleges that are necessary if this important profession is to survive.

The Clinton administration has made much of the key role that librarians will play in creating the new National Information Infrastructure in general, and the National Research and Education Network in particular. Yet bureaucrats and politicians at federal and local level hold back the funds essential for libraries to travel along the information highways. Consequently, while some libraries have superb facilities that place them in the forefront of new ways of information processing, others lack even the equipment that would enable them to offer such basic functions as access to a national set of telephone directories on CD-ROM.

University libraries seem to fare better than those serving impoverished inner-city and small rural communities in this respect. Consequently, there is the very real threat of exacerbating the gap between the information haves and have-nots, and causing a "brain

drain" of librarians who seek better opportunities in the new directions that their profession is going by moving to where the facilities are best.

 # Even the Library of Congress cannot cope

An estimated 20,000 librarians are going on-line regularly through Internet to help identify worthwhile acquisitions and engage in research projects. At least an equal number, however, seems locked into the mindset that their prime role is as the custodians of books, rather than as the disseminators of information. There is remarkable lack of awareness among many librarians about such crucial issues as the changing role of the Library of Congress and whether it needs to be augmented by a virtual "People's Library" on the Internet as a national archive and depository for the tidal wave of electronic publications being created.

Already the Library of Congress typically has, at any one time, a backlog of over 20 million items waiting to be cataloged, a task that could be handled largely by machine if they were in electronic formats. However, most of the e-books, journals, and other documents that are author-published are not going through conventional publishing channels, so they are not archived in the public interest by the Library of Congress. The Library is the extreme example of an organization that desperately needs society to make a major shift away from paper. It also illustrates that libraries that might be good at storing knowledge are often lamentably bad at making it accessible, a task that the new machines perform admirably.

There are probably more answers to more questions available in the Library of Congress than anywhere else in the world, but finding those answers can be very difficult and demands a sophisticated electronic indexing system. Many of the networks and individual databases on the Internet already have those indexing systems, which is why millions increasingly go to these on-line resources rather than to their librarians for answers.

 # Bleak forecasts for librarians who cannot adapt

"If we don't enter the realm of data, we are going to be relegated to low-paying custodial jobs in giant buildings full of unused paper—and we will richly deserve our fates," warns Professor Charles A. Seavey of the University of Arizona Graduate Library School in an article in American Libraries headed "Although we saw it coming, librarians have failed to meet the challenge of the electronic age." Professor Seavey emphasizes that librarians' impressive skills in achieving bibliographic control of textual material risk becoming irrelevant in the new information environment of raw data accessible to anyone with a computer and a modem.

Duke University library's Johannah Shirer challenged delegates to the American Library Association's convention to ponder why so many people are now turning away from libraries to alternative sources of information. Other speakers urged the librarians to prepare to reinvent themselves, to enhance their consultancy skills, to help bring information, not just reading, literacy to their societies, and thereby make their profession more interesting and rewarding.

Librarians' organizations that seem to be slow in adopting the new technologies, and consequently not clearly leading their members forward into this new era, are being hampered by academic traditions. The Association of Research Libraries holds symposia on scholarly publishing on electronic networks—then publishes the papers after a long delay in paperback books costing $20 for a mere 175 pages. These hardcopies cost another $4 to ship in the U.S., or $12 to many of the overseas readers who really need this information to plan for the futures of their libraries and their own careers. Such proceedings could have been published faster, at far less cost, and disseminated internationally much more cost-efficiently in the very electronic formats being discussed.

"I believe such practices are a symptom more of the slow evolution of academe and the need for academics to publish in paper for tenure, rather than our profession being slow to reform," points out the American Library Association's Charles Harmon. Nevertheless, the

American Council of Learned Societies and The Getty Art History Information Program have published on Internet the proceedings at their conference "Technology, Scholarship, and the Humanities: The Implications of Electronic Information." (Internet access is available through Ftp to ftp.cni.org, or by gopher through gopher.cni.org 70.)

A former librarian, Brown University President Vartan Gregorian, drew particular attention in his keynote address to the challenges the profession faces. He emphasized the fact that there is not just an explosion of information, but a fragmentation of it also, with so much specialization that it can be difficult to see the larger picture.

Informing librarians effectively

The American Library Association (ALA) got one false start with the opening and then closing of its electronic publishing and mail service. Now, thanks to some far-seeing staff in several divisions, it produces a number of electronic publications and is active on the Internet. However, only a minute proportion of its 56,000 members asked, in the six months after it was published, for a free copy of the essential librarians' guide to the Internet produced by the ALA's Library and Information Technology Association.

Of course, using the Internet is only a small part of the information that librarians need, because so many of them do not have the modems or the funds to go on-line. Organizations serving librarians have been slow to exploit the cost-efficiency of publishing on floppy disks to the majority of librarians who have access to computers capable of reading floppies. Even the important information coming out of the ALA's Project Century 21 program to help librarians meet future information needs has not been available on floppies, where it could circulate most economically.

This illustrates that librarians get little help from anywhere in being told how to put to really good use the older computing systems that they are saddled with, or which could be theirs for the asking from local companies upgrading their hardware. Such companies can exploit the tax breaks for donations of systems that might be obsolete for many business applications, but have years of useful library life left in them.

 # Librarians become publishers and distributors

The new technology makes librarians not just book custodians and information retrievers, but electronic publishers and e-book distributors. Not having the funding to buy the latest hardware is no excuse for shunning these roles. There is ample evidence just from the examples in this book that publishing and distributing library materials can be done to great effect on even "primitive" computers that librarians can obtain for themselves and their patrons at remarkably low cost. A CD-ROM drive at under $200 added to an old desktop computer can pay for itself in months as an alternative to buying a new set of encyclopedia or allocating shelf space to telephone books.

These same concepts are even more relevant internationally than they are to the libraries of North America. Book publishing and distribution in the former Soviet territories is in chaos, and the libraries are in crisis, unable to cope with the essential role they must play in nurturing democracy and providing the data necessary to feed economical and social development. The shortage of books is so acute that groups gather in Russian libraries to take turns reading aloud from the only single copies available of important works.

Many developing countries in Africa, Asia, and Central and South America are similarly unable to fulfill their social missions simply because of a lack of books and magazines. The demand for publications from the U.S. and Europe is enormous, but our ability to communicate to and influence these developing societies through their libraries is being seriously inhibited by excessive prices and the ineffective distribution of so much printed material. Electronic publishing on floppies and even by radio (examined in a previous chapter) open up exciting opportunities for librarians around the world—once they learn that expensive hardware or significant computing know-how are not required.

Increase efficiency without increasing stress

Librarians who read this book will, I hope, feel stimulated rather than threatened by the personal opportunities that electronic publishing offers them to enhance the quality of their work as well as to increase their efficiency. In a previous book about computing-related health problems, I encountered considerable concern among library personnel that they would become victims of repetitive stress injury, carpal tunnel syndrome, and other physical health hazards arising from interfacing with a computer. These health concerns often reflect a deeper apprehension about computing technology generally.

In fact, there is increasing evidence that repetitive stress is just as likely to result from the physical handling of books and paper records as it is from the typical library keyboarding tasks. Nor do floppy disks appear to cause the breathing problems, skin disorders, or eye irritation associated with mold and fungal spores found on books! Librarians are far more at risk of becoming victims of their too-often self-imposed isolation from the important cultural developments associated with electronic publishing.

The career risks are particularly acute for those librarians preoccupied with their roles as the physical custodians of printed books. Information and communication, not books or periodicals, are the true raw materials of librarianship. Printed books are not sacrosanct icons of culture, but just one of the media players in our cultural development. We have aural and visual traditions for communicating and learning that are just as significant, and now they can blend more readily with the written word into a variety of rich multimedia formats.

Libraries are no longer physical structures

"It is in the library, and in the library alone, that one can learn to the limits of his abilities and to the limits of what is known," proclaimed

the Office for Intellectual Freedom of the American Library Association back in the 1970s. That remains true only in the sense that libraries can no longer be defined in physical terms as buildings housing books and other reference materials. The virtual libraries that exist on-line and on floppies and CDs are now just as much a reality, offering far easier access for millions who are learning to use them without assistance from library professionals.

Electronic publishing empowers writers and independent publishers in ways never possible before. Just as important, these new media also empower librarians to realize their full potential, to spend less of their time stacking books, and more of their minds to ensure that libraries will continue to change lives.

Writers and editors

Content is all-important in electronic publishing, just as it is with the printed word. Consequently, writers, the prime originators of published words, can flourish in this new environment if they seize the creative initiative. Particularly in demand are writers able to conceive and develop products with multimedia potential.

It is now almost a prerequisite when pitching a book proposal to dangle spin-off opportunities in other media before an agent or prospective publisher. It might not even be necessary to make your book the core product. You might have a great concept that should go first as a game, educational program, or in some other electronic format, with print following later if your concept proves viable.

You might need to demonstrate that, if your work doesn't fly in one medium, the development and other costs can be amortized over alternative formats with specific marketing opportunities that help to spread the publisher's risk. I have been helping a colleague recently with a great idea that was originally developed in a totally inappropriate medium—a tape-slide presentation—but which now has potential in its entirety on video, and then can be split up to sell off its photographic elements for multimedia collections.

New skills needed

"Many writers can use word processing software, but will find that they need more types of computing skills once they begin electronic authoring," says author and shareware publisher Jim Hood. "Writers need to know about such things as screen designs and DOS commands before they make the jump to electronic publishing."

There are many ways of acquiring these computer skills, including books, video programs, interactive multimedia tutorials, and Jim's own excellent PC-Learn software, which is widely available on bulletin boards and through shareware libraries. Software is becoming so much easier to use in the new graphical interfaces that only a basic technical knowledge of the processes involved is required. However, in their own interests, writers should try to learn as much as they can about how texts are turned into electronic publications— and then how they are used by readers.

As with writing in any other media, the best learning is by reading and viewing other electronically published materials in your field. Sit down and interact with some of the electronic publications mentioned in this book, and your understanding of what is required of writers, and what you will be able to contribute, should increase immensely.

Research is transformed

It is vital for writers to know how to exploit the new research sources available to them. The major benefit of electronic publishing to writers and other researchers is that so much material is becoming so much more readily available in ways that can benefit our careers. The new media, particularly CD-ROM, are bringing precious archives out of the vaults and literally onto our desks. Fortunately, desks are moving into cyberspace also and becoming virtual environments for work in progress, providing the space that physical desks cannot.

For example, I now have on my already cluttered desk ready access to 60 million feet of archived newsreel footage for a future book

project. That's over three million filmed news segments, from the silent movies of 1919 to recent television newsreel segments. These are all physically contained on a single CD-ROM disc waiting to be released as needed. Much of this material has never been widely seen before, and it will immeasurably enhance a long-term project about the World War II on which I have been working.

One electronic publishing development in particular is helping with this project. Horizons Technology, Inc. (HTI) has been working with another Hollywood company, Fox Movietone News, Inc., to put the unique Movietone News library footage onto CD-ROM as a digitized library of important events, personalities, and social trends. This database can be searched using HTI's fuzzy logic technology, which does not require exact parameters to zero in on what you may be seeking. This is ideal for projects where you can not always define exactly what it is you need. Fuzzy logic searching also helps identify material that is relevant, but which the human researcher, especially in the early days of a project, might not even consider.

These extensions of the creative dimensions of researching, writing, and editing come as valuable bonuses from electronic publishing. As such databases are established, the range of information resources available to us must steadily increase. More specialized databases will be published when opportunities are seen to select and group material in compilations that make sense and are commercially viable. This ability to unlock knowledge and make it usable enables electronic publishing to enhance the writer's power and earning capacity.

⇨ Writers share their resources

One concern by academics about electronic publishing is that future generations might find it difficult to analyze the development of writers. The argument is that it will be impossible to study early drafts of published manuscripts or view research material because this will have been zapped into oblivion by the author pressing the Delete key when his or her electronic notes are no longer needed.

In fact, most authors I know seem, if anything, to be more inclined to hang onto early drafts and research material when stored on disk than when this potentially interesting material is cluttering up their workspace. Many authors don't want their early efforts to be seen by others, or to reveal their sources, but if you do, you might be able to arrange with your publisher to pack much of this material onto a floppy and make it available to anyone who asks.

➡ Editors need new skills, also

Editors, just as librarians and writers, are particularly challenged by the new technology. Although self-publishing electronically seems to limit career opportunities for editors in some respects, new doors open as others close. A significant amount of electronic author-publishing will be by those who realize that they lack writing skills and have the motivation and funds to employ freelance editors. Informed authors and publishers alike appreciate the benefits derived from competent editing, and there always remains in this litigious society the need to check for accuracy and defamation.

Editors, like writers, will need to be informed better about marketing, distribution, and multimedia issues. There are very attractive careers opening for editors with the expertise necessary to handle multimedia projects. For example, a new category of publishing staff is emerging already: acquisitions editors specializing in multimedia. They might not be called editors, and they might work for software houses instead of publishers, but their function is to identify and purchase or retain creative talent. When you identify someone performing this role, nurture your relationship with him or her; it could be crucial to your future.

The evolving role of the editor is illustrated by the way that "Letters to the Editor" newspaper and magazine pages are taking on a whole new meaning. Readers by the thousand leap at the chance to communicate directly with the editors of their favorite publications. Almost all of the computer magazines, and an increasing number of computing-aware publications in other fields, now blur the lines between their established print products and their new on-line reader services.

Omni is typical of the trend for magazine editors to host on-line debates with readers about their plans for future issues. As a result, an article might begin as an on-line debate, appear in printed form in a magazine, and then continue as a dynamic document with a life of its own on-line. An interesting example is *Omni's* "Bordercrossings" article by Janet Stiles, which began when Janet initiated an e-mail discussion on relationships between the sciences and the humanities. After the article appeared in print, a special Bordercrossings folder was opened on the Omni Magazine Online bulletin board, giving readers the opportunity to extend the debate on this important topic.

As such activities expand, all journalists—reporters as well as editors—need to become far more interactive with their readers and to take paperless publishing into account when working on assignments, even if their main medium remains print. This adds a new dynamism to journalism never possible before.

Hypertext challenges editors

It might fall heavily on editors to be the architects of hypertext, with the monitoring and creation of dynamic links between items of information becoming an important editorial skill. Electronic publishing has ethical implications, also, that only impartial editors might be able satisfactorily to resolve. For example, in an e-magazine, editorial and advertising content can no longer be readily distinguished by the page formatting conventions established in print.

As hypertext offers attractive opportunities to generate advertising revenue, the degree to which editorial becomes blended with sponsorship, advertising, or other interests demands strict policing by editors. The editorial function might include ensuring that there are clear indications, perhaps by color coding, where a hypertext link from editorial leads to paid advertising material. We can expect to see this happening in such areas as movie reviews on-line, with a click of the mouse linking you by hypertext to downloading the movie to your home, booking seats at the local theater, or reserving a video from the nearest video store.

Similarly, restaurant reviews and recipes could lead directly into on-line table bookings, while product reviews could generate, by hypertext, either more detailed information from the manufacturer, or the placing of a direct order to be delivered overnight. Knight-Ridder is but one of the newspaper groups that has been actively developing such concepts into practical realities to be available as services to both readers and advertisers in the mid-1990s.

 Editors as quality controllers

The editorial quality-control role is emphasized by John Dawes, chairman and founder of the Author-Publisher Enterprise in Britain, which in 1994 launched road shows to inform writers of the many benefits they can enjoy from publishing their works themselves. A very experienced professional writer in the print medium, John is enthusiastic about electronic publishing, but warns, "Don't think that by publishing on disk instead of on paper you can avoid the publishing disciplines of selecting, editing, rewriting, illustrating, producing, reviewing, promoting, and distributing. If these traditional disciplines from print are not maintained in the new electronic media, we and our readers risk being buried under a pile of rubbish.

"There continues to be a prime need for the selecting and editing phases of the publishing process," he emphasizes. "For any publication to be successful, these must add value to the words, and to the information that the words convey. The editor remains the gatekeeper, only allowing through from the author what will entertain, inform, or otherwise benefit the reader."

Scientists & academics

Electronic publishing is becoming essential for the dissemination of scientific information. Some university and research libraries now spend more of their budgets on electronic publications than they do on conventional print. The only way they can keep up with the flood of information is to go on-line and use the fastest, most efficient, and

most economical way in which researchers around the world disseminate information and document their activities.

Dependent on digitized data

Some researchers already rely almost totally on scientific information in digital format, and only refer to hardcopy to locate papers that predate electronic publishing. For many, not to have daily access to their favorite bulletin boards has become unthinkable, as was shown by the flood of protests in October 1993 from among the 8,000 physicists who use the bulletin board at Los Alamos National Laboratory. The board was only temporarily down as the result of a funding rather than a technical problem, but the reaction from around the world was a clear sign of the importance of electronic publishing among researchers.

"The episode not only demonstrates how much political clout can be generated through e-mail, it also shows just how much physicists have come to rely on the bulletin boards, and the extent to which they have changed the culture of physics," writes a contributor to *Science* magazine.

A further benefit is that scientists can now reach out as never before to communicate to special-interest groups and to the public at large. As more and more research findings become available as electronic files, so our ability to access that information increases.

International problems establishing standards

But there are snags. Scientific publishing is now generating so much material that even electronic formats cannot cope with it. The problem is aggravated by international and interdisciplinary disputes over standards for electronic publishing.

The amount of information being generated internationally by the Human Genome Project is an example of this problem. Researchers in Europe, North America, and other regions might have to create an

international federation of databases just to bring some cohesion out of the cacophony of digital publishing resulting from this project. Much of the material is being published to bulletin boards in different computer languages as well as a variety of human languages.

Some of this information later gets on to CD-ROM, while other material is published to myriad environments on floppies, by direct file transfers, or to special-interest groups in Internet. The National Center for Biotechnology Information (NCBI) in the U.S. and the European Bioinformatics Institute have been trying to get the material indexed and practical links forged between the different sources and databases, so that researchers can find what they need in research fields where speedy access is synonymous with success.

The international scientific community must come to terms with the need to agree on a standard format, a *lingua franca* for databases. The NCBI has made a lot of progress with its ASN.1 format, but so has a European consortium centered on Germany in the development of its Integrated Genome Database with a different format. The opening in 1995 of the EMBL centralized data library in England might help point the way to a common standard, but there are programs scheduled through much of the 1990s in both the U.S. and Europe to spend millions of dollars just on research database technology to find a way out of the enormously complex electronic publishing maze created by the Human Genome Project.

This project has even spawned a new branch of science and a new word for our dictionaries: *bioinformatics*. The probable conclusion will be the emergence of at least two, and perhaps three or four leading database formats favored by molecular biologists in which to publish their work. This will require the formation of a kind of virtual international federation of scientific databases so that they have a means of talking to each other.

The Internet is probably the only way that scientific authors and publishers will be able to keep up with developments in this ongoing battle to establish publishing standards. The lesson from all this is not to paint yourself into a corner with a format that is not sufficiently flexible to enable data to be converted with reasonable ease.

 # Academic and professional pressures to publish

Unless you are close to the academic and scientific communities, it is difficult to appreciate how great can be the pressures to get published, or the rivalries and anger that result from the competitive spirit this engenders. The stress and friction that can be created was dramatically illustrated in the case of an associate professor at Montreal's Concordia College, who posted messages on the Internet claiming that university officials were insisting on being listed as coauthors on papers to which they had not contributed.

The college sued him for libel, the professor's persecution complex escalated, his tenure application was rejected, and in August 1992 he shot and killed four fellow faculty members. Now he is serving a life sentence for first-degree murder. Paperless academic publishing might not solve such problems, but it certainly offers the hope of easing a lot of frustration!

"It seems only reasonable to grant electronic publishing the prestige currently afforded print publishing," says William Y. Arms, president for computing services at Carnegie Mellon University. Unfortunately, this is proving a slow process, being fought tooth-and-nail by some commercial interests vested in print.

If the need to publish in print becomes less important in advancing an academic career or obtaining funding, there will be fundamental changes in how academics view their intellectual products. There could be a distinctive move towards academic publishing for profit rather than prestige. As David Bearman, editor of Archives and Museum Informatics, told a recent electronic conference on this subject, academics in the humanities might need to adjust to "leasing" rather than giving away their intellectual property, in an era when public funding is being withdrawn.

"We will either become part of the economic system that is driving development, or be taken advantage of by it," he says.

⇨ Education

Education really is being transformed by electronic publishing, particularly multimedia. It is changing not just the teaching methods, but the actual classroom environment (Fig. 7-1).

Figure 7-1

Electronic publishing coupled with new portable computing technology are transforming how and where people work. The changes particularly benefit students, giving them easier and cheaper access to text books and reference materials. A rich library can be accessed on- or off-campus, extracts taken, and the books annotated very easily. Sharp Electronics Corporation

Houston Community College, the largest in Texas, has created what it calls "mini-teaching bunkers" in classrooms. When a teacher arrives, perhaps from another of HCC's 46 different locations, he or she docks into the bunker the portable computer carrying all the computerized material needed for the course. The portable hooks up to CD-ROM and laser disk players, network connections, projectors, room lights, and anything else needed to make a complete multimedia presentation, or to access electronic publications virtually anywhere.

Naturally, there are concerns that the trend towards electronic publications, and particularly the graphics-intensive multimedia starting to replace plain text in the classroom, will exacerbate the problems of illiteracy among the young. Much of the best evidence appears to indicate otherwise, however: exposure to multimedia seems to help stimulate interest in the written word.

Certainly having access to a computer is helping to close the learning gaps generally between children from poor and more affluent homes. In a 1993 report, the International Association for Evaluation of Education Achievement found that schools with high proportions of students from low-income and minority groups now have one computer for every 10 to 15 students. This improved ratio enables poor students to come much closer in their performance to classmates from more affluent backgrounds who have greater access to computers at home. This survey of over 11,000 students in 573 schools also found little difference between girls and boys over the degree of use and the proficiency with computers.

 # Teachers and students become publishers

Both students and faculty members at schools all over the world now publish electronically for serious motives—and for the fun of it. You can create a journal and generate an information flow in both directions to help gain a degree or enhance your professional credibility.

Most of these publications are free and cannot carry advertising or be overtly sponsored by commercial interests because this would make them unacceptable to many of the bulletin boards and networks over which they are distributed. However, if your information is not available elsewhere and of sufficient quality, you might well attract revenue for it. *InterText*, a fiction e-magazine published by Jason Snell, a student at the University of California at Berkeley, quickly garnered over 1,000 registered subscribers out of an estimated readership of between 5,000 and 20,000.

Multimedia electronic publishing is enabling schools and colleges to have dynamic syllabuses for many courses, with the students

themselves creating much of the course material as they construct databases rather than just study prepared material that hardly changes from year to year. "They gain insights and understanding in a way that would not be possible with passive viewing," says Barbara Maliska, the first director of Stanford University's Academic Software Development group.

Interactive media as a catalyst for learning

Stanford University is the pilot for the New Media Centers Program, a collaboration of leading software, hardware, and publishing companies founded in 1993 to help campuses use interactive media as a catalyst for innovation. Stanford's SMILE (the Stanford Media Integration Lab for Education) is the first of what could develop into a truly international network of centers that will do much to promote various forms of electronic publishing. The aim is to have 100 such centers operating by 1996, each equipped with the latest hardware, software, and peripherals for multimedia production.

These could be important resources for local publishers or authors to use to create electronic editions of their works, as community access is an important element of the concept. The centers are expected to do a lot of electronic publishing themselves as they develop curriculum materials that they can distribute on a royalty basis to other campuses, or release commercially. Indeed, it is hoped that many of the New Media Centers will become self-funding as they develop viable titles, tap corporate and alumni sources for funding, and act as testing and product development facilities for commercial manufacturers and publishers.

These centers can obtain their hardware and software facilities at very attractive prices, which helps the budgets allocated by participating universities to go a lot further than by trying to establish multimedia labs independently. As an indication of what is involved, the Stanford center has a computer classroom, with individual student stations and a large projection screen for the instruction; a curriculum development laboratory, where instructional programs or publications are created by faculty and students; and what is called a "public

computer cluster" of 50 networked Macintosh Centris 650 systems with CD-ROM drives that the students can use.

The first two courses taught at the center illustrate the range of topics suitable for such multimedia applications: the History of Silicon Valley and Elizabethan Theater. There is an annual selection process for campuses interested in joining the New Media Centers program. You can get details from the organizers at 415-558-8866, AppleLink NMC; Internet NMC @ netcom.com.

Although these centers are geared towards higher education, multimedia publishing projects can be applied at virtually any level of the educational system. Third- and fourth-graders at Argonaut School in Saratoga, California showed the way when they used the America Alive Navigator program to complete the state report projects required of all California students.

Each child chose a state and wrote about its history, industry, environment, and other features. They drew maps and other illustrations, sang state songs, and added audio commentaries. The final publication was copied onto a Kodak PhotoCD in a unique group class project, but with each student's contribution retaining its individuality.

On this CD it is easy to find individual references or student projects, and the disk can be duplicated so that every student has a permanent record of this phase of his or her school career. Such electronic publishing opens up fascinating opportunities to record our lives in a permanent form that can be viewed later and passed on to succeeding generations. This new technology offers many alternatives to the traditional school yearbook and family snapshot album.

Helping teachers meet increasing social obligations

As teachers are forced to play much wider roles affecting the social welfare of their children, they find multimedia a useful tool in these tasks also. An important application of electronic publishing to social problems is helping children to learn how to function in our

increasingly complex and often hostile society. John Walsh, host of Fox TV's "America's Most Wanted" series, featured in a CD-ROM presentation to raise funds for the National Center for Missing & Exploited Children, as well as to teach children how to minimize their risks of being abducted.

Such safety lessons and resource guides communicating to children with animation, video, and other multimedia features will become increasingly important. Teachers can create new career opportunities by participating in the production of these materials, rather than just being involved in their distribution to the children.

Educators create customized materials

Already educators at more than 800 colleges and universities are custom-designing the reading materials for their courses through Primis, the McGraw-Hill electronic database publishing unit. Instructors create their own textbooks by selecting material from the database and adding their own notes. Primis software then automatically creates a unique new book with its own ISBN, title, table of contents, and index. Even in hard copy form, the instructor receives his or her customized text back in 72 hours, and there are significant savings for students.

In 1994, World Library Inc.'s Library of the Future, Second Edition, containing 2,000 literary works, was added to the Primis database of 12,000 textbooks, journals, lab manuals, case studies, and articles.

Produce an e-book to help your business

A book is a powerful tool for sales, public relations, training, employee motivation, and other business needs. Create a book or a series of books, and let the words in its most valued and tangible form effectively replace much of the need to travel to communicate with diverse audiences.

With the personal computer now the universal business tool, *e-books* become the natural medium for many types of communication. Business users are often up-to-date with the latest business technology, so increasingly it is appropriate to create more sophisticated information targeted at this readership. Sound, graphics, and animation are being taken for granted by many business computer users (Fig. 7-2).

Figure 7-2

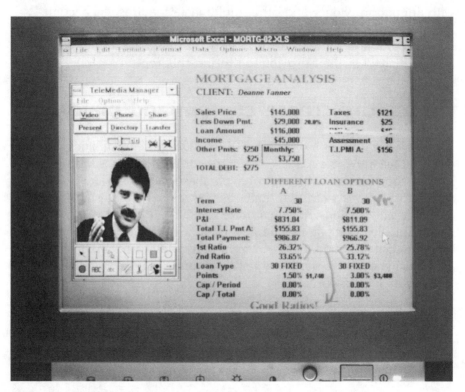

When published material is available in digital forms, it becomes far more flexible and dynamic. Here, a number of people in widely scattered locations are able to work with the same documents using AT&T's TeleMedia personal video system. AT&T

⇨ Market your business information

Database directories are among the most successful electronic business publications. You might already have lists of people, companies, addresses, and resources that are of particular interest to

the business market and could be published as e-books to generate more prestige and revenue than renting them out as mailing lists.

Or you might have particular expertise or case-history details from a project that yield information of value to a business sector. You might be sitting on important technical or marketing information that can be distributed quickly and cost-efficiently on disk to an audience with a defined need to know that information.

When aiming at the business market, remember that new information is worth far more to some people than that same information when it is a week, a month, or a year old. The price that information can realize when it is fresh can be many times what it is worth as it ages. The speed of electronic publishing can enable you to maximize that potential.

Publish to motivate and inform employees

An e-book might do more for less cost than an expensive consultant or other expert brought in to train or brief staff on important topics. You might not even need to create such a book; there might be one out already, bearing the name of an author and a prestigious imprint that you can adopt or customize to enhance your communications efforts.

For example, my book for the American Management Association on computing-related health problems provides a low cost and easy tool for a company to meet new statutory requirements to inform and instruct staff in healthy ways to work. At the same time, giving this printed book or a version of it on disk or over the network to each computer operator would be a tangible expression of corporate concern for employees. It might even reduce potential corporate liability for industrial injury claims, since this book disseminates information that enables the employees to assume much of the responsibility for their own welfare.

If you are publishing an e-book to enhance your professional reputation or for publicity purposes, the results will probably be better if the book has a physical substance. The section in chapter 9 on packaging has many suggestions.

 # Publishing a book is an event

You can exploit the fact that the publication of a book is an event, almost like a birth, steeped in mysticism and wonder, especially for those who regard putting tens of thousands of words together in a logical sequence as a remarkable achievement. Books can achieve an impact just by being, so for particular business or professional purposes, it is essential to bring your virtual book out of cyberspace and give it physical substance.

"'Tis pleasant, sure, to see one's name in print," wrote Byron with typical cynicism. "A book's a book, although there's nothing in't." Mark Twain shared that viewpoint, describing the classic book as one "which people praise and don't read," an illustration of the way that books communicate even to those who do not read them.

Most of our contemporary business gurus are known by their books, which are bought more than read, but still communicate even when unopened as if by some kind of osmosis from all that is written and said about them. A thought can spring from a book and become alive and change the history of humanity—or the course of a company. "How many a man has dated a new era in his life from the reading of a book," said Thoreau.

That's Henry David Thoreau, of course, who died in 1862, never traveled much, yet is still communicating furiously because his books, although little read these days, were rich in pithy quotes. These have fluttered forth with a life of their own and flourished because they were born in books. Books have a permanence and status that other media lack, enhancing the communication prospects of both the thoughts they contain and the authors who wrote them.

 # E-books as agents for change

Just by being a book, rather than a brochure, newsletter, or magazine, a publication can be a powerful force in the business environment. It does not have to be a big book, something quite modest in length can still have a great deal of impact.

A book, either as a physical entity or as a virtual book on disk or over a network, can be a powerful agent to facilitate change in a corporate environment. Consider the example of a modest book created as part of a strategy to foster change in a company needing urgently to adapt to a new market situation, adopt new technology, and get rid of its outdated hierarchical management style. Just such a case is discussed in the following sections. Freelance writers and consultants might be able to abstract from it the basis for pitching a book proposal to a corporate client.

 # The Corporate Book of Change scenario

A new CEO has come on board and is battling both to get her management team to realize that change is essential, and to communicate to the disillusioned workforce, dealers, and suppliers that change is actually happening; that the old, demotivating situation is being replaced by something exciting and new.

When multinational corporations embark on such exercises, the travel involved is usually enormously expensive and time-consuming. It is a particular problem in sectors such as the motor industry, where success might hinge on communicating with and motivating dealerships scattered around the country or the world.

But our smart executive saves most of those air fares, hotel bills, and management time. She decides to create and distribute a book on change as a tangible expression of the new corporate culture. Such a book can be created using almost any of the authoring software described in earlier chapters, and probably needs to be printed as well as distributed electronically to have the desired impact and reach all members of the target audience.

Budget and structure

This book is so important for the company that a realistic budget has been approved, but the unit price for the printed version is not to exceed $5 because this must not be seen as an extravagant,

ego-boosting exercise. The CEO also wants a flexible format so that other volumes can follow on such topics as ethics, conflict, and quality. To meet these requirements, she instructs that the book must meet the following objectives:

➤ Offer clear benefits to the target audiences.

➤ Be motivating and easily accessible.

➤ Have a concise, punchy style and entertaining visuals.

➤ Appear substantial and prestigious despite the budget restraints.

A small management steering committee meets and draws up the following specification as a guide to everybody involved in this project.

The Acme Book of Change: The Challenges & Trauma of Transition at Acme Manufacturing

Formats

A conventional printed book is required so that the key elements of the message can be compiled in a permanent, easily used form accessible to all of the target audience. The page size of approximately 5.5-x-8.5 is sufficiently large to have impact and clarity, but attractively compact and portable. It can be printed in-house from standard letter-size paper, and an envelope for the electronic publications and presentations on disks can be bound in. Between 64 and 100 pages on a cream or light-gray paper stock, perhaps featuring the corporate color and of a type to bulk up impressively to give higher perceived value.

There are alternative versions of the first two pages, so that the book can be customized easily for different audiences: dealers, workers, suppliers, and potential recruits. Special hand-bound presentation copies can be produced for major investors, directors, and other targets for premium copies. These could be calligraphed by computer on the first facing page with the name of each recipient, and there is space for the CEO personally to address and autograph presentation copies.

Content

An introduction from the CEO explains why change is necessary in the organization. The book is a tangible expression of management's determination to initiate those changes to benefit everyone in the enterprise. Then follows a brief history of the organization and an upbeat forecast of a bright future if we adapt to the changing business environment.

Production requirements

To ease production, there is a standardized run-of-book layout which is elegantly simple, and works as well on screens as on paper. One or two quotations on various aspects of change are the dominant upper element on each page. They may be set in a conventional typeface (such as Times Roman or Bookman) about 14 or 16pt, with a 24 to 48pt calligraphic-style initial drop letter to distinguish the quotes from the rest of the text.

Below each quote is a commentary on the quote, relating it directly to a particular situation within the corporation. The commentaries come from management, union representatives, and a cross-section of employees. They form a tangible expression of all personnel internalizing the new corporate culture.

Visuals will help the impact of the book and need not add seriously to the cost. Each quote and commentary will be illustrated by a visual typifying the area of the corporation to which it is linked, or by a portrait of the member of the corporate team making the commentary, or by both. Photographs of the people featured can be turned into easily reproducible line art after scanning them into an image-manipulating program. Suitable visuals can be screened and printed very lightly underneath the text as a background.

The 60 pages in the book will be printed in two lots of 30, folded, saddle-stitched, and trimmed at the same time to achieve some of the economies available for print runs of 1,000 copies or more. Then, drawing from this stock, smaller quantities will be bound as needed to meet demand, using one of the many desktop binding systems available.

 # Customize your books to your readers

It is useful to be able to take preprinted standard copies of a corporate book and customize the binding to use the book for specific purposes or target audiences. In the case of a book on disk, you can customize the opening title screen, the slip cover, and the label for the disk very economically.

Your book might, for example, be adapted to stockholders by a management team seeking support against a hostile takeover bid. Then, with a different presentation and introduction, the same book can be circulated internally to inform employees about the takeover and maintain morale during a critical period.

This approach is a much more efficient way to reach a widely scattered workforce than having managers traipsing from one location to another giving live presentations. However, remember that a book is not in itself interactive. There are many circumstances in which the publishing of a book should be supported by other activities using appropriate media for the responses that might be generated—a telephone hot line or written questionnaire, for example. Publishing through interactive employee kiosks can also be very effective.

Either a printed or electronic book can easily be made interactive by adding some kind of questionnaire requiring a response. In the case of an electronic book, there are several programs that can prompt reaction by question-and-answer screens or by using tutorial structures.

 # Reaching external audiences

If a book created for internal uses really comes together well, consider extending its application to various external audiences who need to be informed about a new policy or other significant corporate event. Review copies can be sent to media contacts as part of the external PR effort. A book can stimulate more editorial coverage than a straight media release would achieve.

The same text could be produced and distributed very economically as an audiotape. A professional actor with a strong, mature voice could read the quotes, and the featured members of the organization would each record their own commentaries. You could amplify their views and make a tape that compliments the book by interviewing each contributor in turn and producing a documentary on the topic of change in the corporation.

 Getting the most for your money

The cost to produce either a printed or e-book like this can be very attractive. You can get the best of paper and paperless publishing with a hybrid production, in which the book also provides the packaging for more extensive documentation on disk. If you construct your printed material so that it applies to your entire target readership, you can then easily and economically customize the disk contents for particular groups.

For easy and economical sources of content, turn to dictionaries of quotations in print or on disk. For example, a classic shareware program called Wisdom of the Ages can do a simple search from the keyboard to find great quotes appropriate to almost any communications task. Keith D. Mohler (800-800-1997) has also put together a great selection of 12,000 quotes called Quotes on Line, published on disk using the powerful askSam search text engine.

We live in times of great change, and are often fearful of departures from our established routines. Any kind of change can usually be turned from a problem into a potential opportunity, and most changes, whether positive or negative, provide opportunities to produce a book.

Packaging and duplicating

I T has never been possible to tell a good book by its cover with any degree of certainty. E-books, which do not have covers at all, present a particularly intriguing challenge when they must be moved out of cyberspace and into the real world, where physical appearances are very important.

Once you have freed a publication from the bulk and other physical restraints imposed by paper, you gain many new opportunities for creatively packaging and presenting it. Effective packaging is vital for many types of electronic publications, particularly those that will rely on point-of-purchase sales, or when they land on the desks of prime prospects needing to be wooed by impressions of substance and professionalism.

Packaging is required for practical purposes as well as to enhance images. Your floppies or CDs must be packaged to withstand the rigors of mailing and shipping services, so that they arrive in pristine condition. Almost invariably, you will need to include some hardcopy documentation in your package. Such documentation typically contains basic details of the systems on which your publication will run and instructions for bringing it up on screen.

⇨ Play with the packaging

You might want to go with very impressive packaging if you have an appropriate market, or an exceptional title such as an expensive reference or coffee-table book/disk combination. A superb example of this is *From Alice to Ocean*, the story of Robyn Davidson's 1,700-mile trek by camel across the Australian outback. It combines a large-format photo book published by Addison-Wesley with an interactive CD for Windows and Macintosh systems from Claris Corporation, both in a shrink-wrapped cardboard tray showing off the beautiful artwork from every angle.

Nestling securely behind the book in the base of the tray is a CD-ROM, also attractively printed on its top surface. The book and disc work excellently together to entertain and provide information about the culture of the Aboriginal people and the geography of the Australian desert. The same CD features audio tracks in which Robyn describes her journey, which can be played on a standard audio CD player. There are even tips about photography on the CD-ROM from Rick Smolan, who took the pictures and is well-known for his *Day in the Life* series of photographic books. Look for this remarkable example of how e-books can be packaged for maximum shelf appeal, giving them the kind of physical substance that people like to have in gift books. No wonder *Publishers Weekly* said that this was a foretaste of book publishing of the future.

Also worth seeking out in stores is an interactive CD-ROM video game in which the packaging is a game as well. Aris Multimedia Entertainment of California packaged its Video Cube: Space title with a complementary game, rather like Rubik's cube, made of cardboard to complement the virtual game played on screen (Fig. 8-1).

Figure 8-1

This imaginative packaging for the Video Cube: Space *multimedia title carries the same theme from the outer box to the inner disk and its container. The box forms a physical Rubik's-cube-type of game that mirrors the one on the CD.*
Aris Multimedia Entertainment

This is a particularly imaginative use of the multimedia publishing format as well as the packaging. The program begins with an animated cube comprising many animated video fragments hurling themselves through space. The reader must unscramble the pictures on each side of the cube to run a series of NASA video sequences accompanied by high-quality music.

⇨ Software in a tin

Excellent packaging might exist already that is appropriate to the topic of your e-book and will attract attention and enhance its

perceived value. A brilliantly simple example of this is The Fractal Design Painter program. It carries a nearly $300 retail pricetag, but is delivered with disks and manuals packed inside a standard one-gallon paint tin. (Your local hardware store sells such tins for about $1.25 each.)

An attractive label turns that mundane tin into strong and attractive packaging for this commercial paint program—packaging so good that it often becomes a display piece for an office or studio.

Seek out or create unusual and economical packaging appropriate to the contents of your title. Without incurring great expense or making your title unduly bulky, there are hardly any limits to the packaging of e-books that will help them to be commercially successful. Authors also get the tactile pleasure that a printed book provides, by something tangible to have and hold.

 # Point-of-sale display

Creative packaging can be a big help when trying to sell through computer stores, bookstores, and nontraditional outlets for publications (Fig. 8-2). Just as printed books have broken into many nontraditional book-retailing categories, so can publications on disk go into specialty stores, hardware and home supply centers, drug stores, souvenir shops, and many other sales outlets that cater for the same consumer categories as your subject matter. The acceptability of your electronic publication by retailers for whom the concept of selling software is novel could be influenced very much by its packaging.

Distinctive packaging that gets exposure in reviews or television appearances will help with any retail, direct mail, or other selling activities in which you are engaged. If you are doing any space advertising in print media, showing packaging that will be remembered helps to convert prospects to sales.

Even for limited, noncommercial distribution, you might want to package your disks in a fun or unusual way that is appropriate to their content, author, and target readers. A floppy-based family chronicle for distribution to relatives and friends at Christmas could be

Figure 8-2

Even very large publications can be packaged and distributed on floppy disks, with a wide selection of containers available that can be readily customized. This Expressions StepCase is an effective way of containing and displaying ten diskettes. MicroComputer Accessories, Inc.

packaged attractively, for example. A completely different approach to the same idea would be taken for an e-brochure and agenda promoting professional consultancy services in conjunction with an up-market seminar.

Virtual packaging for electronic distribution

In some situations, you might not need to create any physical or visual impact until your reader sees your title screen on the monitor. If you rely on distribution by modem, physical packaging might not be an issue at all for you. However, there are equally important

virtual packaging considerations. You must compress your files and present them in formats acceptable to the *sysops* (system operators) controlling the bulletin boards to which you wish to upload.

Practical ease of use and aesthetic appeal are important when your files are eventually opened by your readers, so it is important to make the screens of the title and contents particularly attractive, with the text display easy to read on a wide variety of monitors—including the liquid-crystal displays of portables. The better authoring programs provide various ways of achieving these virtual packaging objectives.

When sending e-books on floppies to shareware distributors or reviewers, the physical packaging should be impressive as well as protective. By adding visual appeal, you can help your work stand out from hundreds of other submissions received every week.

Packaging possibilities for small runs and big images

To get a good sampling of the packaging options open to you, I sought input from three very different enterprises, each illustrating how a small author-publisher with limited resources can cost-efficiently package floppies in image-enhancing ways.

One example comes from Mexico, with a format that enables a business periodical on floppy disks to compete, in a conservative market, with conventional print magazines in retail outlets. The two other sources of packaging expertise have nothing in common except their capacity for great creative designs. Pat Baldwin is a successful self-publisher of the home-based small business genre, while Creative Disk is a leader in printing and packing floppies for big corporations as well as for small independent enterprises.

Miniature marvels

Pat Baldwin's enterprise is small, in more ways than one. Tiny, in fact—a one-woman business in the little Arizona mining town of

Bisbee where she produces miniature books. Pat's books are three-dimensional works of art in limited editions that sell almost exclusively to the 450 members of the Miniature Book Society. To meet the standards for this category of book, each volume must measure no more than three inches high or wide. That is smaller than a 720K disk, but these miniature books could accommodate flash cards (discussed in chapter 5).

These cards could become an important e-book medium, and are being used already for titles ranging from the Bible to phrase books for foreign travelers. Even the texts of large encyclopedia can be compressed to fit onto one of these tiny data storage devices. The fact that there is already an established standard for miniature books makes their format attractive for hybrid, limited-edition, print and e-books on cards.

Even if you do not plan to distribute on electronic media that can be accommodated within the strict limitations of collectible miniature books, the principles for packaging flash cards can be extended to accommodate the slightly larger 3.5-inch disks that are now the most popular floppy and CD formats, and even the larger 5.25-inch floppies.

It would be good for electronic publishing generally if authors and publishers could stimulate a demand for collectible limited editions of outstanding merit and intrinsic physical value. The miniature formats of this media makes blending them with print in tiny works of art an attractive proposition, and Pat Baldwin and I have been working to do this with a commemorative edition for the tenth anniversary of the Shakespeare Authorship Roundtable.

Pat's miniature books sell strongly at upwards of $60 each. Most are more expensive than this, but still her editions sell out quickly because collectors and dealers are not price-sensitive for a quality miniature book, and might well not be either for one incorporating an electronic medium. They can expect their miniatures to appreciate in value more certainly than stamps, coins, gold bars, or real estate. One of Pat's titles that cost $60 three years ago is now trading at over $1,000.

Pat does all the layout, typesetting, illustrations, printing, and binding herself, making very effective use of a PC and color inkjet printer.

She has also written some of the 22 titles that her Pequeño Press has produced.

 # New perceptions on book packaging

The main lesson that Pat's success teaches electronic self-publishers is to throw away all preconceptions of how books and computer software should be physically packaged. (Book packagers, as the industry now uses the term, are specialists who bring together various elements, e.g., writers and artists, for the creation of books that they sell across a number of media platforms. They, too, should flourish in the new electronic publishing environment.)

Pat's miniature volumes go beyond conventional covers, printed pages, and boxes or sleeves. She designs her books so that the content and the packaging physically and visually reflect a common theme. Many open with concertina folds or cut-outs. One has hundreds of minute cut-out butterfly wings that add a whole new visual dimension to the text about butterflies—the kind of approach you might want to consider for poetry e-books. Another deals with collectible minerals, and has a circle cut in the center of all the pages right through the book to display an azurite specimen mounted on the inside back cover. You admire the mineral as you read the text, and the two make a unified visual display.

Origami folds form a gaily colored envelope for a collection of poems, each on tiny cards contained inside. Pat showed me how this concept could be adapted to make unusual packaging for floppy disks. Paper-folding by authors is not a new idea; it is quite common in Asia, where paper was invented and revered for itself, irrespective of whether ink has been smeared across it. Japanese e-book publishers might consider building on their culture's tradition of using folded paper for the ceremonial wrapping of gifts.

In the West, the poet Shelley and author Lewis Carroll were fascinated by origami. *Alice in Wonderland* was one of the first children's classics to appear in several e-book editions, and I am sure that Carroll, wherever he is, would be delighted to hear of plans for one on a floppy, incorporating the original illustrations and packaged

in an example of the origami fishing boats that he folded to entertain the children of the Duchess of Albany.

 # Packaging materials need not be paper-based

Another of Pat's books has the hardest of hard covers that I have ever seen: a ceramic sculpted front cover that she made from one of the new generation of polymer modeling materials. You might be able to create such rigid packaging from a variety of craft materials that would both enhance and protect a floppy disk.

Still another of Pat's titles, about the universe, opens out so that a concertina fold linking the pages forms a canopy depicting the night sky. A bed-time story has a padded fabric cover depicting pillows and quilts, and it nestles in a book stand in the shape of a miniature brass bed frame. Both point the way to new and imaginative treatments for disk containers that appeal to both adults and children. You might well be able to package disks of data, poetry, or fiction in ways that make them far more marketable as gifts, souvenirs, or commemoratives. For business occasions, they offer new alternatives to the jaded selections of corporate gifts.

 # Small markets can yield big results

Visiting Pat's design studio and print shop emphasizes the principle that you can be very successful when self-publishing to very small markets, if you meet the essential needs of those strongly motivated to want your type of publication. Pat needs to tell only 450 people in her database that she has a new book, and the immediate response is usually enough to sell out an entire edition at a satisfactory profit.

Pat also demonstrates vividly that there is no limit to the formats in which a printed book can be packaged. The same goes for disks and any accompanying software manuals, providing that you are not restricted by the dictates of retail display conventions. Printed books have been greatly inhibited by bookstore requirements for titling on the spines for shelf display. This has drastically limited the production

of spiral-bound books, which are so practical for the reader and offer the author an economical binding alternative for short self-published print runs.

Professional packagers can help you

The creative people at Fractal Design Painter went to Creative Disc, Inc. in Campbell, California when they wanted equally powerful packaging for their demonstration disks. The people at Creative Disc are experts in customizing demo disks, a form of electronic publications on floppies that must be produced economically in large quantities, with packaging that protects the disks during mailing or rough handling at trade shows and other venues. The company caters also to smaller enterprises with short runs who can benefit from the expertise and experience gained on the big commercial jobs.

The extensive research undertaken by firms distributing demo disks emphasizes the importance of enhancing the appearance of both the disks themselves and their packaging. An attractively customized disk will rarely be thrown away or even reformatted for re-use. It has a tangible value and should get a message across far more efficiently than, for example, a brochure that has to compete with other printed materials in a day's typical junk mail.

One test-marketing exercise in the Netherlands revealed that 85% of the 5,000 prospects sent a disk promotion about investments took time to examine it, and most of them went on to spend several minutes studying the contents of the disk. That kind of response exceeds the wildest dreams of direct mail marketers. Treat your disk as a valuable medium, and as part of your marketing strategy give very serious consideration to enhancing its appearance and consequent impact on your readers.

"This need not be expensive," disk packaging expert Jim Moreton maintains. "It is economical to customize disks even in small

quantities. For example, high-density 5.25-inch colored disks can have printing on them and be duplicated from about $1.10 each for 500, 90 cents in quantities of 5,000. The 3.5-inch diskettes would be $1.50 each for 500, and $1.25 for 5,000. Customized packaging costs are all over the price map because there are so many possibilities, but the price can still be reasonable."

⇨ Cheap but effective disk cases and mailers

Jim showed me some examples of custom jobs that his company has undertaken. One electronic publisher had a sturdy, high-quality cardboard mailer for floppy disks produced in one color for 75 cents each—less than the retail cost of buying an inferior mailer from a stationery store. For the 3.25-inch disks, a plastic "jewel case" costing only 60 cents each protects the disks and makes an effective container for a printed insert, similar to the way that audio CDs are packaged for retail display.

You can even put your disks into a sealed plastic bag for about 25 cents a piece, and have that form a complete package if you include a printed card insert as a front "cover," and a card stiffener at the back. Author-publishers can do this kind of packaging themselves as a kitchen-table operation, using self-sealing bags or the heat sealers sold for packaging food for the freezer.

You can enclose the finished package in an envelope, printed in one color, for delivery. Most desktop printers and copiers can generate envelopes if they are not too thick. I tackled this task by printing a master off my laser, then duplicating it on envelopes fed through the by-pass sheet input of my copier. In this way, the envelope follows a straight path through the copier and is less likely to jam or get crinkled.

Before buying a large quantity of envelopes, check their suitability for this type of printing. Some have adhesive on the flap that cannot cope with the heat required to fix the image in a laser printer or a copier. Of course, don't use envelopes that have metal fasteners!

253

 # Use color economically

Jim Moreton emphasizes how a customized full-color diskette can enhance your image and credibility, making it stand out from all the other electronic and print materials competing for attention. Research indicates that a typical recipient of a promotion on a customized disk will spend between 26 and 30 minutes interacting with it. The response should be even more impressive if the disk contains an electronic publication that the end-user has actually requested and probably paid for.

Customized disks are available in all formats and a wide range of colors, with surfaces that will take almost any design printed in one or several contrasting colors. You get very impressive results using just a single color, as demonstrated by OmniPATH in Fig. 8-3, with its striking design of black print directly on a white disk cover.

Figure 8-3

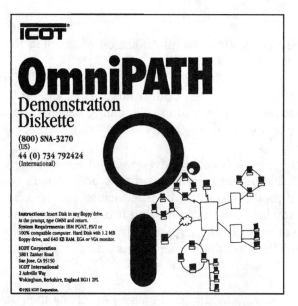

Just plain black printing on a white diskette cover can be very striking, as demonstrated with this OmniPATH *demo diskette produced by Creative Disk.*

If you want a full-color graphic, the economics of volume suggest printing one label that can be stuck onto all the disk formats you are likely to require. Packaging different disk sizes is a real challenge. Creative Disc rose imaginatively to that challenge for Lotus's Ami Pro demonstration disks in both 5.25-inch and 3.5-inch formats. A sepia-colored teaser photograph is featured on the cardboard packaging, and repeated on both sizes of the disk contained inside. The smaller 3.5-inch disk nestles in a slot in front of the larger disk.

Expect to spend a total of about $5 a unit for such packaging and the accompanying disk duplication in runs of about 1,000, dropping to perhaps $3 for big runs of around 5,000. The results for an appropriate electronic publishing venture could make that very cost-effective, and highly competitive with print.

If budgets are tight, however, consider just having your disks generically customized with a distinctive color, title, and your publishing imprint. Then, for small runs of a particular title, add a stick-on label with details specific to that disk. Anything is possible, as Pat Baldwin and Creative Disc both demonstrate, at opposite ends of the publishing scale.

You can contact Jim Moreton at 408-988-8533.

Do-it-yourself packaging ideas

Impressive results can be achieved for short runs by embossing in metallic foil on just a small area of your packaging materials. Your local office supplies store probably stocks kits for this that work with your laser printer or copier. They might also have preprinted color paper, with borders or other artwork, onto which you can print or copy your black text. You can also get foil printing on the disk itself, which can greatly enhance its perceived value.

Many newer personal copiers have the ability to take toner cartridges in different colors, enabling simple multicolor printing to be done on the desktop. Create your packaging design with paint or drawing software that will generate color separations, one master for each color. Alternatively, create the masters by deleting the other colors

and printing one with the red content, one for the blue, and so on. Use good-quality paper that will take the repeated handling and heating through the copier.

Color photographs offer a cheap solution

For small runs, consider also the low cost of repeat prints of a single photographic negative obtained through the special offers regularly made by consumer photographic processing facilities. Your best deal might be using coupons from your neighborhood grocery store. A color print can be stuck onto your box, folder, or whatever other packaging you are using to give it a lift, or added to the insert that you slip into a transparent plastic case or envelope.

Going a little further, you can create your titling and other information to make up the complete cover or outer packaging artwork, then shoot a negative of this and have it duplicated as an appropriately sized print. You might be going down two or more generations, so keep the layout simple, with the different color areas clearly defined and the whole shot crisp with plenty of contrast. This approach can work well for fictional as well as nonfiction works, allowing lots of scope for moody and creative photography.

Color copiers offer fast, economical solutions

Color copiers continue to get better and cheaper, and can be the means to very cost-effective packaging, particularly when you need to get orders out quickly. Most copiers produce standard letter-size sheets, and you might be able to fit several covers or packaging inserts onto one sheet, greatly reducing the cost.

One low-cost way of achieving this is to generate your final color master through the expensive and very sophisticated copiers operated by services catering to advertising agencies, architects, and other professional design services. Most cities have at least one such

facility. Use this high-quality color copy as the master for same-size reproduction runs on a lower-grade color copier at a local store, where the price might be under 40 cents for a sheet containing four, six, or eight package covers.

Disk labeling

Disks look a lot better if labeled attractively. Each disk in a multi-disk package should be numbered clearly, and bear the title, copyright notice, and other basic publishing details. On the first or only disk, give a clear installation instruction, usually the one required to start the batch file that launches your e-book on screen. These days, it is hardly necessary to give all the details about putting the disk in the drive and getting to the DOS prompt, or using Windows' Program or File Manager Run commands. Simply put on the label something like "Type GO to start" (assuming GO is the name of your batch file).

Many shareware programs generate reasonably attractive disk labels, or you might prefer to design one with your graphic, word processing, or desktop publishing software. Duplicate it by printing or copying it onto adhesive labels to attach to the disks—labels that will not degenerate when copying, nor are likely to come off and jam your readers' drives.

Disk duplication services usually offer label-printing facilities, and for do-it-yourselfers there are lots of programs available that enable you to create labels from your own printer.

Packaging for business and professional markets

By defining your markets and your readership at the beginning of your electronic publishing project, you should have clear ideas of what kind of packaging is most appropriate for a particular work. An academic or scientific audience will accept clean and simple packaging more readily than the market for an e-book on the movies or repairing bicycles.

All that might be necessary is to use your word processor to create a single-sheet design that gives the title, author, concise summary of reader benefits and contents, and the name and address of the publisher. This one-page layout can then be copied or printed in a single color onto an envelope, box, file folder, or other packaging used to protect and distribute your disks.

An author-publisher who is well-known in his or her field might get maximum impact for back-of-the-room sales at seminars with a simple but elegant package just bearing the name of the e-book or other publication, and the name of the author. That can be more powerful than a thousand words or great graphic images on an expensively printed box.

If you are a researcher or professional regularly distributing material on floppies, consider investing up-front in a stock of high-quality disk mailing envelopes preprinted with your name and other basic details. Then, prepare a simple insert to describe the particular disk you are distributing at any given time.

E-magazine hybrid provides effective packaging and protection

A good example of an electronic business publication with the visual appeal and physical substance to compete with print on magazine racks is the Mexican e-magazine *Indize*, a pioneer in the field that grabbed the attention of its target readership wherever it was displayed. Its deceptively simple layout makes extensive use of clip art graphics, spot colors, and charts and graphs that can be created in spreadsheet and desktop publishing programs.

Printed on high-quality coated card, the cover shown in Fig. 8-4 provides professional and practical packaging for the disk inside, plus many tidbits of information that encourage newsstand browsers to buy. Every month, it provides important new economic data that can

Figure 8-4

The front cover of the Mexican electronic business journal Indize *is an attention-grabber on the newsstands. Printed on stiff card, it provides practical packaging for the floppy disk inside containing the latest economic data. Extensive use is made of clip art, charts, and spot color. The envelope containing the floppy is held in place inside by the two staples used in the simple saddle-stitching.* Exagono Sistemas SA de CV

be processed and published onto disk far faster and more efficiently than into a hardcopy magazine. Director general Lorenzo Mariscal and his team supply a small magazine around the floppy using quality heavy paper and light card stock. This package both protects the disk and provides powerful point-of-sale appeal.

The accompanying illustration of a typical *Indize* edition show how this is done. Note, on the cover, the text and visual flags that announce this is more than just another print publication, but contains a computer disk that is rich in topical economic data. The message comes across clearly, even if you do not read Spanish.

The back cover of *Indize* is a model of clear text and visual information that sells both the electronic journal inside and the additional services offered by the publishers. The back cover is a potentially powerful medium for communication in any publication. Use it well, whether you are publishing your electronic book or journal, or in a box or envelope.

When you open *Indize*, you are presented immediately with its most valuable element: the computer disk containing all the latest economic data. The first facing page has the bound-in sealed disk envelope over it, but not completely concealing it. Always package your disk in a sealed container to protect it from dust, potentially damaging handling, and theft. The envelope flap should issue an invitation to open it.

When the envelope is opened, the *Indize* disk and a printed insert containing detailed instructions for operating the software are revealed. Flip the disk envelope back without opening, as you would the opening title page when browsing a book or magazine, and the contents and essential details about the publisher are revealed on the first facing page of text. Small graphic symbols identify the contents of both the disk and the printed pages that follow.

There are 12 printed pages in the issue shown here, with a trim size approximately 25cm tall by 19.5cm wide. This is slightly smaller than *Newsweek* or *Time*, with which it often shares shelf space, and enables *Indize* to slip easily into mailing envelopes for distribution to subscribers. The hardcopy magazine-style packaging provides

sufficient protection for the *Indize* data disk to withstand the rigors of Mexican mail or messenger delivery.

If you are packaging your publication in the U.S. with a similar format, you might save considerably by using standard (8¹/₂×14 inches) card stock. When folded once, this comes down to 8¹/₂×7 inches, a practical size for display, mailing, and to protect the disk inside, even if it is a 5.25 floppy.

Indize makes good use of clear, simple, computer-generated graphics, including maps, charts, and logos. It is worth spending plenty of time creating a good logo for your individual publication, or for your publisher's imprint if you intend to produce a number of electronic books or wish to draw attention to your business name. The *Indize* logo is used as part of the address on the subscription card.

This Mexican publication was well ahead of anything similar in the U.S. when it was launched in 1992, and is an excellent example of simple, effective packaging to emulate.

Duplicating disks quickly and economically

The worst way to duplicate disks for distribution is to have a master in one drive and do a disk copy to another. At the very least, put your disk contents onto the hard drive so that the copying goes faster.

If you have lots of disks to duplicate, duplicating services that advertise in the back of computer magazines such as *Byte* might do the job almost as cheaply as you can, and save a lot of time and hassle. There are, however, various ways of duplicating disks yourself rather than having this done for you, with the main advantage being that you can gear production to demand without having to commit to a particular volume that you might not sell or need to revise.

Only if you have long runs will you want to lay out a considerable sum on dedicated automatic disk duplicating hardware, but any PC

with appropriately sized floppy drives will do the job if you don't mind having to keep on feeding the disks in. I know of shareware authors and distributors who set up a spare computer within sight of the television and get the kids to do it.

A computer with a fast hard drive and plentiful RAM makes the job go faster, as will using double-speed drives. If you are only making a few copies, you can simply load the publication onto your hard disk, or onto a virtual disk in RAM if you have sufficient memory, and copy it to formatted floppies using standard copy commands. However, it is usually faster, more reliable, and more convenient to use one of the special copying programs available as commercial titles or shareware. One of the most versatile is DiskDupe from Micro System Designs (408-446-2066) with a number of features particularly helpful for electronic publishers. It runs well on older hardware that you might want to use for copying. In fact, it might be better than a dedicated duplicator in many publishing situations because all your master files can be stored on the hard disk for fast and easy access to produce copies on demand.

DiskDupe's creators, Max Dunn and Paul Perry, have packaged a lot of user copying experience into the latest version, including invaluable automatic and sensing features that minimize the risk of bad copies and consequent fulfillment and after-sales support problems. If you have disks already formatted, you can get up to 200 copies an hour with DiskDupe's automatic sensing feature, which ensures that, despite frantic disk swapping, you do not inadvertently remove one that was not copied. There is even the facility through DiskDupe's pull-down menus to do the drive cleaning necessary every 500 disks.

Instruction manuals and other booklets

You will almost certainly include some documentation with your disk. This poses the challenging task of trying to get a description, together with instructions and other information, into a small printed format that can be packaged easily with the disk. You might also be

generating orders by initially stimulating inquiries through editorial, space advertising, direct mail, or other promotional activities and want a similar printed document to mail economically to prospects. Sometimes the same printed material will cover both needs.

If you have a desktop publishing program or a recent version of one of the powerful word processors, you might already have templates that make formatting and printing small booklets far easier than traditional methods. The fastest, easiest, most economical way that I know of to create small booklets is a program called ClickBook (from BookMaker Corporation at 800-766-8531). It costs under $70, works with any Windows application, including the word processors, and virtually any printer. Compile your booklet text in your word processor or text editor, choose one of 18 booklet formats (such as the one shown in Fig. 8-5), and ClickBook does the rest.

Figure 8-5

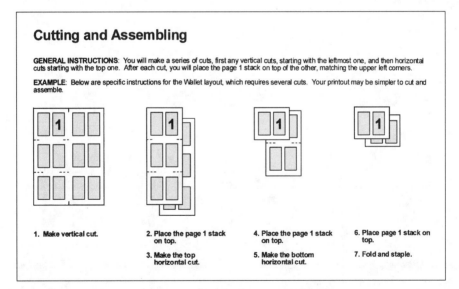

Cutting and Assembling

GENERAL INSTRUCTIONS: You will make a series of cuts, first any vertical cuts, starting with the leftmost one, and then horizontal cuts starting with the top one. After each cut, you will place the page 1 stack on top of the other, matching the upper left corners.

EXAMPLE: Below are specific instructions for the Wallet layout, which requires several cuts. Your printout may be simpler to cut and assemble.

1. Make vertical cut.

2. Place the page 1 stack on top.

3. Make the top horizontal cut.

4. Place the page 1 stack on top.

5. Make the bottom horizontal cut.

6. Place page 1 stack on top.

7. Fold and staple.

ClickBook makes it so easy to create booklets and small manuals to accompany electronic publications on disk. The program automatically takes a word processed document and formats it into the different pages, working out the pagination for you. These simple cutting and assembling instructions show the Wallet *layout from a standard letter-size page, which is a useful format to travel along with floppies.* BookMaker Corporation

It sorts out the pagination, determining which page should be on the reverse of another when the standard sheets come off the printer and need to be folded, cut, and stapled. It is not appropriate for long documents, but for the typical paperwork that accompanies an electronic publication on any form of disk, or for audio and video tapes as well, ClickBook does a great job.

Use it to generate as many copies as you want, when you want them, straight from your printer, if your initial requirements are low volume. If you are going into a fairly long print run, the same program can create masters which you can then print cheaply at an offset print shop, or with a copier. There are also booklet compiling programs available as shareware which, if your requirements are modest, might do a perfectly acceptable job for you at even less cost.

Guard and nurture your intellectual property rights

THE legal wrangles over intellectual property rights in the new media have already begun. The National Writers Union in New York has gone on record as believing that the rights of hundreds, if not thousands, of writers are being violated by publication on CDs and in electronic databases, without either their permissions being obtained or appropriate royalties being paid.

Ten members of the union filed a federal lawsuit in late 1993 against some of the biggest names in publishing, claiming that their copyrights were being violated. Many writers, artists, and photographers who have not already specifically signed away electronic rights will find that they have little recourse because their print contracts, going back many years, have clauses permitting publishers to use works in new editions, or in compilations, without print or electronic media being specified. Most book contracts have, for a long time, embraced electronic rights without additional royalty advances to authors.

Until recently, most authors never even considered that nonbook rights to their works might have any value, apart from the remote possibility of an audio book edition, or a movie or broadcasting option.

⇨ Test cases

A number of test cases over the next few years will eventually help to clarify some of the gray areas of the copyright law in these respects, but expect confusion to reign for a considerable period. Already, author contracts are being drawn up to embrace potentially lucrative electronic rights, without it being clear how these will be implemented in an increasingly uncertain publishing environment. Even the definition of publishing itself is changing.

In the case of new works for which the creator has not specifically signed away rights, or which did not result from assignments on a work-for-hire basis, the author's situation is legally clear. You own the rights to your creative works immediately when you create them, whether you have registered the copyright or not. Under the international conventions, you don't even need to affix a copyright

notice, although doing so and going through a registration procedure can greatly strengthen any claim that you might have to make. Of course, enforcing your rights, particularly against a fly-by-night or deep-pocket publisher, can be an expensive exercise in futility.

⇨ Windfalls and pitfalls

While some aspects of electronic publishing represent a threat to the owners of intellectual property rights, it can also be a blessing. Responsible publishers are generating additional incomes for writers, artists, and photographers, while some compilations are actually making it easier to identify the owners of copyright material and ensure that permissions are obtained and appropriate fees paid. When MPI Multimedia in Illinois compiled their CD-ROM Kids in History and three other titles, for example, they tracked down and obtained permission where necessary to use over 1,000 individual film and video programs, and over 12,000 hours of stock and archival footage.

Artists have had windfalls from the new media when reputable publishers have included them in electronic compilations. For example, Andean Pan flutists and other Bolivian artists have been receiving royalties from Aris Entertainment's multimedia CD title Tropical Rainforest—income and exposure that would probably not have come their way otherwise. Some of the more responsible publishers of multimedia clip art, texts, and video collections have gone to enormous lengths to establish rights and obtain appropriate clearances. Inevitably, others have not bothered, so there is a great deal of material being circulated that could cause potential problems for end-users.

The specialists in publishing who deal with intellectual property rights frequently get together to learn—as is their legitimate intent—how to maximize the profit potential of those rights for the publishers who are their employers and clients. One of the most important of these gatherings is the annual rights directors meeting at the Frankfurt Book Fair, which, like similar events, is becoming dominated by electronic rights issues.

The typical author, writer, artist, and photographer has little knowledge of the issues and trends being discussed, but guidelines are being set which could have a major impact on your profession and income. Already, you can see the results in author contracts being drafted to protect commercial publishers' interests in electronic media by broadening the range of rights which the publisher, rather than the author, controls.

At the same time, many publishers are seeking to extend contract periods and not relinquish control of rights back to an author as quickly or readily as before when a book goes out of print. It used to be fairly easy to decide that a particular title had reached the end of its commercial print life, and it made better business sense to remainder (sell off at a knock down price) any copies left in inventory.

Some contracts and publishers' practices go further and permit the author to have the litho film from which the book was printed—if the printer can actually find the film, which is often not the case in practice. In the past, with scarcely a second thought, helpful publishers' staff members have given their confirmation that, under the terms of the original publishing contract, all the rights have reverted to the author. The assumption when only print revenues were at stake has been, "if *we* can't make any more money out of this title, the author is even less likely to make a success of it." In fairness, the attitude among some publishers has also been, "although it's costing us money to keep this title in print, it is a creative work in which the author has a substantial personal stake which may well not have been paid off by our efforts, so we should give him or her *every* opportunity to try to make more of it than we have been able to do."

Now, everything is changing—particularly the concept of a book going out of print. If it exists as a title in an electronic format, it need never go out of print, nor impose significant costs on the publisher to keep it available for the occasional sale. The whole marketing and distribution functions for a backlist are very different in the new media than they are in print.

For valid business reasons, many publishers now want to control all rights, particularly electronic rights, for as long as they can. In this fast-changing technology and with the fickle consumer trends it

generates, it is very difficult to decide when a title has reached the end of its commercial life. Nor, with the billions being wagered on the information superhighways, do publishers want to risk losing control of material that, in some form or other, might become profitable in the future because of the unpredictable demand for product to flow along those highways.

Only a small fraction of the hundreds of services or channels that will be piped into homes will be able to afford expensive productions featuring live actors. There could be a strong demand for a new kind of piped television, essentially computerized multimedia projects authored by individuals or small independent companies catering for niche markets. An author with specialized knowledge of a particular subject and a PC might spend a year turning one of his or her books into such a production and generate substantial revenue from it. The original book might then gain a new lease on life in print.

It will be a brave soul in a publishing house, therefore, who returns rights to authors as readily as in the past. Such an individual risks being criticized for letting go a work that had unsuspected earning potential in another medium.

⇨ It's not a perfect world

In a perfect world, many authors would be quite content to have a powerful and well-informed publisher shepherding his or her title through the rights minefields of multimedia. But this is not a perfect world, and publishing staff are only human, preoccupied with putting their best efforts into the bestselling, newest titles, and leaving the backlist largely to fend for itself.

So, as an author, you might find yourself locked into a situation where your manuscript has reached the end of its print cycle—which is all that you have been paid for—and you can do nothing to get it moving in another media direction. The publisher is unable or unwilling to explore the earning potential that you feel, rightly or wrongly, your work still has in other media. You might feel that, in its present form, or with the updates that you are able to give it, your work could really fly in the new media, but you are unable to do

anything because you have a contract that effectively imprisons your work, and any derivatives of it, in your publisher's dead files.

 # Rights signed away by time rather than results

There have already been movements in the publishing industry to establish ten years as a minimum period for which a publisher should secure rights. There are very good arguments for this coming from publishers on both sides of the Atlantic, who point out that it always used to be common for authors to sign away their rights for the same lengthy periods that the copyright in a work could be protected. Only in comparatively recent times has it become the norm for authors to do deals for fixed terms of five or ten years, with contracts that gave both publishers and authors ways out of the relationship if the work did not prove profitable in print.

Consequently, authors need to be very aware of what is going on in the new media. Remember that your works might have publishing opportunities in places and in media that you just cannot anticipate. A title might well stand to make more in other media than it does in the print editions that are covered specifically in the author contract.

 # Agents are not necessarily a protection

Unfortunately, many agents are not as knowledgeable about the new media as they should be, and because of the lack of regulation in this profession, it is easy for almost anyone to set up a literary agency to try to get into the action. Consequently, as an author or other creative artist who feels fortunate to be handled by an agent at all, you might be saddled with one who does not fully comprehend the potential importance of the clauses in a contract that relate to electronic media rights.

After considerable experience with agents, and speaking to other authors who have had unfortunate experiences, it is often difficult to assess where many agents put their long-term interests: their author clients, or their publisher clients. Regulated real-estate agents have

much better defined responsibilities to sellers or buyers than publishing agents. The situation is made worse by the pressures put on agents by publishers not to rock the boat with nit-picking contract amendments in the current very tight and competitive market.

It behooves you, then, to be particularly careful when signing contracts, even when your agent has approved them, and not to hesitate to seek a second legal opinion.

Danger signs

Watch out for unacceptable restrictions on your work, not just the particular work specified in your contract, but on any restrictions put on your ability to use the expertise reflected in your book to create other intellectual properties for other media. You might find your professional ability to communicate severely compromised by the wording of some boilerplate contracts.

Bear in mind also that the rights staffs at publishing houses are themselves coming under increasing pressure to cope with a flood of complex requests to use intellectual properties in a variety of media and applications, particularly collections on CD-ROMs. Not only do they have problems coping with these requests, in some houses there is the tendency not to even process the more obscure and less lucrative requests that come in, nor to effectively police unauthorized publications and infringements of their own and the author's rights. This situation can cost you lost revenue, and might also deny opportunities for your work to be published in places where, even if the revenue is minute, the exposure can be beneficial.

Many print publishers have not even coped effectively with the rights issues created by the advent of photocopying, so they are even less equipped to deal with the far more complex issues raised by electronic publishing media, in which the intellectual property is used in a virtual reality form.

Literary agents spelled out some of these dangers in their 1993 position paper, but the Authors Guild and the American Society of Journalists subsequently took a much stronger stand on behalf of

writers in their joint position paper. Get a copy of this, and any later such documents, if you are a member of either of these organizations. The paper includes suggested clauses to add to contracts that protect your electronic rights if the publisher's contract fails to do so.

Members of the Society of Authors in Britain, and other organizations for writers in other countries, offer contract-review services that members can consult on such issues. In general, experts advising writers rather than publishers recommend that, if you contract to assign your electronic rights, you should be compensated appropriately by advances and royalties, just as you are for printed works. You should also try to retain some control of the media, the form, and the content in which your work may be used if your publisher wants to grant licenses to third parties. Plus, of course, when your rights are sold to third parties, you should get a proper share of the spoils.

There are, among the new entrepreneurial entrants into electronic publishing, those with few scruples and no long-term sense of commitment who will see writers and other creative artists as "marks" ripe for the picking. There obviously will be large numbers of both winners and losers as a result of this new electronic publishing wave. You need even more savvy awareness of what is going to reduce the risk of being among the losers. Be careful, therefore, about any actual or implied contractual relationship that you enter into regarding your intellectual property rights. The warnings about publishers apply at least as much to agreements with electronic bookstores and similar on-line services.

 # Plagiarism in science and academia

Fears of plagiarism are a particular problem for scientists and academics. It is obviously much easier for intellectual thieves to clip other people's ideas and results from electronic documents and patch them directly into grant applications, papers, and project reports than it is to abstract them from printed journals. As paperless publishing enables so many longer papers to become available, on subjects that

would not normally get into hardcopy, so the vein of intellectual effort to be mined by plagiarists gets richer, and offenses harder to detect.

You can add various types of identification coding to an electronic text that can help identify if it has been copied—the digital equivalents of watermarks on paper. There are no fully effective technological solutions to this plagiarism problem, however; it must be tackled as part of the overall issue of ethical behavior in the professions. The old trick of helping to establish copyright by mailing a hardcopy of your manuscript to yourself by recorded delivery in a sealed envelope can be a worthwhile protective measure before letting your research results or knowledge loose on the Internet.

If you want to keep abreast of what is happening in the field of intellectual rights, there is a wealth of material obtainable via Internet from the electronic conferences and back issues of the American Association for the Advancement of Science's Professional Ethics Report, and the newsletters of the Office of Research Integrity.

The international scene

A particular point for you to consider is that your electronic works now become more likely to be incorporated into compilations or titles in ways that you cannot anticipate and in places far away, without your knowledge. The national boundaries defining markets in print publishing become far less significant with virtual publications that can move internationally so easily. Consequently, it is becoming less practical to have an agreement releasing, say, North American first rights only, and assume that you still have United Kingdom, Germany, or Japan clean and clear for other rights negotiations. Your e-book might have been widely distributed in Japan more quickly than it circulated in the U.S. or Canadian markets.

There is a particular hunger around the world for material to add production values and bulk to CD-ROM titles. Quite apart from monetary considerations, you might not want your words or pictures to be part of some of these works. You might already have signed away your rights to control these situations, which could prove to be

more of a problem in North America than Europe. Intellectual property rights in Europe have always tended to give writers more in the way of "moral rights" over how and where their creative works are used than in the U.S., but this could change. There is a lot of variation among older contracts that did not anticipate the significance of intellectual property rights in electronic formats. The key is to check on old contracts, and carefully review new ones.

Some countries will pose particular copyright problems. These are easily identified because they also have rotten records for pirating books and software. Expect, for example, those Chinese with computers and access to on-line services to get hold of the increasing number of English texts available electronically, then to pirate them on disk and on paper. In Europe, too, if your works are pirated in, say, Italy, you have realistically much less chance of protecting your rights than in Germany, France, or the U.K.

Corporate licensing

If you supply works that are likely to be used in controlled corporate or institutional situations rather than by individuals, you might well be able to implement some kind of electronic metering system to ensure that you are paid royalties properly. The campaigns conducted by the Software Publishers Association and the Business Software Alliance have been quite effective in making organizations more conscious of the dangers of piracy. It is now routine for corporations to conduct audits of the software being used on networks and individual workstations, and to have procedures in place to ensure that proper licenses and royalty payments are processed. The Association of Shareware Professionals also has considerable expertise in corporate licensing situations, and is well worth joining for this, and its other activities to protect and guide those distributing software as shareware.

As the large software publishers have found out, you run comparatively little risk of your work being pirated if you supply an evaluation copy to a large organization or a responsible small business. If they want to carry on using your material, you will usually be able to strike a mutually acceptable licensing deal. Depending on the type of work and how it will be used, there might be a one-time

fee, periodic payments possibly linked to technical support and the provision of updates, or an access royalty every time an employee or member uses your material.

 # Locks and keys

Hardware and software locks and keys are available to perform the required metering, but the cost and added complexity might outweigh any risk inherent in a straightforward, written agreement based largely on trust. If you are marketing some form of database, however, you might be able to borrow a monitoring technique used quite effectively by the renters of mailing lists.

Many address lists are now supplied in electronic formats, not preprinted labels as was usual in the past. Lists already digitized are far easier to copy if a renter wants to keep on using the list without making further payments. Most lists, therefore, include monitoring addresses to which the owner of the list has direct access and will be able to tell immediately if the list is being used without payment, or in some other unauthorized way. You might decide, in your nonfiction work, to supply an information resource or some other kind of contact that helps you monitor how your title is being used.

You have a built-in protection against theft and piracy if your work is physically substantial, comprising large files. There just might be no incentive or financial advantage for someone to try to download a 100,000-word book with a standard modem handling 2400 bits per second—the telephone and on-line charges could be more than the cost of purchase. This will not always be so, however, particularly as faster modems become more widely used, file compression improves, and optical cabling make very fast transfer rates practical.

Watch out for royalty snags with authoring and reader programs

It is impossible to give timeless advice on how to cope with all the licensing issues that could arise over the software that you might incorporate in your electronic publications. In most cases, the

provider of your e-book authoring or compiling program will state very clearly the conditions under which you can distributes the "reader" program module.

Some of the shareware and commercial programs, typified by Writer's Dream and Common Ground, have adopted a policy of placing very few restrictions on their reader modules. If you are a registered user of the authoring program, they encourage you to distribute the reader without badgering you for additional contracts, permissions, and royalty payments. Others, like Adobe's Acrobat and IBM's BookManager are, at the time of writing, far more restrictive. Some software publishers say they will negotiate each case on its merits and not set clear guidelines, which poses real difficulties if you spend a lot of time compiling your e-book in a certain way, and then find that you are going to have to pay an inordinate amount in software royalties for every copy that you sell.

Multimedia publications present particular problems because it's much more difficult to recompile if you do your original production work in an authoring program that proves later to present practical or legal complications. You might even create a title with no intention of distributing it beyond the corporate environment for which you have licensed reader or viewer software available. Then new circumstances arise, you want to distribute more widely and generate sales revenue, and you run into problems. When selecting your authoring program, therefore, take very serious account of the policy and prices for the reader modules to ensure that they are as compatible as possible with your ultimate marketing and distribution objectives.

For example, the legal issues raised by Compton's NewMedia patents on search systems for multimedia CDs were not clear as this book went to press. Patent, trademark, and copyright disputes can drag on for years, as has the legal battle over "look and feel" graphical user interfaces. It might be best to select software that is less likely to create any difficulties, even if it is somewhat less powerful than the alternatives.

There were even some early legal skirmishes over rights to the very term *electronic books*. At one stage, Sony distributed material claiming the phrase as a trademark, but quickly pulled back from that

position. Now it seems universally accepted that the term is a generic description of a type of publishing, and its use should pose no problems for you. However, if you create words for your titles—*diskzine* for a magazine on floppies is a good example—you might well find that someone else has established a prior right of use.

When registering marks or business names, or copyrighting material, you might want to strengthen your degree of protection by incorporating words such as Electronic Books along with your business name or publishing imprint.

Be cautious, but not obsessive

Although this is all valid cautionary advice about some of the rights issues raised by electronic publishing, there is the danger of becoming so concerned about protecting your literary properties that you are unable to exploit properly the new opportunities being offered. I support the advice that Ted Husted, a distinguished pioneer in electronic publishing, gives authors that they should not be overly concerned about piracy. It does not happen as much as many people think, and you cannot do much to prevent it anyway.

The publishing world has come to accept multiple, nonpaying, readership of printed books and magazines, and will have to accept that many, if not most, of the readers of electronic publications will use copies for which they have not paid. You can, however, try to gain from this greater exposure by building incentives for further sales and revenue. Such an incentive is built into Ted Husted's authoring program Dart, which he distributes very liberally. As you become familiar with the program and learn more about it, you will find many good reasons for becoming a registered user and staying in touch with Ted Husted and his UserWare software publishing enterprise.

One of the most attractive incentives to register is that UserWare sponsors the Digital Co-op, which helps to coordinate authors' and publishers' cooperative marketing efforts. Compile your publication and send it on a disk to UserWare, or upload it to the Digital Publishing Association's bulletin board and notify UserWare, and they

will place it for you on CompuServe's Electronic Publishing section. It's this sort of extra effort to help customers or readers that pays big dividends in the long run by building their loyalty.

Clifford Skoog, of El Cerrito, California is an example of how you can allow your intellectual property to be distributed and used freely as a way of attracting registered, paying subscribers, while protecting your rights at the same time. Clifford markets his PC-Shakespeare computerized Shakespeare concordance and study program by releasing a freeware sample comprising six of the plays. He requests a $5 donation if the sample is used in a course for academic credit, and this is credited against the $40 price for the full program.

Economical site licenses are available to encourage use of the program in schools, colleges, and other institutions. PC-Shakespeare demonstrates the wisdom of being prepared to give away a generous sampling of your title to ensure that it really demonstrates its value to potential users—but make very clear up front just what rights, if any, you are relinquishing.

Do not donate into the public domain any works that you want to protect in any way. Even if you do not solicit payments, you might still want to establish the right to control how your words are used. You need not give up anything, even the right later to impose charges, if you distribute a fully functioning and complete title on-line. Just state clearly in the opening screens exactly what rights you claim, and under what conditions you authorize the use of your creative efforts.

Shareware files can circulate for years, so it might be a very long time before your e-book gets to many of your prospective purchasers or subscribers. In these circumstances, when releasing a complete, fully functioning edition as shareware, make your registration pitch on the merits of purchasing the latest, much revised, edition.

The e-book of your life

CHAPTER 10

BOOKS have played a unique role as a means of trying to perpetuate ourselves. Booklore is rife with examples of people who have been buried with books; others have written works with the hope these would ensure some kind of immortality.

Many wills are attempts to continue to influence, even control, people and events after the author's death. Autobiographies and memoirs reach out for a permanency beyond the author's lifespan. Much of writing and other creative work is motivated by a need to put the meanings of a life into a permanent form. "Every artist writes his own biography," said the British psychologist and author, Havelock Ellis.

Diaries can play these roles also, despite the fact that in these high-pressure times they are called "agendas," as if their only function is to monitor appointments and other time-sensitive commitments. Diaries have always been a means to secure a form of immortality and permanence for the author, as well as being working documents to develop ideas and think through problems.

E-books provide a new form of personal expression in a medium that is almost as difficult to define in physical terms as life itself. When you relate an autobiographical e-book to the concept that a form of immortality can be achieved by capturing one's thoughts and attitudes within computer files, fascinating possibilities emerge. The ultimate e-diary or e-autobiography would be so comprehensive that it would pass a kind of Turing test, in which you would feel you were communicating with a real person when interacting with it via a powerful computer and artificial intelligence software.

The e-book of your life can take many formats in addition to the obvious autobiographical record. These new publishing media offer many different ways to use your creativity to add new interests and dimensions to the record of your life—particularly if you have spent a lifetime developing skills, knowledge, or expertise that should be passed on to others.

Electronic diaries

Keeping electronic diaries has become very easy in a variety of programs, with PIMs (personal information managers), particularly appropriate for the task. Otherwise, any word processor or text editor will do; often, simpler is better if it is run on a portable that is readily accessible whenever thoughts need to be captured.

Even the author of a diary who guards its secrets while alive might wish to have it published after he or she has died. Sadly, however, many of these records of lives are lost or destroyed. Perhaps, because of the practicality of archiving digital diaries, we can envisage a central depository of diaries on disk, with it becoming routine in a will to instruct your heirs to whom, and when, access may be granted, and if efforts should be made to publish it at a prescribed future date when its encryption codes will be automatically unlocked. Such a virtual cryogenic depository of thoughts and attitudes would be inexpensive to set up and operate on-line, providing the Internet's cyberspace community with an intellectual graveyard from which rebirth is not only possible, but routine.

The fact that the diaries of Samuel Pepys and Ann Frank survive to give us unique insights on important periods in history only underlines the unknown losses that have occurred because physical diaries did not survive fire, floods, holocausts, rodents, or decay. Also, contemporary diarists can be inspired by the possibility that their writings might have value that they cannot yet define. C.S. Lewis, the English diarist, would never have guessed how capturing the most intimate moments of his private life would help to create *Shadowlands*, one of the most acclaimed films of 1994, and inspire international interest in his other writings long after his death.

The impact that electronic media can have on the art of the diarist is a fascinating topic. Unfortunately, the best book on diaries, Thomas Mallon's *A Book of One's Own, People and Their Diaries*, has gone

out of print. Perhaps there might be an electronic version before long, so that we can share Mellon's insightful analyses of why people keep books of their lives to help to perpetuate those lives.

➡ Therapeutic benefits

Being able to express your own life experiences in the written word can be therapeutic. Many authors have done this in either fictional work, or in their own diaries or memoirs. Publication of the final text along with access to the writer's research material, notes, and explanations of his or her motivations can greatly enhance the comprehension and enjoyment of readers, and is readily achievable in electronic formats.

For example, David Cornwell, who writes best-selling spy novels as John le Carre, revealed to *People* magazine the benefits he gained by expressing his long suppressed feelings about his father in *A Perfect Spy*. "I felt as if I'd taken myself through some kind of wonderful, refreshing therapy," he said.

The therapeutic effects of the writing process can be greatly enhanced with the knowledge that it will be possible to publish electronically. Just knowing that the publishing ability is there somehow adds a greater sense of purpose and a rationale to the writing process, making it seem less introspective and self-indulgent.

It can be particularly rewarding later in life to focus on the influences of childhood. As another author, Humphrey Carpenter, points out, "a children's book can be the perfect vehicle for an adult's most personal and private concerns." So the most fruitful time of even a long and active life to mine for a book might well be the early days of childhood.

➡ Creating family chronicles

An e-book can be the most practical way to compile a family chronicle as a permanent record that can be updated with births, deaths, marriages, and other significant events. Several software programs can help you write the story of an individual life or the

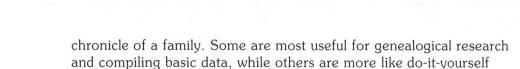

chronicle of a family. Some are most useful for genealogical research and compiling basic data, while others are more like do-it-yourself autobiography kits, prompting with questions about births, employment, and special family events.

Some resume-generating software programs provide similar prompts to structure and build the story of a life. Use the software to create a resume to try to get a job, and keep on using it to develop a resume of a life to publish within a family and leave to your children and grandchildren.

An e-book autobiography or family chronicle can be greatly enhanced by ancestor charts, or family trees. You can make these more interesting if the names of the people involved are accompanied by scanned photographs. These can be enhanced, turned into line drawings, and sized by image-manipulating software, then put into position on the chart.

A really great program for doing this kind of graphic publishing and lots of other graphic work is Visio from Shapeware Corporation (206-467-6723). It is marketed to the business community to help managers and technical people who cannot draw produce impressive visuals for printed or electronic presentations. Its low street price and easy drag-and-drop method of working with shapes and electronic stencils makes it an attractive tool, also, for individual authors to add a wide range of graphics to their titles.

A multimedia autobiography or family chronicle can include sound files of voices and video clips as well. Kodak's Photo CD software and third-party programs can turn a collection of slides or still photographs into a really comprehensive multimedia e-book of an individual life, a marriage, or an entire family.

⇨ Tap into your expertise as well as your experiences

You don't need to have been famous or have led an eventful life to write about your experiences. You might have a particular expertise

that can be communicated effectively to others by letting them share the stories of your life. This can be an ideal retirement project, with the potential to generate significant income.

"I am very excited about electronic publishing—I'm afraid I will be left behind if I don't learn about it," 65-year-old John Damiano, of Springfield, Pennsylvania, says. "I was a chemist before I retired, and many ideas come to mind for electronic publishing in the chemical education field to help supplement my social security and pension checks."

John's first step to develop his retirement publishing project was to register his SoftBook Publishing business name in his state. Establishing a registered name and a clearly identified and protected publishing imprint gives an identity and form to such an enterprise. What otherwise might appear merely a dream or passing whim takes on serious intent. Such official registration enables you to focus your own efforts, as well as improve the attitude of others to your electronic publishing projects.

Choose the name carefully, as John did, so that in editorial publicity, advertisements, and other promotions it conveys substance and creates an image that distances the authoring from the publishing. Using your own name as the basis for the business name and imprint makes registration easier, but it has practical disadvantages. A distinctive name for the imprint, like "SoftBook Publishing," enhances the image, and consequent marketability, of the publication by helping to disguise that it is self-published. This might seem like pandering to the entrenched perceptions that have bedeviled self-publishing for so long, but we must be realistic about these things.

John demonstrates also that you can get into the business with minimum expense. There is just no need for him to have software on the cutting edge of the technology. I sent him a copy of Writer's Dream that will work excellently on the system he bought in the late 1980s, a basic computer by today's standards that he funded with a five-gallon jug of coins saved over the years.

Publishing poetry
and drama as multimedia

CHAPTER 11

P OETRY is such a personal and intensely creative process that many poets will be eager to express their passion for this literary form by using the many multimedia opportunities now available to extend their creativity. Poets are the most frustrated of all writers by the restrictions imposed on them by the commercial realities of print publishing. As the American humorist Don Marquis said, publishing a volume of verse "is like dropping a rose petal down the Grand Canyon and waiting for the echo."

The scope for poets and dramatists (that other very frustrated group of writers) to create works that take full advantage of the distribution possibilities of the electronic media are many. Their works can be replicated and distributed on-line and on disk for very little cost to overcome the frustrations of never being able to achieve publication or performance.

Software is now available to make creating these works much easier. Ben Jonson said about the labors of poets and dramatists, "Who casts to write a living line, must sweat." This chapter looks at some very interesting software for poets that takes much of the sweat out of their more mechanical tasks. Dramatists, too, have some great programs available that remove the drudgery of formatting scripts for stage, film, or television production. You can find them in the word processing categories of almost any good shareware collection.

The most exciting developments for both categories of writers are in multimedia. Multimedia enables poets to express themselves visually as well as aurally, and dramatists to mobilize casts of virtual characters and become one-person dramatic production units.

Poetry in multimedia and on-line

If talented poets really use the new media, they will play an important cultural role in introducing the joys of poetry to a generation unfamiliar with its unique attractions. There are so many new forms to explore, and old traditions to develop.

Concrete, emblem, or pattern poems, in which the visual shape of the text is also an expression of the content, are ideal for publishing in electronic forms. Many poets have strong political and social messages that they wish to communicate, and the distribution channels open for e-poetry provide opportunities to influence public policy as Harriet Beecher Stowe's *Uncle Tom's Cabin* and Upton Sinclair's *The Jungle* did for earlier generations. Epics and odes are other poetic forms that lend themselves to expression in multimedia formats.

Interactive poetry

"Everglade," Rod Willmott's hypertext poem, has pioneered a new form of nonlinear poetry in which hypertext links lead the reader from one stanza to another. The reader uses the hypertext links to make a choice where to go next with the poem, so that every reading can be a new experience.

Some poets and authors object to the reader being able to exercise this kind of independence. It might even cause serious concern to a creative writer that his or her work will be released without any controls over how it might be manipulated. If this worries you, various software locks and encryption keys might help prevent your files, and consequently your words, from being corrupted. Personally, I think this is an exaggerated fear. Ever since words were chipped into stone blocks, there has been parody and plagiarism. The electronic media makes this easier, but not, I suspect, much more likely.

Introducing young people to the joys of poetry

You don't need to be a proficient poet to participate in electronic publishing. Those who love poetry and want to spread the good news have wonderful creative opportunities to compile and expand collections of favorite works. Out-of-copyright poetry can be a great basis for creating an original multimedia e-book. The poetry

anthology can take on a new form in projects like one I am engaged in to pay tribute to the Lake Poets, Samuel Taylor Coleridge, William Wordsworth, and Robert Southey.

These three wrote a number of memorable poems while living in the English Lake District in the 19th century. Their poetry has had a significant cultural impact throughout the English-speaking world, but you can only fully appreciate why this if you have seen this unique mountainous region, with its soft light and muted colors. There are fascinating facts behind the motivation for Wordsworth to write how he "wandered lonely as a cloud" through this landscape. The pictures, sound effects, and music that can be incorporated with the verses in multimedia presentations will help explain to new generations of readers the impact on him when "all at once I saw a crowd, a host of golden daffodils."

I doubt that the Lake Poets would have any objection having their work transferred to these new media. Southey tended to be rather prim and proper about the sanctity of books as objects, but Wordsworth was more concerned with the content than the packaging of literature. He horrified Southey by cutting the pages of a new book with a dirty butter knife in his hurry to get to the words, while Southey was a dedicated bibliophile who guarded his library and would not allow Wordsworth into it.

"How dead Southey is become to all but books," Wordsworth commented sadly. That is a scathing indictment of the attitude that values books as objects distinct from the creativity that resulted in the compilation of the words they contain. If a work really has merit, its creative integrity and true worth will survive and perhaps flourish if it moves beyond its original covers into new shapes, forms, and media.

I want contemporary kids who cannot relate to poetry at all to know Wordsworth's verses as the friends they were to me when I was growing up, even if I have to add human interest and interactive gimmicks, like encouraging them to download the recipe for the ginger cookies that Dorothy Wordsworth would make for her brother when he returned from his long walks through the Lake District countryside.

Retailing poetry

When poetry and drama are given these additional production values, they stand a much better chance of getting into retail outlets. Bookstores are opening their doors to interactive entertainment software, and some of the results are encouraging for retailers, publishers, and writers alike.

The Voyager Company, the publisher that has done most to advance electronic work in the Macintosh environment, has been working during 1994 with Apple Computer and four other electronic publishers to put titles into a cross-section of bookstores on both sides of the Atlantic.

"The best bookstores are wonderful places to browse a wide selection of works, and typically provide a high level of customer service," comments Voyager's Bob Stein. "We wanted to bring that comfort, selection, and service to buyers of interactive software. It makes sense, because these products are as much like books as they are like software, and the shopping experience should be similar."

The test marketing exercise has been accompanied by promotional events and a training program to help bookstore staff understand the new media and be able to give demonstrations to customers.

Shakespeare goes multimedia

In a work that embraces poetry and drama, Voyager is publishing a multimedia Shakespeare series. The aim is to overcome the traditional problem when publishing Shakespeare of being able to cater for the larger market of general readers, while also satisfying serious students and scholars.

The confines of the written words and even of the dramatic production of Shakespeare's works are broken wide open in the first title of the series, *Macbeth*. While reading the play, you can at any time use all the complementary material in the form of additional text

notes, audio, and even full-motion video. A click on any line in the play brings up on that page a video performance by the Royal Shakespeare Company.

Clicking on underlined words produces boxes with help and definitions. You can search and make notes, access background essays and details of Shakespearean characters, see video clips of other productions of *Macbeth*, and even select a role and participate in readings with professional actors by using a karaoke feature.

"I've always wanted to have an edition of Shakespeare that lets me see the works both as plays and as beautiful and intricate poetry," explains producer Michael Cohen. (In addition to publishing e-books, Voyager supplies the excellent Expanded Book Toolkit for electronic publishing in the Macintosh environment. For details, call 800-446-2001.)

"Better brain rewards than drugs"

If you resist electronic publishing because you fear the detrimental effects that the technology might have on the academic and cultural qualities of literature, then it is worth studying the pioneering poetry software created by Michael Newman.

Michael was a protégé of W.H. Auden and, influenced by that distinguished poet's emphasis on technique, has initiated a significant breakthrough in automating many of the technical aspects of writing poetry. The whole concept might worry literary purists, but it is not as academically disturbing as it might sound—unless you are the kind of writer who believes that your pure thoughts might be corrupted by committing them to paper with any instrument more technologically sophisticated than a lead pencil or a nib pen.

There are, on the other hand, many who believe that, if Shakespeare were living today, he would be using a word processor. These people will rejoice in what Newman has achieved. By exploiting word processing technology, he is offering an open door into the wonderful world of poetry for present and future generations. Whether we like it

or not, most literate people will make computers their medium of choice for expressing intellectual creativity, and this kind of software will have increasing appeal. It encourages more people to write and enjoy poetry, giving writers greater confidence in their ability to be creative in the various poetic forms, and perhaps triggering an aspect of individual creativity that lies dormant for most people.

To be able to create software that helps people write poetry, Newman has had to study the structures and technicalities of the poetic medium, and explain them to users of his Poetry Processor software packages. The explanatory documentation that accompanies the software is a quick course in the history and structure of the various poetic formats.

Michael Newman dreams that his programs might prove to be agents for social change. He hopes to get his poetry software used in prisons to help young, predominantly black, drug offenders develop their vocabularies and reading and writing skills.

"These young offenders have often have tremendous rhyming skills, as demonstrated by the rap phenomenon," Newman explains. "They already have right-brain capabilities, and this software could help them, through writing poetry, develop the more logical left-brain functions necessary for them to get jobs and lead more productive lives. Poetry software could reach these youngsters as no team of do-gooders can, and I believe that poetry stimulates a special endorphin reaction that gives better brain rewards than drugs."

Could two phenomena of the 1990s—rap and personal computers—combine to stimulate young people to write poetry and become more useful members of society? This is a fascinating concept, and Newman got an encouraging response when he proposed the idea to new Clinton White House team. The problem, as with the development of other aspects of electronic publishing, is one of accessibility. Hardware must continue to plunge in price and become more portable so that the creative software that helps people read and write electronically becomes widely available and practical.

Michael Newman thinks that, to unleash the full power of poetry as an agent for social change, his software must become available as low

cost *firmware*, programmed onto microchips that can be incorporated into the new portable handheld computing devices. He continues working towards that end. In the meantime, if you have a PC, he will help you become a poet right now. If you are a poet already, a little technological help might enable you to become a better or more productive exponent of prosody.

Poetry Processor displays on-screen whatever structure you have chosen, whether it be free verse, or the distinctive rigid format of a classic Shakespeare sonnet. You are guided to fit your words into the appropriate rhyme and rhythm. There is even the option to load an existing poem in the format you are using to act as a model framework for your own creation. That's a great help if you want to parody an existing work.

Michael Newman has created another program called Orpheus A-B-C (not to be confused with the Orpheus hypertext publishing program). This Orpheus is a computerized course in classical poetry that can be used at various levels. Children can enjoy it as a game, or it can be of great help to serious students of literature at degree level and beyond.

The registration fees and system requirements for these packages are very modest: around 300K of RAM and any version of DOS after 2.1. For more information, call or write

NewManWare
84 Front Street
New Haven, CT 06513

12

Opportunities for photographers, artists, and musicians

E LECTRONIC communications are evolving rapidly from being almost exclusively letters and numbers to having strong visual and audio elements. Consequently, the opportunities for photographers, artists, and musicians in the new media are at least as attractive as they are for writers.

Visual artists face even more difficulties than poets in getting their work published in print, because the cost of reproducing color is enormous unless amortized over very long runs. It is not unusual for even a black-and-white photographic book with very little text to cost over $10,000 in print preproduction work, often a lot more. Even after such an up-front investment, there is still a lot of work to be done and expense incurred before the project gets as far as ink being pressed onto paper.

Consequently, the self-publishing option has not been a viable one for all but the more affluent artists. Now that situation has changed with the ease that paintings and other forms of expression can be converted into high-quality digital images. Musicians can even use music-reading software to publish electronically, as in Fig. 12-1.

➡️ Achieving creative satisfaction

Of course, the format for playing back those images is physically very limited by the small size of the monitor screen. Thousands of artists are finding, however, that the new work-for-hire and self-publishing opportunities that attracted them to experimenting with digital imagery has led to significant creative satisfaction despite the screen limitations. Software paint and drawing programs such as Fauve Matisse help by creating working environments in which artists used to traditional materials can feel more comfortable.

HSC Software's InterActive typifies how creative people in any of the arts can sit down at a quite modest PC running Windows and build on whatever existing skills they have to become multimedia artists and publishers. Writers can work with photographic, line, and paint images; painters can add words and movement to their pictures;

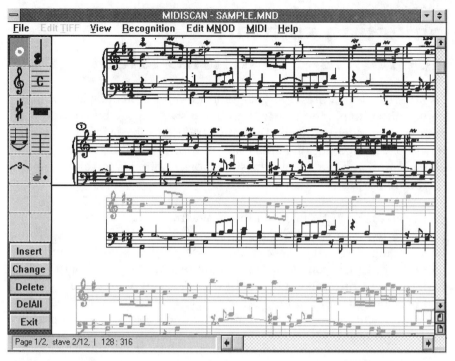

Figure 12-1

Publishing music electronically has now become very practical with programs like MIDISCAN for Windows. This music-reading software can be used immediately without any musical training or become a powerful communications tool for experienced musicians, composers, and arrangers. Musitek Corporation

musicians can create their own imaginative e-book equivalents of music videos. InterActive offers royalty-free runtime distribution, although as with any other authoring program, you still need to check whether it has the flexibility and licensing requirements to meet your particular publishing needs.

In the next few years, a wide selection of the computerized equivalents of *livre de peintre* limited-edition books will appear, in which poets, artists, and perhaps art dealers cooperate as they did when the genre first appeared in Paris in the 19th century. These new versions of the *livre de peintre* will have an important function as catalogs to promote original canvases and prints.

 # Selecting software appropriate to artistic talent

As an artist, try to preserve your skills in natural media when you move to the computer, rather than being swept away by the new technology. Much early computer-generated art is obviously a product of the plastic age, lacking spontaneity, form, and life. That is changing now, but a lot of published work continues to reflect more the computer's skills than the artist's.

The scope for artistic talent in these new media is enormous, particularly for those who carry through and develop the skills they have acquired in traditional media. Consequently, selecting the software in which you work really is important. As you experiment with different programs, you might find that you work more creatively and efficiently in a program that is simple or effectively mimics traditional watercolors or oils than in the most popular or expensive drawing program.

A particularly comprehensive resource for artists moving to digital media is the book *Digital Imaging for Visual Artists* by Sally Wiener Grotta and Daniel Grotta, published by Windcrest/McGraw-Hill.

 # Photographers have a digital medium perfect for their needs

In their book, the Grottas point out that, for artists and photographers shopping for hardware to move to the digital media, "separating the hype and hyperbole from the truth is a time-consuming, trial-and-error process best left to disinterested experts who are not trying to sell anything to you." Their book caters for professionals, so they fix their upper price limit for individual hardware components at $20,000. If you want to make nowhere near that kind of investment to get started, both photographers and visual artists can achieve excellent results on complete hardware systems

under $2,000, and software costing only a few hundred dollars at most.

One reason that you can great results so economically is that the Eastman Kodak Company is spending many millions to try to establish its Photo CD system as a worldwide standard that eventually will replace, to a significant degree, the traditional photographic materials on which the company has built its success. If this doesn't work, Kodak and other companies who have formed alliances with it are in big trouble. Consequently, there are tremendous commercial forces pushing Photo CD forward to make it as safe and universal an electronic publishing format as possible.

To use this system, you can take your pictures with existing photographic equipment. Then, send your films to any one of a growing international network of licensed laboratories that will quickly and economically process them into digital images on a CD disk. If you have a library of existing images that you want in digital form, they will process those also from color slides and prints for as little as under $1 an image.

You can import and manipulate Photo CD images in many authoring programs. In 1994, Kodak's own Photo CD Portfolio Authoring software arrived, enabling the desktop computer user to combine images with text, graphics, sound, and interactive features to create Photo CDs that can be played back on computers or television sets.

Photo CD gives authors the reassurance that they will be able to use competing photo finishers to duplicate their CD titles. They will not be limited to one or two services with little incentive to compete on price, or be forced to buy their own expensive hardware, which can soon be devalued and outdated by the speed with which this technology is moving forward. This is changing the economics of CD publishing, making it far more cost-effective for small enterprises and individuals.

Of particular interest to authors and art directors needing stock photographs, or agencies and professional photographers wanting to market their work, is the Kodak Picture Exchange (800-579-8737).

The Exchange is essentially an on-line database of photographs, an enormous resource to bring together those with pictures to sell and those seeking to purchase the rights to use a particular type of image. It could transform the marketing of freelance photographs and eliminates much of the cost and risk inherent in shipping expensive slides and prints.

⇨ The Photo CD formats

There are four main Photo CD formats. The original Master Disc is aimed at amateurs and professionals working in 35mm. It holds about 100 images with resolution about 16 times greater than that achieved on current NTSC broadcast television receivers. The images can be played through any Photo CD-compatible drive directly to a television or computer, and they can act also as negatives to generate prints up to poster size. The Pro Photo CD Master Disc is aimed at professional photographers and stores high-resolution images in larger film formats as well as in 35mm.

The other two formats are the media that have such strong potential for publishing. Portfolio Discs are appropriate for publishing any kind of picture stories with text and other multimedia features, including stereo sound. Authors have considerable flexibility in making use of the space on the disk. They can preserve high-resolution standards or save space by reducing resolution to make room for graphics and audio. The cost is attractive enough for small-scale publishing, right down to e-books of family events such as weddings.

The Kodak Photo CD Catalog disc format can be used to get as many as 4,400 images onto a disk at lower resolutions still acceptable for many purposes when viewed on monitors or television sets. These disks contain image search and retrieval software, but the images are not suitable for making photographic quality prints.

Kodak and its associates also support the smaller 80mm disk format which is becoming a standard for portable computers and personal

digital assistants. These small disks become an even more attractive publishing medium when you know that they are backwards-compatible with drives for the standard 120mm format.

Digital still and video cameras

If you want to capture your own photographic still images electronically, make sure that the camera you choose can download the images to a computer. You can get conversion kits that will enable the early electronic still cameras, notably the Canon Xap-Shot, to generate suitable digital images. Analog to digital converters, popularly known as *frame grabbers*, also allow single video frames to be incorporated easily into electronic or print documents. Quality is very much dependent on the performance of the digitizer board. It might be low, but still acceptable when the images are used small, as might be the case in a catalog or as a window to supplement a screen of text. In 1994, the Apple QuickTake digital camera launched a new era of affordable, high-quality blending of photography with electronic publishing.

You can use a camcorder to capture images, feeding directly into your video capture card or storing the images on tape for later transfer. This is often not as easy as it sounds, however, but there is now a very interesting alternative for the electronic publisher. VideoLabs' FlexCam is a miniature desktop color camera mounted on a flexible gooseneck arm, which can have a microphone incorporated in it. You can scan documents or capture moving or still images of pictures or three-dimensional objects, focusing down to as close as a quarter-inch to achieve a 50× magnification. Prices for the various models start at around $600, with PAL, NTSC, and S-video versions available.

This could become a very important tool for the publishers of electronic technical documents and scientific papers. Its applications are really only limited by your imagination. It's like having an electronic eye sitting on the desk beside you, always ready to import any image that you want to incorporate into an e-document.

 # Turn quality problems into creative opportunities

When you first start to include visual images into electronic publications, you might become frustrated with the difficulties of trying to achieve the standards you have come to expect from print media. The loss of quality will be greatly influenced by the capabilities of your hardware and software, as well as by the characteristics of the original image.

Often, quality will perceive to be improved by using the image smaller—it will also take up less disk space. Or you can turn a problem into extra production values by creatively processing appropriate photographs into impressionist renderings, which can be particularly effective for use as backgrounds. Such illustrations work well for poetry and fiction.

This process can be carried out entirely in the computer using image-editing software. You can also experiment with modifying your original by projecting the slide onto shower-curtain glass or semi-opaque plastic sheeting, and then photographing the image from the other side using a videocamera, still electronic camera, or a conventional camera with the film processed as a Photo CD.

If your original is a print, shoot a copy through textured glass placed over the print. (This is more difficult than working with slides.) Various lenses and filters can also turn a mundane photograph into an artistic impressionist image, which can be imported into the computer for incorporation in an electronic publication without needing to be of high resolution.

13

Electronic fiction

PUBLISHING fiction electronically poses special challenges not faced by nonfiction authors. Nevertheless, e-books are becoming viable media for a few fiction writers. Novels, short stories, and other fiction will increasingly be available electronically as portable hardware, particularly PDAs, stimulate the acceptability of recreational reading from a screen.

Of course, as thousands of frustrated, unpublished novelists and short-story writers release their works into cyberspace, it will be necessary for all writers going electronic to woo readers more assiduously. As Oliver Goldsmith pointed out for an earlier age of literature, "As writers become more numerous, it is natural for readers to become more indolent."

⇨ Science fiction flourishes on-line

Science fiction attracts many readers on-line because enthusiasts for the genre include an unusually high proportion of computer users interested in participating in new technological developments. An outstanding example of publishing contemporary science fiction electronically is the ClariNet CD Hugo and Nebula Anthology. The 1993 edition comprises five complete novels and the Hugo and Nebula Award nominated short fiction works, all on one disk costing under $30. The equivalent printed versions would cost over $230 at publishers' list prices.

That's not all in this remarkable package of fiction writing. The disk also contains a wealth of background information, artworks nominated for the Hugo awards, and video and sound clips of authors.

⇨ Mass-market fiction

Mass-market fiction is not going into e-book format so quickly or successfully because the large market for it is not developed yet. But that could change. FloppyBook's Paul Peacock confidently forecasts that the mass-market fiction blockbusters will do well with disk

releases, particularly when the fast-moving software publishers start shaking up the traditional print publishers.

"The PC software industry is moving faster than a speeding bullet, while the print publishing industry is sitting on its hands," says Paul. "Imagine if Microsoft released Stephen King's next novel on CD-ROM. They could offer him high royalties per copy, the best editors and marketing effort that money can buy, and the ability to augment his words with scary noises and special visual and audio effects. They could coordinate the release of the book onto different platforms: CD-ROM, Franklin and pop-in-cards, floppies, paper and hard cover books, etc. The potential earnings would be far higher than conventional publishing."

King has, as mentioned in an earlier chapter, already experimented with promotional releases on-line. Such experiments with on-line marketing, however, do not address the problem of creating a fiction work that is more attractive electronically than it is in print, and then getting readers to pay for it.

"Write an electronic book that gets the story started, introduces the characters, tells a complete story, but leaves more to be told," is one of author and electronic publisher Steve Hudgik's suggestions for fiction writers tackling these practical problems. "The reader can then call an on-line service, perhaps using a 900 number, and download more of the book."

Steve also suggests writing fictional works that can be adapted to changing political or economic situations. For example, provide an incentive for readers to call an on-line service to download updates that expand or change the book so that, when it is read again, the story is different. Such a facility would be fascinating if, for example, it had been applied to the Cold War spy novels of John Le Carre.

"Some people just do not want to wait," Steve says. "Once they get into reading something, they'll want to finish it. The ability to have a story change with changing current events can be a great hook. You might build a base of regular readers who'll call anytime a significant event happens in the world—such as the 1993 American bombing of Iraq—just to see how those events have affected the story."

"What is required is more than an interactive story, but a structure requiring skill on the part of the reader in order to actually set the direction that the story takes," he continues. "I don't think that interactive stories in which the reader just has a choice in which direction the story moves have much of a market because part of the fun of reading fiction is not knowing what is going to happen. However, another way to take advantage of the power of a computer—and to differentiate electronic from printed works—is to create stories that develop differently each time that they are read."

Interactive novels establish a new genre

A breakthrough electronic book worth studying by fiction writers that uses some of these techniques is *The Madness of Roland*, by Greg Roach, published by Hyperbole Studios on CD-ROM. Available for both Macintosh and Windows platforms, it could well establish a new fictional genre.

This novel, based on a medieval French legend, describes how the central character, the noble Roland, descends into madness. The story can be read from the different viewpoints of five other characters. Each of them is represented graphically by a Tarot card, providing gateways through which readers can move at will to view the development of the story from these different viewpoints.

You can also read the book in a conventional linear way, or click the mouse button to get historical, intellectual, and visual commentaries on what is happening. It is a radio play as well as a book and a movie because the story can also be accessed through audio files of professional actors reading it aloud as the text flows by on screen.

Such high production values as those in *The Madness of Roland*, are difficult to achieve, but remember that some of the most successful movies have not had any extravagant special effects. It is possible for individual authors to create interactive multimedia novels from their own desktops with quite modest resources. A good story, effectively told, is still the key to successful fiction publishing in any medium.

Games as a new medium for fiction writers

Computer games on-line are tending to move away from pure text to become more visual, like the multimedia video games marketed by Nintendo and Sega. However, there are large numbers of hackers and word-oriented intellectuals in the cyberspace community who do not need pretty pictures to stimulate their brain cells. Opportunities still exist, therefore, to create imaginative textual fiction; just don't expect to earn much from it.

The MUD (multi-user dungeon or dimension) phenomenon is still evolving on-line. MUDs and their derivatives include virtual communities created by their participants, offering many challenges to the fiction writers who participate. However, to make money from electronic fiction, the best bet at present is to create storylines and write scripts for multimedia games. These are a multibillion-dollar publishing business already, with new hardware and the information highways promising to continue fueling growth and consequent demand for new creative input.

 # Eliminating the out-of-print problem

Perhaps the most important contribution that electronic publishing will make to fiction is to keep alive and available the classics and worthwhile contemporary works not available in printed form. As a fiction author, you can ensure that there are always copies of your works available, and you can duplicate and distribute them as you will.

Certainly classical fiction is being kept alive by such ventures as the Reading for Pleasure shareware service on disks. "We're trying to provide an affordable library of cyberbooks, without requiring a lot of extra hardware," managing editor Cindy Bartorillo explains. They are among many independent publishing ventures willing to consider

worthy fictional works from contemporary fiction writers. The contact address is

Reading for Pleasure
103 Baughman's Lane, Suite 303
Frederick, MD 21702

On a larger scale, World Library, Inc. (800-443-0238) has made a major contribution to preserving the greatest fictional literary works in portable, searchable, and economical form. Its "Library of the Future, 3rd Edition" CD is a treasure trove of over 3,500 books, stories, plays, poems, religious works, historical documents, and scientific papers.

Writing tips, tricks, and techniques

OLD writers do not have to learn many new tricks when moving into the new electronic media. If you did it right in print, you stand a good chance of performing equally well in the electronic media with minimum learning curves. There are really no new rules to learn, just reinforcement of the old ones. Dr. Johnson's advice to "read your own composition, and when you meet with a passage which you think is particularly fine, strike it out," applies just as much to writers tempted to be pompous and verbose in word-processed e-books as it did when the medium was a quill pen.

The task of self-editing becomes more difficult when you know that you have lots of space left on a disk, with no cost or bulk constraints about adding more words. All writers now working in electronic media without the old space constraints should have pinned over their monitors Mark Twain's admonition that "few sinners are saved after the first twenty minutes of a sermon."

Imposing any rules on writing other than the need to conform to the basic grammatical structures that make the language work can be inhibiting and counterproductive. Communications of all kinds fail, however, if they break any one of a few basic rules. This chapter provides the only basic guidelines about writing that you really *must* observe if you want your electronic publications to be successful.

⇨ Keep it simple

Simplicity is of prime importance. The misconception that long and obscure words, and complex sentences and paragraphs, will impress the reader might persist among those with literary pretensions, but it has no place in any form of results-oriented publishing. This is particularly the case in the electronic media, with the monitor screen being even more unforgiving than the printed page to those who write with pomposity or unnecessary complexity.

The results that you seek from your publishing enterprise might be profit from registrations or sales, influence among those to whom your book is targeted, or enhancement of your reputation. Or you might just wish to entertain and inform people with no thought of

personal gain. If your communication does not get these desired results, however elegantly you might feel it was written, the fault might be in the marketing and distribution, as well as in the writing. Examine each aspect critically. Perhaps even the basic concept is off target, and there just is not sufficient demand for your publication.

Despite hypertext and other features that enable readers to progress through your text any way they wish, it is still advisable to keep your structure simple. Progress logically from one point to another by organizing what you want to say in the simplest, easiest to understand manner. This is important even in sophisticated multimedia presentations.

Keep the sequence simple

Novels, movies, and seminars are all familiar examples of sequential, linear media. Despite all the hype about hypertext, many electronic publications that are not random-access works of reference will be approached by their users in the traditional sequential, linear way. Users expect that they must catch your information train at the departing station and stick with it to the destination, with limited flexibility to retrace the route. In theory, of course, you can re-read a section of text or rewind a tape, but this should never be necessary to help comprehension and is less likely to happen in an e-book than one with printed pages. Assume that readers or viewers will not bother to go back if your meaning was unclear on the first pass. It is more likely that they will jump off your information train and catch another that offers a less demanding journey.

Within the logical, linear sequence, pay particular attention to the points at which you introduce information that your readers cannot be expected to know already, but will need for the next steps along their journey. To do this without breaking up the smooth flow of the narrative is one of the most challenging tasks in writing—which is why some writers dodge it by hiding away such information in footnotes. Do not use footnotes in electronic publications; they just don't work. Nor should you assume that your readers will automatically take hypertext jumps to supplementary information that they need for comprehension.

In a two-way conversation, questions are asked constantly as one person says something, and the other asks more questions to get more information. In the medium of writing, the reader does not have the immediate opportunity to ask questions, so the meaning must be clear all the way through. Facts and background must be presented in the order necessary to anticipate and resolve any questions that the reader might need to understand one thought before moving on to the next.

Don't get into a time trap

There are many situations when restructuring—departing from the natural chronological sequence—makes a written document easier to understand and more fun to read. For example, a scientific or technical presentation might become boring if the research and applications stages are described strictly in the sequence in which they happened. Instead, state the benefits of the research up front, and then go back to describe how the research work progressed to lead to the new product or service.

Take care not to advance from one paragraph to the next without providing the technical information that the target audience needs to understand each paragraph. Always keep your target audience in mind, so you will not bore them with too much background explanation of what they already know, nor confuse and lose them because you do not explain things they cannot be expected to know about.

The outlining capabilities now included in sophisticated word processors can help with these tasks. Multimedia authoring programs usually incorporate some kind of timeline or storyboard facility as a way of assembling all the different elements. If you do have visuals, audio clips, and the like, a storyboard becomes essential. Even if your title does not include multimedia features, use an outliner to create the text equivalent of a storyboard. This can be the best way to structure the text.

Revise, revise, revise!

Devote as much time as you can to revising. Do so on a screen with a display format as similar as possible to the one your readers will use.

That is contrary advice to using a word processor to prepare text that will be printed as a hardcopy. In that case, you should do your final revisions on an actual print-out.

Get someone who will give you an impartial opinion, and whose proficiency at a computer is about the same level as your average targeted reader, to go through your e-book before releasing it. If you have created it on a fast, powerful system, check its performance on a slower computer with less memory.

Entertain as well as inform

Even if your subject is serious, work hard to maintain reader interest. Entertain as well as inform as much as possible. Motivate the audience to open your e-book and then stay with your words and pictures. I always organize my material with the strong lead up-front as the creative starting point in the writing process, as well as the first contact with the audience. This applies as much to a business letter or report as to an article for a magazine or newspaper, or to an e-book. Every type of communication must compete for attention with the plethora of other material directed at your target reader, so it had better start strongly, with at least one attention-grabbing point in the first few lines.

In newspapers, which are random-access media, every story must start strongly to attract the reader's attention. The heading and lead sentence must be strong, active, and above all, relevant and important to the target readers. This rule can be applied to almost everything that is published electronically. Technical service bulletins, for example, tend to look boring and usually start off with dull labels as headings before diving into a mire of equally ponderous text. There is some myth among engineers that technical papers will not get taken seriously unless they are dull. What nonsense! And what a shame it will be if these attitudes are carried over into the electronic media that are beginning to play such an important role in conveying technical information.

In addition to using attention-grabbing words in the headings and opening paragraphs, make particularly good use in these opening

sequences of sound, color, or other enhancing features that you have available. Some purists might sneer at such devices as animated cartoons or sound effects in technical material, but they achieve their business objectives if technicians are alerted to problems and servicing requirements, and are motivated to improve workshop productivity and customer satisfaction. In virtually every field, service personnel are on the receiving end of a flood of routine bulletins and booklets. A simple but high-impact message is needed to cut through the clutter, grab their attention, and communicate a specific course of action for them to take.

⇨ Practical tools for writers

I have tried an enormous variety of much-touted tools for computer-based writers. The most useful is still a word-processing program with which you feel comfortably proficient. You might feel that you function very well in an older DOS version, or in any one of many basic text editors, but the new, sophisticated, word processing applications for the Macintosh and Windows can make you far more productive. Their improved screen displays, greater proficiency at checking grammar and spelling, and the ease with which you can edit and manipulate text encourages revision and leads to a higher-quality product.

If you handle a lot of research material, it is very helpful to have a word processor that enables several windows of text from different documents to be open at the same time, so that you can cut and paste from them into your manuscript. I used this technique extensively when handling the vast amount of research material collected for this book.

Using an old portable running askSam database software, I just dumped into a text database the details and comments from all the thousands of bits of paper that contained my original sources. Not bothering to make corrections or tidy up the phrasing (except for factual accuracy), I accumulated very large files of unformatted data that I then compiled into one word processor file.

I drafted the manuscript with two files open at any one time: one was the file for the current chapter, the other the collections of notes. Using the word processor's keyword search function, I selected and cut from the research file the sections that I needed at the time, and patched them into the manuscript. It was a much faster and more convenient way of working than being knee-deep in paper notes. I found it even better, when working on a more powerful multitasking computer, to have those notes in askSam for Windows and manage them there, while also having open my Windows-based word processor.

New and better ways to handle research materials

Electronic publishing is a particularly appropriate medium for substantial works containing large amounts of information. Managing that information can be a nightmare for authors and researchers swamped in seas of paper, and probably also tangles of information contained in computer files. In this era of multimedia, many writers must also cope with information resources on tape, film, or CD, as well as paper.

There has to be a better way than the traditional methods of organizing research material into hanging files and folders, with cross-references on index cards. Many of the apparent solutions offered by computing technology just do not work because database and personal information manager software neglect the needs of writers. Most writers tend to gather information randomly, without any real idea of how it will be structured until the actual creative process of writing is under way. Computer databases are not sympathetic to such disorganized habits and want you to straight jacket your information into rigid "fields" right from the beginning.

However, askSam is one software program that fits the particular needs of writers like a glove. It is unique in the way that information can be dumped into it in a completely random fashion, then retrieved by whatever way you want to organize. If, for example, you have

clearly defined chapters on different topics, you can do searches that will bring together into one report all your research information relevant to the chapter on which you are working.

If you are writing a long and complex novel, you can have the entire manuscript in one file and move through it very rapidly to check on some previous aspect of a character or a plot. Cutting, pasting, and making changes during rewrites, become much easier than with most word processors. As well as providing powerful hypertext facilities, askSam lets you embed graphics in your text, and link to other multimedia elements.

There are DOS versions of askSam that run on very modest hardware with minimum RAM and without hard disks, although they require considerably more effort to learn than the new Windows version. Either a DOS or Windows version will process data that can be captured and output in the simplest of ASCII text files, the *lingua franca* of electronic publishing.

Of particular interest to electronic publishers is that you can create and distribute publications that incorporate askSam's sophisticated search software, so this program is also an authoring system. You can license the search module and obtain permission to distribute it with your own electronic publication. If you want to go that route, talk to the askSam people for licensing rates, which vary considerably according to the application. The askSam people are very helpful and can be reached at

askSam Systems
P.O. Box 1428
Perry, Florida 32347
800-800-1997

Robert Lissauer is a good example of a writer with a very heavy research load who used askSam to manage his information so that it could be compiled into a massive book. Robert's passion is music, and he spent six years gathering music trivia, with the help of askSam, into the six-pound *Encyclopedia of Popular Music in America*, containing details of nearly 20,000 popular songs.

"I foresaw that if I were to use index cards to register the information garnered through my research, it might take 25 years to complete the task," says Robert. Instead, he got his book completed in a quarter of the time.

Another askSam enthusiast is Fred B. Eiseman Jr., who lives an idyllic writer's life, spending six months each year in Bali. He has six books in print about this Indonesian paradise.

"All of my field notes for all of these books are stored in askSam files," says Fred. He normally takes a laptop into the field and enters data directly into askSam files, or transcribes handwritten notes into askSam when he returns. "Whenever I go into the field, I make sketches of significant items that I am studying. When I get back to my base, I scan the sketches with my Logitech ScanMan hand scanner, convert them to GIF files with HiJaak, and store them with the askSam file on the same subject so that the sketches become part of the field notes."

Fred also uses askSam for his Balinese-English dictionary, for cataloguing slides, indexing maps, helping to manage his finances, and for his "to-do" list. His Bali askSam files contain sixteen million bytes of information!

Find those elusive files

When handling a book-length manuscript and lots of research notes, an author can go mad trying to find files identified only by the cryptic DOS filenames. Your basic equipment should include a good file finder. Some are built into word processing applications or included in collections of utilities such as Norton Utilities.

If you are working in Windows, I recommend Eclipse FIND (800-452-0120). It builds an index of every word in every one of your files, and then, given the minimum of information, finds the file you seek with amazing speed. It even finds things you forgot that you had.

Go fishing to eliminate writer's block

Another program tailor-made for writers is IdeaFisher, now available in a Windows version as well as for DOS. It negates any excuses that "writer's block" is getting in the way of finishing a project.

I was amazed to find, at my first experience attending a California writers' conference, that the session on how to deal with the emotional stress of writer's block was standing-room-only. You owe it to yourself to get past this myth of the writing craft, so that you can focus your intellectual energies more on enjoying the process and doing it as well as you can. I have met hundreds of professional writers over a long career, and can't recall any who seriously concerned themselves with the writer's block issue. When their creativity, like their digestions, occasionally stiffened up, they would exercise their intellects with a good book or conversation, or take a brisk walk to get the juices flowing again.

However, writing does tend to be a lonely, isolated occupation, which can become stressful. When you are self-publishing, that sense of isolation can become considerably worse, particularly if you are used to a conventional work environment in which your creativity is stimulated by contacts with others. The need for creative stimulation from others could be as important in evolving your marketing plans as it is in actually creating the works that you are trying to market.

Going on-line to the writers' and publishers groups on GEnie, CompuServe, the Digital Publishing Association, and other bulletin boards is one possibility, but can be slow, expensive, and frustrating. Easier and better in many respects is a software program that could have been custom-built for self-publishing authors. IdeaFisher is the nearest thing to an electronic collective mind for authors that I have ever encountered.

The program was conceived—and its enormous development costs financed—by Marsh D. Fisher, co-founder of the Century 21 Real Estate Corporation. Marsh was yet another frustrated writer who had tried with little success to learn comedy writing techniques. When he retired in 1977, he began a project which could do more good for

creative writing (and marketing) than any number of Nobel literary laureates in recent years.

Marsh employed over 250 researchers and funded hundreds of thousands of hours of investigation, compiling, and computer programming to put together a unique database of information and questions designed to get creative juices flowing, however they might be blocked.

"We really now have a unique thesaurus of ideas," Marsh says. "You can use it for almost any kind of creative process or problem-solving need." Marsh has launched Windows and Macintosh versions of IdeaFisher, with nearly 800,000 idea associations, and the price has become very affordable. For details, call 800-289-4332.

15

Good news for disabled writers and readers

CHAPTER 15

THE business community, as well as the general public, should be enthusiastic about electronic publishing if for no other reason than the benefits it brings to disabled readers and writers. The business community is being forced by legislation to offer more equal facilities for the disabled, and electronic publishing can be a big help in meeting these new requirements. Telecommuting and other applications of corporate paperless publishing almost invariably make it easier for a business to conform to the Americans with Disabilities Act, often offering cost-efficient alternatives to converting offices or publishing employee documentation in other forms. We should become a better society as a whole as the information highways open up and the disabled can travel along them on equal terms with others.

Apart from these more altruistic aspects, in hard commercial terms, the disabled comprise a big market for electronic publishing products. There are an estimated three million people in the U.S. with impaired vision or other conditions, such as hand loss, that make it difficult for them to read print. The National Library Service for the Blind and Physically Handicapped (800-424-9100) already does much to enrich these lives through audio books. Electronic publishing can do even more because every digitized text is a dynamic, flexible document that can be more easily converted to make it more accessible to those with different disabilities. In particular, the advances made in synthesizing speech from digital texts is amazing; every e-book can be a talking book.

To keep abreast of products and services for the visually handicapped, and perhaps find a market for your own creations, contact

The National Association for the Visually Handicapped
22 West 21st Street, Sixth Floor
New York, NY 10010

 # Literacy considerations for the blind and vision-impaired

Visually handicapped people who have made the considerable effort to learn Braille, together with the business interests that serve them,

will continue to champion this touch medium, despite the advances made in voice-activated computers and software that translate text into speech with increasing proficiency.

There is a case to be made for preserving Braille because the new computer technology that puts the emphasis on audio is resulting in significant increases in illiteracy among the visually handicapped in the U.S. Of course, if you define illiteracy as an inability to read text paper, that is a problem. If you think of illiteracy in terms of a general inability to obtain and communicate information, however, then paperless publishing is a wonderful development for blind people that, for these times, might be ranked with the significance of Dr. Braille's invention.

Of course, the two should happily coexist. It is now far easier and cheaper to create a Braille text from a digitized document than one that exists only in printed hardcopy, so far more publications should become more readily available to millions of blind people around the world for whom Braille is the most appropriate reading medium.

There are far more people globally with low vision than those actually classified as blind. The deficit in their ability to see interferes with their daily lives, but rarely results in blindness. For them, the ability to customize a digitized document to display at an enlarged size, with greater contrast, or in a clearer typeface, can be a blessing beyond the capacity of those with good vision to appreciate fully. Already, with library budgets under so much pressure, e-books are a welcome and economical addition to the provision of large-type books so appreciated by the growing numbers of elderly people with vision problems.

Visually impaired authors and readers need not despair that the move to graphical interfaces generally, and Windows in particular, will negate many of the advantages offered them by electronic publishing. Several companies are developing software that generates audio messages for the pull-down menus and icons that the blind cannot see, or enlarges graphical images as well as text for those with limited vision.

The federal authorities are doing their best also, with the Clearing House on Computer Accommodation, run by the General Services Administration, offering a free tutorial on audiocassette to help visually impaired people use Windows programs. (Call the Clearing House at 202-501-4906 for details.)

If you are publishing to the visually handicapped market or have a personal or institutional need for detailed information about adaptive technology, the unique resource is *Solutions, Access Technologies for People Who Are Blind*, published by the National Braille Press (617-266-6160). Appropriately, it is available as an electronic book on disc, an audio book on cassette, in Braille, and as a conventional hardcopy.

Help for the hearing impaired

Electronic publishing can be used also to help the hearing-impaired. The ability for deaf children and adults to interact at their own pace with stories and games that creatively use visuals and text offers many opportunities for learning in general, and specifically for training in such skills as lip-reading and speech.

If this field interests you, keep track of what Matsushita Electric of Japan (Panasonic is one of their famous brands) is doing with its CISTA (computer-integrated speech training aid) technology. Over 100 schools in Japan and several in the U.S. have been involved in developing this system in which hearing-impaired children teach themselves to speak. Sensors analyze key elements of a child's speech pattern and, if a word is spoken properly, the child is able to make things happen on the screen—score a basket in a basketball game, for example.

This is but one of many developments of basic games concepts not only helping disabled people, but also being incorporated in electronic publications with learning and entertainment objectives.

16

Scanning & compression

CHAPTER 16

S CANNING and compression are two technologies that, sooner or later, electronic authors and publishers need to use. It is crazy to waste the time and human effort needed to retype documents existing only in hardcopy when they can be scanned and digitized by computer. Similarly, it makes good sense once a publication exists in virtual form, to exploit the fact that it can be squeezed into far smaller files by a variety of compression techniques.

These technologies are vital in the development of many forms of electronic publishing, but they are not as easy to use as they might at first appear.

⇨ Reducing the hassles in OCR and scanning

Don't be seduced by the obvious attractions of optical character recognition and the somewhat confusing claims made for the technology by those selling hardware and software products. You will be very lucky if you can take that one typed copy of a manuscript, feed it through a scanner and OCR program, and get clean, accurate text on your monitor. In many cases, it might be quicker to retype the text, since only clean documents, well-printed with a limited range of typefaces at particular point sizes, on white paper without fancy formatting, will get close to the claims of 99% OCR accuracy.

If the hardcopy being scanned has complex formatting and includes a range of typefaces or fonts, or a mixture of graphics and text, the OCR program can soon become confused and inaccurate. If the spacing between the letters is less or more than normal, the characters have unusual features, the type used is smaller than 9pt or bigger than 28pt, or the pages were typed using a fabric ribbon, error rates can increase considerably. Particular problems are posed by printing on colored or textured paper, or by that overworked contemporary design device of running text over images, particularly screened photographs.

If the hardcopy has lived an interesting life and acquired stains and smudges, the task of the scanner and OCR software becomes

increasingly difficult. Even an actual accuracy rate of over 98.5% yields a mistake in about every line of scanned text, and it is not practical to expect all those errors to be caught by even the best spell checker. Every 1% difference in OCR accuracy makes an enormous impact on the quality of the document, and if you get less than 90% accuracy, the results probably offer no advantage in time or cost over retyping.

If, for example, you are trying to compile an electronic book from a collection of newspaper clippings—perhaps tearsheets of features you have written—the multiple columns, lack of contrast, and probable use of visuals will be just too challenging for most OCR programs. You might be able to improve things a little by making crisp new photocopies, but that extra generation of copying might add as many recognition problems as it resolves.

But it is not all bad news. OCR is improving rapidly, and if you have a suitable hardcopy, the results can be very impressive. There are refinements to OCR programs, such as the AccuPage facilities with Hewlett-Packard scanner software, that can enhance contrast and other important aspects of the image. Before you spend a lot of money on a scanner and software, however, try them first to make sure that they will live up to your expectations.

When image quality is poor and retyping is not a viable proposition, you might consider scanning hardcopies of documents into graphic images and then using a file- or document-management program to publish them. Although document imaging is seen mainly as a solution to the business community's problems in managing its paper, the technology does have a place in certain publishing needs where it is not practical to digitize the text on the hardcopies.

If you are still working on a typewriter and think that you might want to create digital copies at some time in the future, it would be a sensible long-term economy to use a carbon rather than a cloth ribbon. Typing from a cloth ribbon, along with all but the best dot-matrix output, does not fare as well in the OCR process as nice, crisp, laser copies. Similarly, carbon copies and faxes are not handled well by scanners or OCR software.

Scanners differ greatly in their capabilities

For serious OCR work involving significant quantities of material, a flatbed scanner (Fig. 16-1) is almost invariably easier to use and will give more accurate results than a hand scanner. The flatbeds are coming down in price as they increase in proficiency, and for many independent authors it might make more sense to invest in a scanner/laser printer combination than a copier, particularly if there is a low-cost copying service nearby. Some office supply stores use their copying facilities as a loss leader to pull in customers.

Figure 16-1

A flatbed scanner is more expensive than the typical hand scanner, but almost essential when scanning high-quality visuals or lengthy documents for optical character recognition. Sharp Electronics Corporation

An alternative to either hand or flatbed scanners is the type with roller mechanisms that take up very little desk space and are more portable than the flatbeds, while tending to be easier to use and more

accurate than the handhelds. However, the roller scanners cannot cope with bound books.

The best solution for many individual scanning needs is one of the services that converts paper documents into electronic documents. These are springing up in cities where there is sufficient demand. If there is not one near you, you can mail or ship your texts to a distant service, such as the Larry Whitaker Association (619-259-7911). Expect to pay about 50 cents for an average-sized image, and $1.50 to scan a standard letter-size page of text until competition is brisk enough to bring down prices.

 # Capturing screen images

Once your image is in a digital form and you have manipulated it on screen to your satisfaction, you might want to capture it to incorporate in your publication, or to print out as a hardcopy. Screen captures are widely used in the printed documentation accompanying software.

You will rarely get satisfactory results using the print screen command from your keyboard; screen capturing usually requires a dedicated program. I recommend Hotshot Graphics from SymSoft (702-832-4300). It is versatile, easy to use, and gives you the capacity to manipulate images that can be useful when preparing and marketing e-books.

 # Compression is essential, but can be problematical

Compression will be the key to the development of many forms of electronic publishing. While it is comparatively simple and reliable to compress and decompress text files to make them conveniently portable, the process becomes far more complex and unreliable when working with graphics. The potential problems increase by leaps and bounds with the need to compress the animation sequences and full-

motion video that are becoming important elements of electronic publishing.

 # Video compression technology

Even the massive storage capacity of a CD might hold only 30 to 60 minutes of digital video, compared to hundreds of text-only books. Distributing video or more than a few still images on even high-density floppies is impossible. Video files also take up impossible amounts of hard disk space on typical personal computers. Compress those files to get more into a smaller space, and you can run into all kinds of system compatibility and monitor resolution conflicts when they are decompressed by your readers.

If you want to build video or large numbers of graphical images into your electronic publications, you will nevertheless be compelled to use compression techniques, probably those built into your multimedia authoring programs. Compression techniques vary in their efficiency and reliability. Beware particularly those that limit the marketability of your publications by requiring very specific systems on which they can be played back.

Lossy compression methods achieve far smaller files than the *lossless* compression techniques intended to guarantee that no data is lost when the file is decompressed by the user. The lossy methods work by eliminating some of the data in the original, uncompressed images. For example, the lossy compression program might eliminate some of the variations in brightness for certain colors that would not be obvious to the viewer's eyes. Or, when there are repetitions in a sequence, such as a vehicle moving across the screen, the lossy compression program will try to make intelligent guesses at which parts of the picture need not be changed for every frame.

In image compression, the tiny *pixels* that are the basic elements displayed on your monitor are grouped into blocks before compression. These blocks are, in effect, an averaging of the color and light characteristics of the typical 64 individual pixels within the block. When decompressed, the image might be distorted and very different from the original, with results that cannot be guaranteed if

your publication is going to be played on a wide range of computer systems.

The multimedia market is expected to grow to $25 billion a year by 1998, a five-fold increase since 1992, and much of that growth will be made possible by continuing developments enabling publishers to squeeze still and moving images, particularly video, into their titles. It is a technology which, even if you don't begin to understand it, you must still take into consideration in your planning.

Fractal compression

Although all forms of image compression are improving by leaps and bounds, *fractal transform image compression* seems to have inherent advantages that give it an edge. Indeed, one of the pioneer researchers in this field, Taylor Kramer, chief technical officer of Total Multimedia (TMM), maintains, "Fractal video compression is the enabling technology that will unleash a torrent of creative products for educators, magazine and book publishers, electronics companies, and movie and music producers."

"We envision a future in which electronic publications will be routinely enlivened with video and multimedia illustrations now that fractal compression is available for DOS, Windows, and Macintosh systems," he says. "The publisher just needs to compress a video sequence once, and it will play back reliably on all these systems."

One pioneering electronic publishing use of fractal compression is Microsoft's Encarta multimedia encyclopedia, in which thousands of color images are squeezed onto a single CD-ROM. You can experience this compression technology in works from other leading electronic publishers as well, such as Compton's New Media, Grolier, and Software Toolworks. The costs are comparatively high, but you can now get fractal compression software packages from TMM (805-371-0500) for under $1,000, with a license fee or royalty negotiated on any commercial titles in which you use it.

IBM researcher Benoit Mandelbrot conceived fractals in 1975 as a way of mathematically defining irregular shapes. *Fractals* are actually

coded mathematical instructions that enable your originating computer to display a picture. As such, they are much easier to compress into small portable files that will fit on a disc than are the digital elements that make up the picture. When these instructions reach their destination, the computer mathematically expands them again to enable it to display your pictures on whatever monitor it is using.

It is really not the picture that it is being compressed, but the digitized instructions for creating the picture. Compare it to mailing a friend the recipe for mixing and baking a cake, rather than having to make and send the cake itself.

The process differs completely from the physical visual steps in enlarging or reducing a photograph. There is no messing with the pixels themselves in fractal compression, so the process tends to be much faster and more accurate than with other methods. Image files might shrink to one-hundredth of their original size and decompress quickly to give a faithful image on a wide range of monitors, irrespective of their resolution specifications. The decompression process is invisible to the reader, but for complex images, it might take a few seconds. That delay you experience when running multimedia, then, is not just your computer seeking the relevant information from the disk, but decompressing it also.

The implications of fractal compression are enormous for the videotape as well as print media. TMM's Taylor Kramer predicts that cost and durability alone must make movies migrate from tape onto CD-ROM because, thanks to fractal compression, the expense of duplicating a show onto a CD-ROM will be one-tenth the cost of putting it on tape, and the disk will last 100 times longer. Movies going onto CDs will stimulate demand for playback hardware, as happened with video. That's good news for e-book and multimedia publishers because it will increase our markets.

If it were not for compression technology, some of the most interesting applications of electronic publishing would not be possible. The educational sector provides many examples. One of the most interesting is a history course created in the Hueneme School District in California. Using TMM's fractal compression technology, the

children interact in English or Spanish with a multimedia program on the Lewis and Clarke Expedition that includes extracts from the diaries and clips from the movie *Dances with Wolves*.

Over 7,000 students at nine elementary and two junior high schools in the Hueneme district have been exposed to these new multimedia forms of electronic textbooks, and the results have been very encouraging. Test scores have improved to some of the best in California, despite the fact that Hueneme spends less per pupil than the state average. Attendance and discipline problems have become significantly lower, also, since multimedia entered the Hueneme classrooms. This multimedia system runs on a variety of networked PCs, including some older and less powerful systems that can only cope with sophisticated full-motion video because of fractal compression.

Zipping your texts

For electronic publishing that does not involve video, the most universal file compression system is PKWare's PKZIP to compress, and PKUNZIP to decompress. You will find copies of these shareware programs wherever shareware is distributed. By using this popular system, your files will be acceptable to bulletin board sysops and on-line services everywhere. If you are running Windows, another shareware program, WinZip, is much easier to use. The excellent WinZip costs $29 from Nico Mak Computing Inc., P.O. Box 919, Bristol, CT 06011-0919. An evaluation copy, together with the LHA self-extracting archive ideal for e-books, is included with the Writer's Electronic Publishing Kit offered to readers in the coupon at the end of this book.

You must license these compression programs to use them for your publications; there are full details in their documentation files. Several other shareware compression programs do not require licensing fees—and some of these are very good. However, choose carefully because not all are as acceptable on-line, nor as reliable. One of the safest choices is called LHA, widely available on bulletin boards and in shareware collections as *freeware*, which does not require licensing.

In certain publishing situations, you might be able to use the compression facilities available in MS-DOS 6 onwards, but only with high-density disks and for distribution to systems running DoubleSpace.

⇨ Beware of viruses

The last thing you want is for the electronic publications you distribute to provide a hiding place for computer viruses, those destructive programs that attach themselves to program and data files as they move from system to system. There are hundreds of different viruses now circulating, some of them very virulent, destructive, and difficult to detect.

Scan your disks and on-line downloads coming into your system. Also, make sure that any disks that you distribute are clean. Labeling them as having been scanned and virus-free can be a help to sales. The shareware versions of Viruscan and VirusShield are well proven anti-viral protection. MS-DOS 6 and later also feature competent scanning software.

Writing and publishing rewards beyond money

CHAPTER 17

INEVITABLY, there has been considerable emphasis throughout this book on publishing for profit. It is an important and valid objective for writers and publishers to generate income—either big bucks, or just sufficient income to continue a love affair with their vocations. But for virtually all poets, and also for most writers in other categories, the need to write is not primarily motivated by expectations of significant monetary rewards. Almost any other occupation pays better!

Comparatively few active writers spending more than 15 hours a week on the craft earn their livings primarily from their words; some estimates put the proportion at well under 5%. Millions of others take writing seriously as a leisure pursuit with little, if any, thought of monetary gain. Most writers accept that it is unrealistic to expect to make significant money from writing—just the supply-and-demand economics of the publishing industry make that a near impossibility.

Writing, along with painting and music, are universally popular creative pursuits, nonfiction writing included. You do not have to be working on a novel, poem, or short story to be creative with words. Some of the highest-quality writing these days is to be found in nonfiction works rather than bestselling fiction.

Amateur painters and musicians seem more ready than writers to accept that the creative process can be a satisfying end in itself. An exhibition in a gallery or a public performance are attractive possibilities, but not the prime motivation for painting or for mastering a musical instrument. In contrast, virtually all writers feel the need to be published!

The need to be published

Publishing does more than just create an end-product. It gives a sense of purpose, a focus and a climax to the whole writing process. The fact that it is so difficult to publish in print is responsible for much of the frustration and disappointment that writers may experience—a cause-and-effect chain reaction that just keeps making things worse. The popularity of writing increases the demand to be published, which steadily reduces the chances for even commercially viable manuscripts to get into print.

However straitened a writer's financial circumstances might be, if you have had manuscripts accepted, you know that the thrill comes from the news that your creative work will have the opportunity to be seen by others and that consequently it is perceived to have merit. The size of the advance and royalties are important, of course, but the champagne comes out to celebrate the very fact of publication.

For many writers, the challenge of organizing thoughts in a creative process that captures them forever would be sufficient reward if there was a tangible end-product that could be shared with others. There are rewards beyond money that represent the very essence of writing and are too often forgotten in a society where money is the universal measure of merit. The frequent assumption is that writing that has a monetary value placed on it by going through a commercial publishing process is the only really worthwhile writing.

This attitude is spreading through many important fields of human endeavor. Advancing a career in academic and scientific research is becoming over-dependent on the professional prestige associated with publishing reports of one's work. Now that commercial criteria have become important factors in much scientific publishing, the publication of research becomes more important than the research itself, as professional eminence is accumulated by researchers prepared to play the game of diverting much of their effort toward the publishing objective. Grants and big salaries go disproportionately to those who publish and publicize prominently, while much worthwhile activity is being devalued because it is not published.

Electronic publishing could transform this situation, with researchers able to disseminate their findings directly to colleagues through unrestricted information highways (Fig. 17-1). Their readers will have sophisticated search facilities to ensure that they are not swamped by the resulting information torrent, and the lack of peer review might not prove as big a problem as some adherents of traditional publishing maintain.

If for no other reason, the advent of electronic publishing is a milestone cultural event. It must help to change contemporary attitudes about monetary values associated with print publishing. For the first time, a form of publishing is not dominated by the

335

Figure 17-1

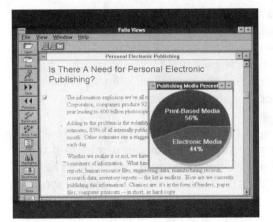

Scientific and academic publications on disk are greatly enhanced by the ease with which illustrations can be closely tied to the relevant sections of text, rather than stuck in one place on one page. This screen from a Folio Views publication demonstrates this kind of flexibility, preserving the familiar appearance of a printed document while adding search features.
Folio Corporation

overwhelming financial considerations of producing and distributing in print, with the consequent need to generate large revenues.

⇨ Self-publishing is not inferior

Attitudes will also change from the present perceptions that self-published works are inferior because they failed to meet all the criteria for commercial print publication. The Author-Publisher Enterprise in the United Kingdom is so successful in enhancing the image of self-publishing that secretary John Dawes says they risk their resources being swamped by "aspiring writers" eager to get themselves into print. As the message spreads that author-publishing *per se* is valid, interest in electronic publishing accelerates on both sides of the Atlantic. Electronic publishing is the most practical way to cope with the demand from literally millions of writers to publish in any form available to them, especially one with such strong cost advantages.

⇨ Farewell to the rejection slip

Because of the dominance of financial considerations from the very earliest days of print publishing, the rejection slip has become a symbol of failure and frustration for writers everywhere. The very

term "rejection slip" has become an established part of the vocabulary of writing, a form of misleading shorthand for a piece of paper that is usually just a convenient and economical means of reporting a decision by an individual or a small group of people. A rejection slip simply means that a particular work does not conform to a set of criteria. That criteria might have little to do with creative quality, but is weighted instead heavily towards corporate profitability.

When you consider the harm that rejection slips do to writers, they should carry a warning notice, like cigarette packets! If a Surgeon General took seriously the emotional well-being of writers and society's need to nurture writing talent, we might see rejection slips carry such wording as:

> Warning! This rejection slip could be harmful to your health and creativity. It does not necessarily reflect any qualified, literary, critical assessment of your submission. It is only an expression of our opinion that we cannot make sufficient money out of publishing it for profit.

The negative impact of the rejection slip is amplified for the author because it might well be the only response he or she receives to hundreds or even thousands of lonely hours of effort. It is easy for authors yearning for some form of recognition to lose sight of the fact that rejection by a commercial print publisher is a subjective decision. The rejection slip should not automatically be viewed as a judgment, a failure. It might not even reflect an informed opinion.

Indeed, most rejection slips are issued for manuscripts that never even go through a proper editorial decision-making process. It is quite likely, particularly if not being handled through an agent, that a rejected manuscript is judged on no more than a cursory editorial glance because of the volume of works submitted by writers seeking to be published.

Even the most responsible, caring publishers with editors actively seeking and nurturing worthy writing talent can do little to change this unsatisfactory situation. Therefore, there is more than adequate room for conventional, commercial publishing to cohabit congenially

alongside electronic author-publishing. Such self-publishing electronically can be either for the same profit motives that dominate print or for nonmonetary rewards.

⇨ Writers have more control— and more responsibilities

Writers can now stop bleating about the deficiencies of the print publishing industry; they have been given the technological edge to become the agents of change. Writers can create opportunities for their works to be published successfully through the new electronic media.

While these opportunities for a writer to publish for profit, for pleasure, or both, are guaranteed, success or failure now becomes far more the writer's responsibility. This can be beneficial, because writers have greater incentives than ever to make their work the best it can be. Also, more direct contact with readers should make writers more conscious of their needs, and consequently less self-indulgent. Even if you are not looking to make a profit from your writing, you must hone your skills at capturing and holding your readers' attentions in the increasing competition for their time. Persuading a reader to spend time with your work can be as challenging as getting them to spend their money.

As we say farewell to the tyranny of the rejection slip, authors must now come to terms with the remaining reality: rejection by readers. All published writers have been at least partly protected from reader criticisms by the skills of their editors!

With few exceptions, the revenue generated by the vast majority of electronic author-published works will be a minute fraction of the gross sales of even a modestly successful commercially printed title. This presents another challenge to established publishing values. Successful electronic titles can generate higher returns to the authors from far smaller receipts than would print editions. The drastically reduced production and distribution costs, and the fact that the lion's share of the revenues will not be absorbed by the retailer, printer, publisher, and agent, permit lower prices to readers and potentially higher net receipts for authors. The other side of the coin is that the risks and actual costs of production, marketing, and distribution fall directly on the author. Even if drastically reduced, these can still be significant.

 ## No more excuses

The knowledge that they will actually be able to publish will provide the stimulus for many would-be writers to get started, and help remove temporary blockages during the actual process. In print publishing, the likelihood that most books and poems would never get beyond the manuscript stage has been a tremendous disincentive to start or complete a work. The present and future certainty that what you write can at least end up in a permanent, readily reproducible, published form provides enormous encouragement.

 ## The published writer syndrome

We should see major changes also to that artificial distinction between "published" and "unpublished" writers, which in print gives an often unfair competitive edge to writers who have managed to get published at least once.

I have had the good fortune to have been published many times in a 40-year career, but that does not exalt me and my work into some elitist category. I know that there are unpublished writers who turn a neater phrase, create more meaningful characters, construct better plots, and communicate technical information more effectively than myself. That they have not had the time, the opportunity, or the good fortune to "get published" does not diminish the quality of their creative work one iota. If "published writers" are ever tempted to get arrogant because the system has worked for us, we should think of such enormous creative talents as Vincent van Gogh who were rejected by their contemporary marketplaces, but have created enduring works.

Electronic publishing levels the playing field for the writer who has not been able to get into print for reasons other than poor-quality work. It should make all writers realize that each work must be judged on its own merits. In electronic publishing, writers will not get published simply because of what they have got into print previously.

Expanding creative opportunities

The new media will have enormous cultural significance in making possible the dissemination of works with minority appeal, unusual structures, great length, or those which for some other reason are impossible to publish profitably in print. The book, which has been so crucial for the cultural evolution of our species, can now expand and develop without the artificial constraints imposed by the rigidities of commercial print publishing.

In addition to writing now being subject to fewer financial restraints, it takes on new dimensions of creativity, also. If your book might benefit from music, audio effects, moving pictures, or sophisticated hypertext references, you can explore these complementary areas of authoring right on your desktop with very few monetary or practical restrictions. To illustrate these principles, consider an example of how just one writer is being creatively empowered in his work by electronic publishing.

Gary Scott Bryant, of Newbury, Massachusetts, was one of the first writers, who, when he heard of this book project, was so hungry for the information that he contacted me and said, "I must have it." Since then I have gradually learned more about Gary's writing, and have been helped to realize just how wide are the horizons now open to a creative writer.

Gary's authoring project is unusual, but the principles he is using apply to virtually any category of writing. The former U.S. Navy submariner began writing after a near-death experience made him reappraise his values and what he wanted to do with his life.

"Now I live to write—it's as simple as that," Gary says. "I do any jobs that I can find that will enable me to continue writing, because I need to write to express the truth."

For 12 years, ever since his experience, Gary has been working on a book called "Seventh Sojourn" that has developed from an autobiography into an epic of nearly a quarter-of-a-million words in which he explores an enormous range of religious and mystical concepts. He worked and saved so that he could go to the Middle East to research first-hand, and then write with greater perception about ancient Egyptian beliefs.

Gary's writing led him in directions where he needed to expand his text with music and pictures. So, after working initially with the Writer's Dream software, he went on to expand his creativity with other multimedia authoring programs.

Fascinating as it is, there are no print publishing categories into which Gary's massive project can readily be accommodated so that its commercial potential can be evaluated. Consequently, no acquisitions editor is likely to offer him a contract; he's just not playing by the rules of commercial publishing. His book does not make a likely candidate for conventional book marketing plans. The salespeople would not even be sure where to advise booksellers to shelve it, and no ISBN classification could define it accurately.

The print production costs would be enormous, and no print house has the technology to cope with the multidimensional nature of the work as Gary expands his writing beyond the words and pictures that a printed book can accommodate. He has gone on to amplify the text by creating large-scale oil paintings, in addition to music and more modest visuals. I expect a call any day for advice on how he can scan or videotape these canvases to transfer the images onto floppies. The next step will be virtual reality programming.

"The high-tech advantage"

Maybe Gary never will complete "Seventh Sojourn," for it is a life's work. But he will always be able to publish and share his vision at any stage that he chooses because he has been empowered as an author with what he calls "the high-tech advantage."

"These ideas about electronic self-publishing are limitless," he says. "Don't give up. Never has there been such a demand for humanity and truth. False beliefs took advantage of the press in the early days of printing, but today we have a possibility to make amends with this new high-tech advantage given directly to authors. There is so much to gain, and so little to lose."

Writers, poets, artists, photographers, scientists, academics, researchers, hobbyists, thinkers, politicians, entrepreneurs, professionals, students, teachers—everybody! You now have the high-tech advantage. It empowers you to publish. With the authoring programs discussed in this book and included on the disk, and your personal computer, *you can publish now*.

Appendix
Programs on the disk

⇨ Dart, the award-winning e-book program

Dart (Fig. A-1) was the winner for two consecutive years of the
Digital Publishing Association's Quill Award for the best software.
The kind of e-books it creates might be compared with the ubiquitous
paperback. Indeed, Dart's creator, Ted Husted of Fairport, New York,
says it is intended to be "the simplest device of its kind."

Ted understates Dart's power. It is rich in features and, if you take
the trouble to spend an hour or two studying the documentation, it
might prove to be the only publishing program you will ever need.

Dart's pedigree is impressive. It is a direct descendant of Iris, first
released as shareware in 1988. The latest version of Dart reflects
how Ted has remained focused on the need for a universal computer
file viewer that runs on virtually any PC—an essential specification
for authors who, above all, want their words to be read by as many
people as possible.

Figure A-1

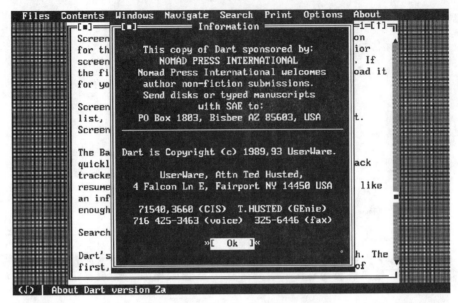

*Dart is loaded with features, and when you register as a user, the "About"
window can be customized with your own message recording your copyright
or promoting your services and other titles. Registration also brings the right
to use Dart for your own publications without further royalty requirements.*

⇨ Hypertext hot words

In addition to its proficiency at handling "plain vanilla" ASCII text files
that can be created by virtually any word processing or text editing
program, Dart also has its own version of hypertext with "hot word"
links. The program automatically creates a table of contents and index,
enables you to emphasize text with boldfacing and underlining, and can
compress text to save disk space and protect your data.

As an author, you can compile your manuscript with varying degrees
of electronic indexing, cross-referencing, and hypertext linking.
Formatting a document to meet your particular publishing needs is
comparatively easy, requires no knowledge of programming, and is
described well in the Dart.#02, Dart.#03, and Dart.#04 files which
are decompressed when you unzip Dart to install it on your computer.

The readers of works published with Dart will not need any printed documentation, but you will benefit if, in any printed material you supply and in your opening screens, you encourage readers to make full use of Dart's search and navigation features and the built-in editor with which they can make notes. These features are added-value advantages for any publication—they make you and your works look professional.

 ## Features for portables

When promoting a publication compiled with Dart, emphasize also that it has a special mode for LCD monitors. Portables with LCD screens will soon be the computers of choice for the majority of electronic book readers, and Dart's clear black-and-white mode for LCD screens is a strong selling point.

Another major attraction for many readers is the automatic bookmark feature. When you close the electronic book, Dart remembers where you were in the text and what you were doing, so that you can restore your electronic desktop automatically. That's another particular boon for portable users who switch their systems off and on frequently to conserve battery power.

Wide range of uses

Dart is an honest, unpretentious, yet capable program that wins friends easily. Iris and Dart have done all the mainstream electronic publishing tasks of creating newsletters, magazines, textbooks, and fiction and nonfiction books. The U.S. Air Force has also used them to distribute internal reports, the IRS and IEEE for technical abstracts, the Clinton campaign staff for literature that helped to win the presidential election, and lawyers for hypertext compilations of legal depositions. Dart's easy search and cross-referencing have made it an ideal format for such applications as an annotated version of the Americans with Disabilities Act and the U.S. Bankruptcy Code.

How to start Dart

To start the program, go to the Dart directory on the floppy, and type Go. For a detailed overview, read the Dart.#01 file first.

Once you register for the modest fee of $34, you can distribute your own e-books in Dart format without further royalty payments, so your readers can use all its features when reading your publication. Your Dart publications will run well on any IBM PC compatible with only 196K of available memory, a single floppy disk drive, virtually any color or monochrome monitor, and MS-DOS 2.1 or later.

To register Dart, send $34.00 to

UserWare
4 Falcon Lane
Fairport, NY 14450-3312

Upon registration, you will receive your own personalized copy of the latest version of Dart and announcements of upgrades and new releases as they become available. There is a 60-day money-back guarantee. What a bargain!

Attention Macintosh users

The nearest equivalent to Dart for Macintosh systems is John J. Gaudreault's Waldo. It is a HyperCard-based combination publisher/reader in one program. Waldo loads plain text files formatted with ASCII to which authors or readers may add a variety of HyperText links. There are no royalties to be paid for publishing with Waldo and the registration fee is only $10 for the shareware version. The Waldo OpenBook option, for $30, enables e-books to be published in a "locked" format to make them integrated units combining the programming with the text.

Any Macintosh (Classic or better recommended) with a hard disk and HyperCard 2.0 will run this program. A version for Windows was in preparation during 1994, and John Gaudreault has another program

called UserWare to Waldo to convert Ted Husted's Dart and other UserWare applications into Waldo documents.

This program is not included on the DOS disk (due to the fact that it's a Mac program). To register and obtain the latest versions, send $10 for Waldo and another $30 if you also want OpenBook to

Artway
P.O. Box 3442
Omaha, NE 68103

MultiMedia Workshop and Writer's Dream

Multimedia programs keep getting more sophisticated and demanding in their system requirements, leaving millions of people with older computers out of the excitement of this new form of electronic publishing. Many of the commercial programs also generate such big files that they complicate publishing and distribution of your titles. Jeff Napier's MultiMedia Workshop (Fig. A-2) is included on the disk because it produces compact, very portable files with modest system requirements.

It is easy to install and run MultiMedia Workshop under Windows, but if you have just a basic PC with at least 512K RAM and a graphics card, you can use it as well. If you do not have a hard disk, decompress the files using another system, copy them onto floppies, and then use those copies on your system.

A great e-book program as well

As a bonus, in the Dream directory on the disk you will find Writer's Dream (Fig. A-3), Jeff's very easy e-book compiling program that was the runner-up to Dart in the first Quill Awards. It is remarkably easy to create electronic publications for distribution on floppies with Dream, and it now has features that enable it to run executable files and create interactive tutorials (Fig. A-4). The reader for this program

Figure A-2

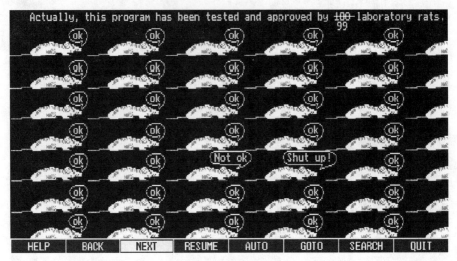

Multimedia Workshop has big advantages in being able to use visuals and other multimedia elements without creating files that are too large to be practical to distribute on floppies. This screen is from the demonstration section.

Figure A-3

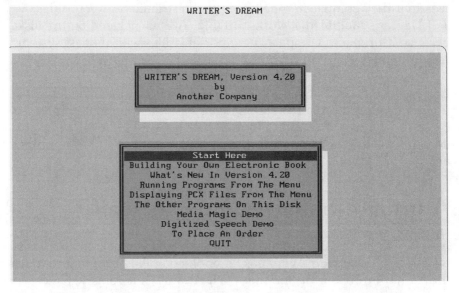

The opening screen for Writer's Dream is a welcoming display of the title and the first section of its contents listing. The program uses itself to explain how it works. Then, when you build your own book, this screen changes to incorporate your title and chapter headings.

Figure A-4

```
                    DISPLAYING PICTURES

        Using  the  capabilities  explained  in  the  preceeding
    chapter, you can use just about any  program  which  displays
    graphic  images  with  Writer's  Dream.   But,  we  also have
    built-in capability for .PCX files, the most common  graphics
    file format.

        To display a  .PCX  file,  you  simply  list  it  in  the
    conten                                                  iter's
    Dream                                                     the
    small      What are you looking for?                     ture,
    waits    .tif FILES                                      tton,
    then re

        PCX.EXE  works with almost any .PCX image from monochrome
    CGA to Super-VGA.   There  are  a  few  images  it  will  not
    display, because the .PCX standard is very  flexible,  and many
    paint  programs take great liberty with the format, resulting
    in  screwey  proportions  or  incorrect  video mode.  And, of
    course, PCX.EXE cannot display a 256-color VGA on a  Hercules
    monitor, for instance.

        PCX.EXE will also run as a stand-alone  program  for  use
    Use arrows & Page keys. Press [F1] for Help & Options. [Esc] to Quit.
```

Your readers have very easy and logical ways to search through your text published in Dream. Typing the letter S anywhere brings up this help panel, into which the reader types a word or phrase and finds all matches within that chapter. Typing G searches the entire book.

is very compact, so you can add production values to e-books of up to 100 chapters that might still fit on to a single floppy.

MultiMedia Workshop also includes a royalty-free runtime show program that you can distribute with your presentations. This takes up only 45K, so that you can get as many as 100 pictures and the show program on a floppy. Jeff Napier was a pioneer in electronic publishing; his first-hand knowledge of the real world is reflected in programs that get great results on the largest possible number of computers—a basic requirement for many electronic publishers.

⇨ Installing Workshop

To start creating and publishing with MultiMedia Workshop and Writer's Dream, go into the Workshop directory on the disk, copy all the files there to a new directory you have created on your hard disk, and type Install. The compressed files will automatically

decompress and that directory will contain a fully functioning Workshop.

If you have Windows, you can also install Workshop to run from Windows. After copying the files to your hard disk, start Windows, then follow these steps:

❶ From the main program group, click on the group in which you want to include the Workshop.

❷ Select New from the File menu. For Program Description, type tmw. For Command Line, type c:\workshop\tmw.exe (assuming that c: is your hard disk, and "workshop" is the subdirectory to which you have copied the MultiMedia Workshop files).

❸ Click on Change Icon. In the Icon filebox, type c:\workshop\tmw.ico.

Double-clicking on the MultiMedia Workshop icon will start the program. Run the Demo.exe file on the disk to get an on-screen demonstration of what you will be able to achieve with this software. (It might not function properly, and the sound effects will be distorted, if you are multi-tasking other programs at the same time. The Multi.doc file explains what to do about this.)

⇨ Installing Dream

To install Writer's Dream, go to the Dream directory on the disk and type Go. The book you open will tell you all about creating e-books with Writer's Dream. You can see the program in action because it is used for its own instructions and for the Workshop's on-screen manual.

To register, send $29.95 to get the latest registered version of Writer's Dream or $99.95 for the MultiMedia Workshop (plus $3 U.S. postage; Canada $5, Overseas $7), or call for more information:

Another Company
P.O. Box 3429
Ashland, OR 97520
1-800-444-2424

Software to market your manuscripts

The Publish directory contains a complete software package to enable you to publish and market your manuscripts in a way that guarantees readers must pay you for your words and data. For all practical purposes, you can electronically publish without risking that your works will be pirated.

This is a special arrangement for readers of this book with SoftLock Services, Inc. of Pennsylvania.

Type Install in the Publish directory, and you will be introduced to a very flexible form of software locking. It enables you to encrypt and "lock" all or parts of your publication. Your readers must pay first to get access to these sections. You should leave unlocked any text that will motivate potential readers to purchase, such as your table of contents, an abstract, review comments, and the kind of cover "blurb" that goes on printed books.

If this concept appeals to you, all the information you need to protect your work is in the directory. Send your finished version to a fulfillment agency for listing in on-line catalogs, including Internet facilities. You do not sign away your copyright. SoftLock has an 800 number by which your readers pay by credit card to get an immediate, decoded copy of your publication.

The agency takes $1.50 per key code released and a 20% commission on any copies that it sells on your behalf, and the rest is remitted monthly.

Give your e-book or database a clear, descriptive title, so that it can be located most efficiently by Gopher, Archie, and other Internet search procedures. If you create a single page (2K or smaller in ASCII) summarizing your e-book's merits, SoftLock will consider placing this on their bulletin board and Internet address. Your summary, which should contain all the strongest elements in your sales pitch to readers, will be given a special code. It will be

downloaded automatically to prospective buyers to help them reach a final decision.

If you have any queries, call SoftLock directly at 1-610-993-9900. Identify yourself as a reader of this book and they will supply any further information that you may require.

 # It pays to register

Please remember that these programs on the disk are all shareware, provided for you to evaluate. If you want to keep on using them, and particularly if you publish with them, you must register with the authors.

There are many practical advantages in registering, as well. I have selected these programs because they are well-supported and constantly being updated and enhanced. Consequently, you can feel confident with any of the four that the time taken to become proficient with them will be well-spent. Registration helps the authors continue to add features and provide excellent electronic publishing tools.

Index

About the Author

Colin Haynes is an award-winning author, broadcaster, and investigative journalist who has been writing professionally for nearly 40 years. His articles have appeared in *Newsweek*, the *New York Times*, *The Times of London*, *Cosmopolitan*, and many specialized publications around the world. His book credits include the *Computer Virus Protection Handbook* (Sybex, 1991), named one of the three best how-to books of the year in the 1991 Sixth Annual Computer Press Awards. He is also author or co-author of *Computer Viruses, Worms & Data Diddlers* (St. Martin's Press), *Portable Computing* (American Management Association), *Healthy Computing* (Amacom), and several other books.

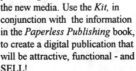

Author's Research on-line, or on disk

Would you like a digital copy of my research notes for this book?

One of the fascinating possibilities opened up by the new media is that authors can easily make available to their readers their research notes, and other material that might be helpful.

If you really want to get involved in these new media, it may help you to have access to the large quantity of research notes that I accumulated while writing this book. I staggered away with over 80 pounds of materials from just one Comdex! Also there are shorthand notes from interviews, extracts from letters, and other source materials.

I have continued adding new information as it has come to hand, creating searchable ASCII files that comprise an informal and evolving database on paperless publishing.

These research notes are being archived in the virtual salon that SoftLock Services has created on the Internet. That way, they are available for any readers who want to explore them.

"Our salon at Downtown Anywhere on the World Wide Web is conveniently located in the center of cyberspace," says Dr. Jonathan Schull, SoftLock's president, and inventor of their innovative technologies. "We are creating an environment which should intrigue anyone interested in electronic publishing, digital commerce, and the evolving marketplace of ideas."

Anyone with a World Wide Web browser like Lynx, or Mosaic, can get there using the address **http://www.awa.com**.

If that sounds like gibberish to you, then dial **1-800-SOFTLOCK** with a touch-tone phone to order the files compressed on to a 3.5" HD floppy. Or just call **1-610-993-9900** during normal business hours on the US east coast to speak to a human helper.

You will find *PaperPub* as a compressed file that you can load into - and search with - your favorite word processor or information manager, or run with the programs *Dart* or *Writer's Dream* on the disk with this book.

There is a nominal contribution of $5 towards the costs, plus $1.50 for the shipping of a floppy, or the downloading on-line. You can pay by Visa or Mastercard. Don't forget to give your *Paperless Publishing* SoftLock ID Code number at the top of this page.

Please let me know what you think of the book - and paperless publishing generally. My address is below.

Happy - and successful - writing and publishing.

Colin Haynes

1257 Siskiyou Boulevard, Suite 179, Ashland OR 97520 USA

DISK WARRANTY

This software is protected by both United States copyright law and international copyright treaty provision. You must treat this software just like a book, except that you may copy it into a computer in order to be used and you may make archival copies of the software for the sole purpose of backing up our software and protecting your investment from loss.

By saying "just like a book," McGraw-Hill means, for example, that this software may be used by any number of people and may be freely moved from one computer location to another, so long as there is no possibility of its being used at one location or on one computer while it also is being used at another. Just as a book cannot be read by two different people in two different places at the same time, neither can the software be used by two different people in two different places at the same time (unless, of course, McGraw-Hill's copyright is being violated).

LIMITED WARRANTY

Windcrest/McGraw-Hill takes great care to provide you with top-quality software, thoroughly checked to prevent virus infections. McGraw-Hill warrants the physical diskette(s) contained herein to be free of defects in materials and workmanship for a period of sixty days from the purchase date. If McGraw-Hill receives written notification within the warranty period of defects in materials or workmanship, and such notification is determined by McGraw-Hill to be correct, McGraw-Hill will replace the defective diskette(s). Send requests to:

> Customer Service
> Windcrest/McGraw-Hill
> 13311 Monterey Lane
> Blue Ridge Summit, PA 17294-0850

The entire and exclusive liability and remedy for breach of this Limited Warranty shall be limited to replacement of defective diskette(s) and shall not include or extend to any claim for or right to cover any other damages, including but not limited to, loss of profit, data, or use of the software, or special, incidental, or consequential damages or other similar claims, even if McGraw-Hill has been specifically advised of the possibility of such damages. In no event will McGraw-Hill's liability for any damages to you or any other person ever exceed the lower of suggested list price or actual price paid for the license to use the software, regardless of any form of the claim.

McGRAW-HILL, INC. SPECIFICALLY DISCLAIMS ALL OTHER WARRANTIES, EXPRESS OR IMPLIED, INCLUDING, BUT NOT LIMITED TO, ANY IMPLIED WARRANTY OF MERCHANTABILITY OR FITNESS FOR A PARTICULAR PURPOSE.

Specifically, McGraw-Hill makes no representation or warranty that the software is fit for any particular purpose and any implied warranty of merchantability is limited to the sixty-day duration of the Limited Warranty covering the physical diskette(s) only (and not the software) and is otherwise expressly and specifically disclaimed.

This limited warranty gives you specific legal rights; you may have others which may vary from state to state. Some states do not allow the exclusion of incidental or consequential damages, or the limitation on how long an implied warranty lasts, so some of the above may not apply to you.